Decolonizing Queer Experience

Decolonizing Queer Experience

LGBT+ Narratives from Eastern Europe and Eurasia

Edited by
Emily Channell-Justice

LEXINGTON BOOKS
Lanham • Boulder • New York • London

Published by Lexington Books
An imprint of The Rowman & Littlefield Publishing Group, Inc.
4501 Forbes Boulevard, Suite 200, Lanham, Maryland 20706
www.rowman.com

6 Tinworth Street, London SE11 5AL, United Kingdom

British Library Cataloguing in Publication Information Available

Library of Congress Cataloging-in-Publication Data

Names: Channell-Justice, Emily, 1986- editor.
Title: Decolonizing queer experience : LGBT+ narratives from Eastern Europe and
    Eurasia / edited by Emily Channell-Justice.
Other titles: Lesbian, Gay, Bisexual, Transgender plus narratives from Eastern Europe
    and Eurasia
Description: Lanham : Lexington Books, 2020. I Includes bibliographical references
    and index. I Summary: "Decolonizing Queer Experience draws from research around
    the post-socialist world to argue that understanding LGBT+ experience in the
    region cannot be limited to oppression and violence. Using a decolonizing lens, the
    contributors explore performance, identity, and political affiliations as essential parts
    of LGBT+ communities"—Provided by publisher.
Identifiers: LCCN 2020039729 (print) I LCCN 2020039730 (ebook) I
    ISBN 9781793630308 (Cloth)
    ISBN 9781793630322 (Pbk) I ISBN 9781793630315 (ePub) Subjects: LCSH: Gays
—Europe, Eastern. I Gays—Eurasia. I Decolonization—Europe,
    Eastern. I Decolonization—Eurasia.
Classification: LCC HQ76.3.E852 D44 2020 (print) I LCC HQ76.3.E852 (ebook) I
    DDC 306.76/60947—dc23
LC record available at https://lccn.loc.gov/2020039729
LC ebook record available at https://lccn.loc.gov/2020039730

Contents

Preface

Vitaly Chernetsky

Recent years have witnessed the rise of a new wave of LGBTQ+-focused scholarship on Eastern Europe and Eurasia, and this volume offers another contribution to this welcome development. The field, if still relatively small in the number of scholars active in it, has grown, and also broadened considerably in terms of disciplinary and national backgrounds of active scholars. It has also undergone a generational change, and thus for scholars from an older cohort like the author of these lines, it is particularly exciting to welcome these recent developments. These developments are especially notable as ten to fifteen years ago it seemed that the field was witnessing an abrupt break in continuity: while research on LGBTQ+-related topics in Eastern Europe and the former Soviet Union was active, it appeared to be pursued only by scholars who had started working on these topics in the early to mid-1990s or even earlier, with few, if any, younger colleagues joining their ranks. Now the situation appears to be the opposite. It is a pleasure to welcome this group of scholars, including contributors to this volume, to this field, and it is exciting to see the diversity of their interests and approaches.

Within this new wave, various forms of social science research appear to be taking the upper hand over the study of cultural artifacts (such as literature and music) and their producers, which was the leading area of scholarly engagement with queer topics for the older generation. Among the earliest publications in what was then the nascent field of gay and lesbian studies of the Russian Empire, the Soviet Union, and Eastern Europe, starting from the mid-1970s, were those focused on articulating and documenting a historical tradition through, on the one hand, compiling annotated chronological lists of notable persons who were claimed for this history, and on the other, through ethnographic approaches to understanding a stigmatized minority through the study of its oral lore, especially its slang—see such examples as Simon

Karlinsky's pioneering 1976 article in the San Francisco-based magazine *Gay Sunshine* and Vladimir Kozlovsky's book *Argo russkoi gomoseksual'noi subkul'tury* (The Argot of Russian Homosexual Subculture, pub. 1986). Karlinsky in particular breached the divide between academic research and community activism, as he was a frequent contributor to such prominent periodicals as *The Advocate* and *Christopher Street*, uniquely for a Slavist. Side by side with those came annotated editions of the collected writings of noted lesbian and gay authors, published in the West as such publication in their home countries was impossible—notably the 1977–1978 three-volume edition of collected poetry of Mikhail Kuzmin in West Germany and the 1979 edition of collected poetry by Sophia Parnok in the United States, then followed by biographic studies of those authors, such as Diana L. Burgin's work on Parnok and John Malmstad's on Kuzmin. Similar biographic research was also growing in music and the visual arts. With the emergence of the lesbian and gay rights movement in some East European countries in the 1980s (most notably in Yugoslavia, especially in Slovenia), research and activism efforts originating outside the region were increasingly operating in dialogue with those emanating from the region itself. With restrictions on travel and research topics disappearing almost completely after 1989, and with the conservative mainstream of Slavic/Soviet studies challenged by the precipitous collapse of the Soviet Union and its satellites it largely failed to anticipate, the 1990s witnessed a rapid rise of this academic field, with multiple panels at influential conferences, prominent presence of LGBTQ topics at summer schools organized in different countries of the region, and an increasing number of publications.

Further development of the field was influenced by a number of overlapping factors. Prominent among them was the profound impact of the AIDS crisis that changed both queer activism and the stance of some in academia toward activist involvement. In Eastern Europe and Eurasia, the arrival of both LGBTQ+ activism and academic research on related topics coincided with the AIDS pandemic, which left its indelible impact on the structuration of the field. Another important factor was the institutional homes that research on LGBTQ+ topics was finding in different countries of the region in the first postcommunist decade: in some of them, this happened in the social sciences, primarily in sociology; in others, it was in philosophy, leading to interesting engagements with queer theory that were, however, completely removed from lived realities; in still others, it was primarily in the humanities and arts, leading to the prominence of art history, literary criticism, and other disciplines, such as translation studies, as venues for queer-themed research. Last but not least, external factors can impact the timeline of such research translating into published results. Thus, Daniel Schluter's pioneering sociological study of gay men in Russia (primarily in Moscow), based on fieldwork undertaken by the author, with considerable risk, shortly *before* the collapse of the USSR, was eventually published only in 2002; by then, given the rapidity of changes in the 1990s, his research became valuable not so much for its immediate implications but for providing us a historical snapshot of that social group as it was beginning to emerge from fully underground existence.[1]

A highly interesting aspect of the field's development was the prominence of self-reflection within it. Many Western participants were acutely aware of the privilege and protection they enjoyed when undertaking research travel in countries of the region at the time when political change was also accompanied by major economic and social turmoil. At the same time, as old communist-era patterns of non-heteronormative behavior were fading in the face of more commodified Western models of LGBT behavior and inclusion, some Western scholars appeared to be looking up to those very fading patterns as a vanishing fluid utopia, conceptualizing this in ways somewhat similar to earlier Western fascination with Native American and Pacific Islander traditional cultures' handling of gender and sexual diversity (see, in particular, Essig 1999; Tuller 1997).

In the 2000s, as the region was entering a period of relative economic prosperity and social stability, attention to LGBTQ+ topics in Eastern Europe and Eurasia faded somewhat; most of the publications were based on research conducted or commenced earlier.[2] However, this was the time when academics in countries of the region finally began serious engagement with postcolonial, and eventually also decolonial theory; within this new turn, queer-identified scholars were also active, but without necessarily prioritizing queer topics.[3] It was only in the early 2010s, in the context of the arrival of the Russian "homosexual propaganda" law in 2013, as well as the rise of the so-called "anti-gender" movement spearheaded by conservative religious circles, primarily in European countries that historically were majority Catholic, including in Eastern Europe, but since then also spreading to historically majority Orthodox Christian countries as well (Kuhar and Paternotte 2017), that we can see a major new wave of LGBTQ+-focused academic research emerging hand-in-hand with the new mobilization of queer activism that is intersectional in its nature and strategies (for more on the relationship between LGBTQ+ issues and leftist activism, using the case study of Ukraine, see the article by Emily Channell-Justice in this volume). This rise has also led to comparative and/or synthesizing book projects that tackle LGBTQ+ issues across Eastern Europe. In literary and cultural studies, it yielded, among others, the volume *Go East! LGBTQ+ Literature in Eastern Europe* (Ljubljana University Press 2020), edited by Andrej Zavrl and Alojzija Zupan Sosič. In the social sciences, it gave us *LGBTQ+ Activism in Central and Eastern Europe: Resistance, Representation and Identity*

(Palgrave 2020), edited by Radzhana Buyantueva and Maryna Shevtsova, an excellent volume whose disciplinary frame is primarily that of political science. The current volume bridges the disciplinary gap between these two by engaging interdisciplinarily across the humanistic social sciences, from anthropology and history to sociology of culture and performance studies. It also broadens the geographic reach by incorporating contributions on Central Asia, which until recently has been largely left out of consideration in these broader projects, even though the region has been witnessing an exciting rise in innovative cultural practices and social activism that engage with LGBTQ+ persons and topics, while simultaneously tackling a plethora of political challenges, many of them recognizable to students of other cultures and national political discourses.

As someone who has tried for decades to foster greater dialogic engagement between scholarship on Eastern Europe and Eurasia, on the one hand, and, on the other, the contemporary theoretical discourses that aspire to global coverage but often neglect this part of the world, perpetuating an oxymoronic binary between what back in the Cold War days used to be called the First and the Third Worlds, ignoring the Second, I am especially pleased by the breadth of this volume's theoretical horizons. One of the aspects of this engagement that to me feels particularly promising focuses on what I would call the queer theorizations and practices of glocalization.

First introduced in the early 1990s, the term "glocalization" and its derivatives (such as "glocality" to designate a social condition and "glocalism" to refer to an ideology or worldview) have gained greater currency in the latest decade. It has also been theorized as a specific form of hybridity, as not all hybridity combines the global and the local. As Victor Roudometof, a leading theorist of glocalization, notes, ultimately "glocalization is a term that entails transcendence, unthinking, and reconfiguration of the conventional post-1989 understanding of globalization" (2016). Glocalization is thus strongly related to cultural appropriation and subversion and a variety of practices of what is alternatively referred to as creolization and/or *mestizaje*. Eastern Europe's new social movements, from Serbia's Otpor to Ukraine's Euromaidan offer telling examples of productive glocal sociopolitical practices from the region.

Within the study of LGBTQ+ communities and cultures, I would point to such instances of promising explorations of glocal potentialities in LGBTQ+ contexts as the work of the anthropologist Martin Manalansan who has been researching Asian and Pacific Islander queer communities, both in the homelands and in the diaspora, and the late Jose Esteban Muñoz, a Cuban-American performance studies scholar whose pioneering theorizations of queer futurity and queer sociality derive from his reconceptualization of queerness, moving away from identity politics to focus on "disidentificatory performances" vis-à-vis white colonialist normativity that enable minoritarian subjects (queers of color in his research) to challenge cultural hegemony, and I am thus especially pleased to see them included in the theoretical corpus with which the contributors to this volume engage.

Ultimately, it is this readiness to engage with diverse scholarly discourses and the refusal to be intimidated by enduring local cultural taboos and prescriptions (and in fact, boldly exploring them instead, as in Syinat Sultanalieva's contribution to this volume) that invites readers of this volume to embrace the promise of queer futurity in Eastern Europe and Eurasia. Here is hoping it is followed by many other inspiring contributions.

NOTES

1. Based on Schluter's dissertation, defended in 1998.

2. The LGBTQ-focused parts of my book *Mapping Postcommunist Cultures: Russia and Ukraine in the Context of Globalization*, can be considered part of this group of publications.

3. Notably, at the crucial event of the first such major institutional engagement, the summer school in postcolonial studies in Minsk in 2001, the main foreign instructor was the late Mark von Hagen, a leading historian of Russia and Ukraine and a gay man himself.

REFERENCES

Chernetsky, Vitaly. 2007. *Mapping Postcommunist Cultures: Russia and Ukraine in the Context of Globalization*. Montreal: McGill-Queen's University Press.

Essig, Laurie. 1999. *Queer in Russia*. Durham, NC: Duke University Press.

Kasinec, E., and Molly Molloy. 1990. "Simon Karlinsky: A Bibliography." *Russian Review* 49(1):57–76.

Kuhar, Roman, and David Paternotte, eds. 2017. *Anti-Gender Campaigns in Europe: Mobilizing Against Equality*. Lanham, MD: Rowman & Littlefield.

Roudometof, Victor. 2016. *Glocalization: A Critical Introduction*. New York: Routledge.

Schluter, Daniel P. 2002. *Gay Life in the Former USSR: Fraternity Without Community*. New York: Routledge.

Tuller, David. 1997. *Cracks in the Iron Closet*. Chicago: University of Chicago Press.

Acknowledgments

Emily Channell-Justice

This book would not have been possible without the active cooperation of LGBT+ community members in each of the authors' research projects. In Ukraine, I am indebted to the activists who continue to share their ideas, council, and support of my various research projects. This volume is a starting point for further research that will ask even more of them, but it strives for the hope of a better future.

The work of the nine authors in this volume is what made this book possible. They were committed to this project despite several delays and changes in form. I appreciate their dedication and hard work to bring these chapters together. I also thank Vitaly Chernetsky for his quick support for the project, for engaging with the chapters, and for contributing the preface.

I would like to thank the original participants of the 2018 panel at the American Anthropological Association Annual Meetings in San Jose, CA, "Decolonizing Queer Performance, Practice, Experience: Examples from Post-Socialism." Samuel Buelow, Jennifer Carroll, Roman Leksikov, Alexandra Novitskaya, and Tamar Shirinian presented and engaged with the themes that are central to this volume and have influenced my thinking on LGBT+ issues in the region. Samuel Buelow directed me to several of the eventual contributors. Jennifer Carroll hosted me at Elon University to present material from my chapter, and the engagement of students and faculty there provided me with crucial momentum to continue this work. While not all of these scholars are featured in the volume, this book would never have been possible without their initial support.

I would like to express my deep gratitude toward Kasey Beduhn. This project would not have been seen through to completion without her support at multiple stages of the process. Over several years and despite the challenges of the COVID-19 pandemic, it has been a true pleasure to work with her on this volume.

I thank my colleagues at the Ukrainian Research Institute at Harvard University for their continued support of my research work on contemporary Ukraine. I am especially grateful to Kristina Conroy for both her technical contributions and her general enthusiasm for this project. Grace Van Gorder contributed to the early research for this project. I thank Jacob Lassin and Georgiy Kent for their commentary on my chapter, as well as on others in the volume. My great appreciation goes to Michelle Viise at Harvard Ukrainian Research Institute Publications.

My family has shown unflagging support in all my research endeavors, but their investment in this project has been especially significant to me. Kathi Regan, Don Channell, Allison Racey, Rodney Racey, and Thomas Justice—thank you.

Introduction

Of Constatives, Performatives, and Disidentifications: Decolonizing Queer Critique in Post-Socialist Times

Tamar Shirinian and Emily Channell-Justice

Performance and performativity, as theoretical frameworks, urge us to consider the quotidian, seemingly inconsequential, individual, and bodily movements and acts that are highly politically motivated sites from which to discern processes of subjection and resistance. Whether collectively or alone, with an agenda or not, publicly or privately, performance performs and informs the sphere of the political. As forms that produce the site and space of the political, performance and performativity also place in question the stability of various scales and forms of sovereignty: personal, bodily, sexual, gendered, familial, state, and so on. Understanding subjecthood and subjection as citationality of norms—norms that are, always, produced through relations and dynamics of power—prompts us to ask in what ways a person or a group maintains the right to execute a commandment (Mbembe 1992) and how the very desire or the will to do so is produced. Furthermore, certain forms of sovereignty—namely, gendered and sexual—might come to a standoff with others—for instance, with the state. Performance and performativity, thus, open up the possibilities of understanding sovereignty as a multiplicity—various machines that form assemblages (Deleuze and Guattari 1987; Puar 2007), each producing different forms of affective relation between bodies, groups, actions, behaviors, desires, and forms of violence.

Performance and performativity have now also become central apparatuses to understanding processes of identity and identification. They shape the ways in which the subject becomes a subject through processes of citation, naming, and iterability. As Judith Butler has canonically argued, performativity can be understood as neither "free play" nor "theatrical self-presentation," and it cannot be simply equated with performance. Rather, performativity is a "regularized and constrained repetition of norms," and this repetition is not "performed *by* a subject," but rather must be understood as what "enables a subject and constitutes the temporal condition of the subject" (1993, 95).

The chapters in *Decolonizing Queer Experience* take up these issues of performativity, identification, and sovereignty and do so not in an abstract way, but very much located within the particularities of lives, experiences, worlds, and the relations of power that are unfolding in the post-socialist spaces of Eastern Europe and Eurasia. The chapters in this book outline critical aspects of queer politics, and their colonizing and colonized tendencies as they are performatively performed in the post-socialist world. In this introduction, we will focus our attention to these larger theoretical structures—of performativity, identification, colonization, and sovereignty—and how they are implicated in what the authors in these pages present to us as the complicated dimensions of gendered and sexualized worlds in a relatively new political-economic era.

PERFORMATIVITY OF A GLOBAL IDENTITY AND A GLOBAL CRITIQUE

Identity is a heavily problematized and problematic category of analysis. On the one hand, it names a process through which a subject comes to understand herself as marked by a difference and, thus, has possibilities of creating collective will for the formation of a politics through which to make claims. In this sense, identity might fail as a fully incorporated descriptive of desires and wills (the way I identify myself and thus with others might not fully capture who I *really* am), but is strategically deployable to create socially cohesive sensibilities. On the other hand, identity has the potential of falling into what Tom Boellstorff calls the "logic of enumeration" (2007, 2011) in which more and more categories are produced to fulfill the demands of particular desires and wills. Insisting upon these specifications of individual desire through identity can be politically dangerous. As Butler argues,

> insofar as it is imperative that we insist upon those specificities in order to expose the fictions of an imperialist humanism that works through unmarked privilege, there remains the risk that we will make the articulation of ever more specified identities into the aim of political activism. Thus every insistence on identity must at some point lead to a taking stock of the constitutive exclusions that reconsolidate hegemonic power differentials, exclusions that each articulation was forced to make in order to proceed. This critical reflection will be important in order not to replicate at the level of identity politics the very exclusionary moves that initiated the turn to specific identities in the first place. (1993, 118)

In this sense, identity—which is always fictive, as it is produced by norms rather than being what is prior to norms and acts, thus, as a constraint rather than liberation (Foucault 1978)—makes possible a continuum between potentials of strategic liberation on one end and the dissolution of (collectively) liberatory potential on the other.

Identity prohibits, like the law, as much as it makes possible recognition before the law. While advocacy toward visible identity was not and is not the only mode of political, cultural, and social relation for the experience of homoerotic, homosexual, or queer difference (Gopinath 2005, 2018), it has become the hegemonic mode, taking root in all corners of the globe, including post-socialist worlds.

In 1997, Dennis Altman published an essay entitled "Global Gays/Global Gaze," in which he argued that the use of identity categories like "gay" and "lesbian" in places and spaces outside of the West, especially in Asia, was a form of cultural imperialism. Mainstream movements insisted on repeating and mirroring Western political forms in the East within a complicated history of Western colonization and imperialism. These movements also ended up producing "gay" as a marker of whiteness, tied to colonial, middle-class, Euro-American privilege, creating other complications of politics and solidarity movements between Asian and Western men and women. This notion of gay identity as cultural imperialism has since been heavily debated by many anthropologists and queer scholars outside of the discipline.

A number of ethnographic investigations have offered nuances to the meaning and perception of the "global" or the "transnational" in queer thought and especially within anthropology. For instance, Martin Manalansan argued that rather than understanding a global gay identity as the "McDonaldsization" of queerness, we can, instead, look at how local and global identities merge and create various iterations of difference to the global within the local (2003). Similarly, Tom Boellstorff (2005) suggests that the time for an anthropology of difference might well be over. Instead, he proposed an anthropology of similitude, in which non-Western forms of borrowing from Western culture can be tracked as a dubbing of the global, producing nuanced variations in the local. Boellstorff also argues that when we refer to gay identity in non-Western places as colonization, we rob local persons who might be choosing to identify with those categories of their agency (2005). Lisa Rofel (2007) points to the ways in which a rhetoric of a colonizing Western gaze produces a problematic spectrum of tradition and modernity, wherein which the colonized context becomes a traditional non-modern one marked by radical difference to modernity. These critiques, she argues, are resonant with colonial anthropology.

These debates are no longer purely academic. Activists within local spaces are hotly embroiled in discussions of what queerness means and when it is and is not advantageous to them to borrow ideas, practices, identity categories, as well as money from what Joseph Massad has termed the "Gay International" (2008). Furthermore, as homophobia and antigay legislation become the ground for international criticism, comprising what Tamar Shirinian has elsewhere called "the Illiberal East" (2020), it is now also something being discussed by states and suprastate structures as bases for foreign aid, sanctions, and militarization. Whether or not gay identity, or homophobia, were Western inventions brought into other sites or local indigenous forms has little to no impact on how they are now used by Western states, postcolonial states, and post-socialist states toward their own interested ends (Butterfield 2013; Hoad 2007). The queer political, in other words, is not merely (sub) cultural. It is political, it is economic, and it is historical.

Gay identity in the post-socialist worlds of Eastern Europe and Eurasia emerged both as a descriptor of desire and practice and as a prohibitor that defined the proper subject and placed limits on the possibilities of that subject. Homosexuality and homoeroticism were, even if perhaps forming thriving subcultures in imperial Russia or at least in some metropolitan centers and legalized in 1922 (Healy 2001), criminalized by the Soviet Union in 1934. This criminalization, of course, did not mean an end to homosexual or homoerotic practices in the Soviet Union or in other socialist spaces where they were not always criminalized (Buyantueva and Shevtsova 2020), but meant that there was little to no room for forming (visible) queer subcultures centered around homoeroticism. The end of the Soviet Union gave way for liberalizing sexual and reproductive politics that have now become what Robert Kulpa calls a "leveraged pedagogy," or a "didactic and cultural hegemonic relation of power, where [Central and Eastern Europe—CEE] figures as an object of Western/European pedagogy" and in which CEE is framed as never yet liberal enough and in a constant state not only of "post-communism" (recovering from a political-economic ailment of sorts) but also homophobia (2014, 432). This leveraged pedagogy acts as both a "condemnation, and also a promise of redemption, because of a geographical location and proximity to the self-proclaimed universality of West/Europe" (Kulpa 2014, 432). The specificities of the geopolitical dimensions of Eastern Europe and Eurasia, especially in its proximity as a kind of long-lost (to communism) sibling of Western Europe (Wedel 2001), complicates the politics of a colonizing global gay identity in these contexts. Eastern Europe and Eurasia are not necessarily the Other onto which the West projects its civilizing mission, but a space between the West and the East: not the First World, not the Third, but a middle Second in its relation to both the spatiality of the West (Buelow 2012) and the temporality (Mizielińska and Kulpa 2011) of economic development.

Leveraged pedagogy has produced internal stratifications within local worlds. Gay identity, or particular forms of activism centered around making

LGBT identities visible, perform not only a modern liberal and cosmopolitan sensibility but also come about through the displacement of other forms of social and political difference—for instance, ethnic and religious minority status (Woodcock 2011) or class interests (Rivkin-Fish 2013; Ghodsee 2004) in the post-socialist world. Furthermore, as these kinds of activist identifications are tied to the ability to engage in other languages—like English or other technical and professional languages (Ghodsee 2004)—they often also produce class differences between those who advocate and belong to an activist class and those who are seen as the objects of political action. These internal displacements and stratifications make up forms of discipline and civilizational missions *within* worlds rather than *between* worlds.

Grassroots movements have popularized critiques of liberal frameworks of queer politics that do not account for race, class, and geopolitics. If gay and lesbian, or LGBT, identity has become a global phenomenon, so have discourses that challenge the imperialism through which this has become possible. Most popular within these critiques is Jasbir Puar's now-canonical *Terrorist Assemblages* (2007), which urges queer thinkers and activists to consider the implications of how Western nationalism aligns with homonormativity by situating the United States (as well as Europe and Israel) as a site of sexual exceptionalism based on a rhetoric of freedom and tolerance. The political claim for LGBT persons to be included into normative frameworks of the nation, in other words, is also a demand to become part of imperialist projects in the name of that nation. Post-socialist nationalisms have not, however, taken up the ideological project of homonationalism and instead most often rely on what Kevin Moss refers to as "good old fashioned heteronationalism," producing discourses of homonationalism as a tenuous one within these contexts (2014, 215). As Roman Leksikov and Dafna Rachok have recently argued, the post-socialist world has little in common with the particular politics of the racialized settler-colonial contexts of the U.S. and Israel through which "homonationalism" emerged. This has not, however, stopped them from circulating as popular critique within activist circles in the post-socialist world (Leksikov and Rachok 2020). While we might point out the original meanings of these terms as applicable only to the militarized and expansionist contexts of imperializing and racializing settler-colonial worlds, and insist that the uses of these concepts be faithful to these particularities, we might also approach these varying uses as the ongoing queer nature of queer critique and open up room for its multiple valences, morphologies, and mutations.

These kinds of critiques—between homonationalism and heteronationalism or between homonationalism and what Leksikov and Rachok offer up as "homo-neoliberalism" (2020, 33)—in Central and Eastern Europe have split CEE nationalisms as well as queer activisms between those who desire

European interventions toward tolerance and others who oppose European intervention as an imperialist one that limits local sovereignty (Korolczuk and Graff 2018). Leftist activists condemn Western intervention, and thus their local LGBT activist compatriots, for their demands for recognition by Europe and for their reproduction of homonormativity and homonationalism. LGBT activists condemn leftists for their failure to critique their own nation's heteronationalist institutions and entities. But, as Leksikov has also pointed out elsewhere, the decolonizing impetus of queer critique, taken up by leftist actors in their local post-socialist scapes, might itself be seen as colonial (2017). These invaginating debates between global gay identity and global critique, has, thus, produced a quagmire that has limited the possibilities of effectual forms of collective decolonizing of queer performance, experience, and political practice.

BETWEEN OVERIDENTIFICATION AND DISIDENTIFICATION

It is, thus, clear that more nuanced forms of critique are called for. And the chapters in this volume offer that. Two frameworks in regard to identity and identification are useful here in order to situate these critiques and their political potentials. First is the notion of *overidentification* that Alexei Yurchak discusses in the context of late socialist political performance (2005), which has also been taken up by Dominic Boyer to think about late liberal performance (2013; Boyer and Yurchak 2010). The other is that of *disidentification* as offered by Jose Esteban Muñoz (1999), to think about the complexities of queer of color performances of identity.

According to Yurchak (2005), Stalin's authorship and its official ideology in the early years of the Soviet Union had great impact on the possibilities of political performance of everyday life in the late socialist period. After Stalin's death, political discourse was cemented into what Yurchak calls "authoritative discourse," discourse against which and outside of which it became impossible to speak and act, including for those who governed the system. But, this authoritative discourse, Yurchak points out, had two components: its performative dimension, in which certain utterances and certain practices had to be kept the same, and its constative dimension, or the meaning enacted by those performances. As such, while the performances were kept the same, throughout the decades after Stalin's death various new constative meanings were introduced, allowing for great transformation of everyday life and ideology even if acts and discourse remained performatively constant. One form of political praxis to which Yurchak draws our attention is *stiob,* a kind of parody of authority and authoritative discourse that relied on its overidentification rather than its critique. However, as practitioners of *stiob* overidentified—sometimes to the extent that it seemed even more genuine to authoritative discourse than authoritative discourse itself—they also called attention to the absurdities of official ideology and practice. The aesthetic of *stiob* "avoided any political or social concerns or straightforward affiliation with support or opposition of anything. . . . [T]hose who practiced it also considered any political positions 'uninteresting'" (Yurchak 2005, 251).

Stiob has also become an aesthetic of late liberalism and capitalism. As Boyer and Yurchak have argued, "American stiob is typified by a parodic overidentification with the predictable and repeatable forms of authoritative discourse (incl. phraseology, rhetorical structure, visual images, performative style) in which political and social issues are represented in media and political culture" in late liberalism and late capitalism (2010, 191). This is also true of other late liberal and capitalist contexts as well—such as Europe—where the overformalized and hypernormalized aesthetics of political discourse have become so cemented as to make it impossible to speak outside of its language (Boyer 2013). "The politics of opposition usually presupposes that resistance and critique are best served by challenging the language of authoritative discourse directly," but hypernormalization might be a feature of late liberalism that highlights "an investment in discursive form that is so constitutive of authoritative discourse in the first place that it cannot be described from within its own language" and, as such, demands other forms of critical intervention, including overidentification, or *stiob* (Boyer and Yurchak 2010, 212).

There are particular forms of authoritarian discourse emerging in the post–Cold War era with sexuality, in many ways, at their center. For instance, while global gay identity has been authoritarian in many ways for the last couple of decades—one set of ways in which we can understand sexuality that has become hegemonic—so has the rhetoric of how these systems of understanding sexuality are articulated by their proponents and opponents. While the United States and European nation-states speak in the overarching language of human rights, Russia and those countries aligned with it (especially as they form the Eurasian Economic Union) also speak a particular hypernormalized illiberal discourse. One side mandates human rights for all, and the other mandates anti-homosexual propaganda bills, all as if these two sides were in concert performance. What we also see, here, however, is that critiques of the liberal framework have also become authoritarian discourse. Within local contexts, as the performativity of liberal frameworks hold sway, the performative of their critiques also emerge. As Emily Channell-Justice tells us (this volume), "there must be an adherence to externally imposed norms of modernity in order to create the space for radical critiques of modernity, normativity, and sexuality."

If these are overdetermined and hypernormalized debates and discourses—performances that now travel from one context to another and demand speech and acts in their languages—then we can pay particular attention to their constative dimensions as sites in which these discourses offer critique through their overidentification. Ghassan Hage (2012) argues that anthropology has a particular affinity with radical politics as its form of critique engages experiences and practices of radical difference; at least, this was once anthropology's forte when the field was primarily invested in primitivist exploration. What would it mean, now, to look for cues for performances of queer and decolonizing practice on the very grassroots levels of post-socialist worlds as they might inform radical difference to what has become hypernormalized there and elsewhere? What would it mean to find alternative constative meanings to the performatives that look very much like, sometimes identical to, those in the West? In other words, what would a queer critique that emerged from the political, economic, and historical context of post-socialism look like if we looked within its overidentified similitude to the global to find its particular?

In regard to (sexual and gender) identity positions that seem "too saturated with injury or aggression," Butler suggests that "it may be that certain identifications and affiliations are made, certain sympathetic connections amplified, precisely in order to institute a *dis*identification with a position . . . , one that might, as a consequence, be occupiable only through imagining the loss of viable identity altogether" (1993: 100). It may also be the case, however, that for some bodies—those which are minoritized or marginalized by heteronormativity, white supremacy, and misogyny—identification emerges only as disidentification—as "identities-in-difference from a failed interpellation within the dominant public sphere" (Muñoz 1999, 7). For Muñoz, disidentification "resists an unproductive turn toward good dog/bad dog criticism and instead leads to an identification that is both mediated and immediate, a disidentification that enables politics" (1999, 9). Disidentification is about "recycling and rethinking encoded meaning" (1999, 31), a "shuffling back and forth between reception and production" (1999, 25), allowing us to rethink the processes through which the post-socialist queer subject both receives global notions of identity and participates in the cultural production of her own identificatory process as well as political critique. In this way, we might understand the post-socialist (geo)political scape as offering discourses that go beyond a politics that can only condemn homonationalist tendencies or only take them up in critique of LGBT identification processes. Disidentification allows us to understand how the desire for (perhaps normative) LGBT identification is, by virtue of being situated in and through heteronationalist claims, always oppositional and always the site of challenging the normative. Disidentification, like *stiob* or overidentification, offers us a third term through which to think the processes of identity-work (Muñoz 1999; Gray 2009) that make use of global hypernormalized discourses, but that always resist a total and full compliance and, furthermore, always provide critique of those discourses. While Yurchak and Boyer's work on overidentification makes possible a theoretical witnessing of how that which might look like identification is actually the emergence of speaking against a language from its inside, Muñoz offers possibilities of theoretical speculations toward queer futurity that emerge from the present quagmire that is, we discover in probing it, something else.

There are elements of what we might call overidentification, hypernormalization, and overformalization of liberal discourse, as well as the hypernormalization and overformalization of illiberal discourse running through all of these papers. In bringing to light these complexities of identity within post-socialist (geo)political worlds, these chapters also engender new ways of thinking performance and performativity with and through (dis)alliance with area studies. Dennis Altman suggests that

> if we abandon the idea that the model for the rest of the world—whether political, cultural, or intellectual—need be New York or Paris, and if we recognize the emerging possibilities for such models in Bangkok and Harare, we may indeed be able to speak of a "queer planet." We may even recognize the need to question whether Anglo-American queer theorists are saying much of relevance to the majority of people in the world who are developing a politics out of their shared sexuality in far more difficult conditions than those within which western lesbian and gay movements arose. (1997, 433)

More recently, Jasbir Puar and Maya Mikdashi—looking for a queer theory that emerges from the Middle East, for instance, rather than the United States—argue that

> different contexts have the potential to push conversations in queer theory in surprising directions precisely because they disturb the "taken for granted" background picture of queer theory as American studies. The relationship of area studies to queer theory is multiple, invigorating, and potentially groundbreaking—but only to the extent that both fields allow their archives, theoretical presumptions, key terms, and areas of inquiry to suffuse, confuse, and destabilize each other. (2016, 221)

Interrogating the performance and performativity of queer politics and experience in the post-socialist world, the chapters in this volume reach into actually existing local contexts, rather than outward to the global imaginary, for the constative meanings that are shaping and will shape the gendered and sexual sovereignties of Eastern Europe and Eurasia.

THE CHAPTERS

Picking out the nuances of the debates on globalization and queer politics and how they play out in local contexts give us some building blocks for the emergence of a particularly post-socialist queer theory not determined by the impulse of seemingly universalist discourses that have emerged from a now hypernormalized Euro-American queer theory and its debates. What would this debate look like entirely in the language and dialect of the performativity and constative meanings of decolonized queer politics of post-socialism? The chapters in this volume intend to give readers a place to begin such a conversation.

The first section, "The Categories Themselves," explores the translation of concepts that developed in Western, so-called "modern" societies, and which have of late been imposed on emerging post-Soviet queer communities. As David Valentine suggests in the article that lends its name to the section, categories such as "gender" and "sexuality" are never fixed or fluid, even in the contexts in which they were developed. The use of these terms as "experiential fact . . . becomes dangerous . . . in the reordering of experience through analytic categories seen to be transparent and natural," which works to "reproduce the invisibility and disenfranchisement of people who have had little voice, historically, in the debates and policies that have shaped their worlds" (2004, 219).

The chapters in this section do not only reinsert the voices of those marginalized groups, but they also bring the discussions of terminology to the forefront. Tjaša Kancler's chapter engages with the intersection of trans* theory and activism with decoloniality through an exploration of art projects in the (post) Yugoslav era. Their chapter pushes back against Western-dominated queer theory in academia and recenters a post-socialist, postcolonial dialogue to create new narratives around LGBT+ communities. Tamar Shirinian argues that LGBT+ identity production in Armenia is a queer process, despite the way Euro-American terms tend to be imposed for sexual and gender identity categories. She explores the production of a survey distribution by an LGBT+ advocacy organization in Yerevan and the conversations staff members had about the use of particular categories to include a diverse group of LGBT+-identified people in their data set. Finally, Syinat Sultanalieva delves into notions of "good" and "bad" girls in Kyrgyzstan, relating these to shame and family expectations. She argues that these categories are contingent on temporal and spatial contexts, shifting over time and incorporating queer women's self-perception.

Section 2, Queer in Public, explores instances in which queer communities take up the space they have long been denied, particularly in the post-socialist region. In her study of gay and lesbian experience in Russia, Laurie Essig (1999) notably established that acceptable spaces for public displays of queerness were limited; more recent researchers have tended to focus on the ways LGBT+ people demand to be present in public spaces and have negotiated for their rights and safety. Emily Channell-Justice uses the example of contentious Pride Parades in Kyiv, Ukraine, to consider leftist radical critiques of LGBT+ movements that are organized around demands for rights and recognition. Leftist activists' participation in Pride and their reflections of this experience show that they consider LGBT+ people in their frameworks for liberation while also questioning mainstream forms of gay rights activism. Feruza Aripova investigates the impact of anti-sodomy laws in Soviet Latvia from the 1960s to the 1980s. By using criminal files of men arrested for sodomy, the chapter considers how queer voices can be retrieved from the archives and how anti-sodomy laws influenced how gay men saw themselves in late socialism. Continuing in the legal realm, Roman Leksikov's chapter is a transnational consideration of LGBT+ activist discourse about police and penitentiaries in Ukraine and North America. Drawing from ethnographic research with LGBT+ victims of hate-motivated attacks in Ukraine, the chapter adds to broader themes of the politics of memory and national belonging.

The final section, Decolonizing Queer Performance, explores the ways that certain sites create spaces for new queer performances and performativities. Despite common assumptions of "backwardness" in the post-Soviet world (Kulpa 2014), the authors in this section find spaces for radical reconsideration of expected behaviors through folklore, music, and religion. Zhanar Sekerbayeva uses Kazakh folklore to find potential for gendered transgressions, arguing that Kazakh rejection of queer behaviors came with Russian colonialism rather than being an inherent trait of Kazakh life. The chapter explores how the stifling of these stories excluded not only queer narratives but also Kazakh particularity, which was often subsumed into Russian folklore studies. Kārlis Vērdiņš and Jānis Ozoliņš delve into the life stories of two queer performers in rural Latvia, arguing that queer identity production does not just happen in urban areas where activist movements are generally centered. Through interviews with both performers and a deep exploration of their work, the chapter argues that their artistic output allows these men to reclaim queer spaces by drawing on well-known pop cultural figures. Finally, Polina Kislitsyna's chapter argues that, despite dominant ideas about religion and LGBT+ communities being at odds with one another, Russian LGBT+ people have varied experiences and relationships with their religions. While some of the interviews and life histories show traumatic experiences with religion, others find empowerment and validation through religion, complicating both queer studies and religious studies.

Together, the chapters in this volume provide a unique look at the lives, experiences, and performances of LGBT+ people and communities in the post-socialist world. They draw from ethnographic research, interviews, life histories, artistic analysis, and archives, showing that LGBT+ studies are deeply enhanced with these critical methodologies. And, as stated earlier, this is not a purely academic conversation, but has implications for the daily lives of LGBT+ people in the countries represented in this volume and beyond. The goal of decolonizing queer studies cannot be accomplished with one volume, but is a project that must be taken seriously as the field of post-socialist LGBT+ research expands.

REFERENCES

Altman, Dennis. 1997. "Global Gaze/Global Gays." *GLQ: A Journal of Lesbian and Gay Studies* 3(4):417–436.

Boellstorff, Tom. 2005. *The Gay Archipelago: Sexuality and Nation in Indonesia.* Princeton, NJ: Princeton University Press.

———. 2007. "Queer Studies in the House of Anthropology." *Annual Review of Anthropology* 36:1–19.

———. 2011. "But Do Not Identify as Gay: A Proleptic Genealogy of the MSM Category." *Cultural Anthropology* 26(2):287–312.

Boyer, Dominic. 2013. "Simply the Best: Parody and Political Sincerity in Iceland." *American Ethnologist* 40(2):276–287.

Boyer, Dominic, and Alexei Yurchak. 2010. "American Stiob: Or, What Late-Socialist Aesthetics of Parody Reveal About Contemporary Political Culture in the West." *Cultural Anthropology* 25(2):179–221.

Buelow, Samuel. 2012. "Locating Kazakhstan: The Role of LGBT Voices in the Asia/Europe Debate." *lamda nordica* 4:99–125.

Butler, Judith. 1993. *Bodies That Matter: On the Discursive Limits of "Sex."* New York: Routledge.

Butterfield, Nicole. 2013. "Sexual Rights as a Tool for Mapping Europe: Discourses of Human Rights and European Identity in Activists' Struggles in Croatia." In *Queer Visibility in Post-Socialist Cultures*, edited by Narcisz Fejes and Andrea P. Balogh Fejes, 12–33. Chicago: Intellect.

Buyantueva, Radzhana, and Maryna Shevtsova. 2020. "Introduction: LGBTQ+ Activism and the Power of Locals." In *LGBT+ Activism in Central and Eastern Europe*, edited by Radzhana Buyantueva and Maryna Shevtsova, 1–19. London: Palgrave Macmillan.

Deleuze, Gilles, and Felix Guattari. 1987. *A Thousand Plateaus: Capitalism and Schizophrenia.* Translated by Brian Massumi. Minneapolis: University of Minnesota Press.

Essig, Laurie. 1999. *Queer in Russia: A Story of Sex, Self, and the Other.* Durham, NC: Duke University Press.

Foucault, Michel. 1978. *The History of Sexuality*, Vol. 1. New York: Vintage Books.

Ghodsee, Kristen. 2004. "Feminism-by-Design: Emerging Capitalisms, Cultural Feminism, and Women's Nongovernmental Organizations in Post-socialist Eastern Europe." *Signs* 29(3):727–753.

Gopinath, Gayatri. 2005. *Impossible Desires: Queer Diasporas and South Asian Public Culture.* Durham, NC: Duke University Press.

———. 2018. "Unruly Visions: The Aesthetic Practices of Queer Diaspora." In *Perverse Modernities*, edited by Jack Halberstam and Lisa Lowe. Durham, NC: Duke University Press.

Gray, Mary L. 2009. *Out in the Country: Youth Media, and Queer Visibility in Rural America.* New York: NYU Press.

Hage, Ghassan. 2012. "Critical Anthropological Thought and the Radical Political Imaginary Today." *Critique of Anthropology* 32(3):285–308.

Healy, Dan. 2001. *Homosexual Desire in Revolutionary Russia.* Chicago: The University of Chicago Press.

Hoad, Neville. 2007. *African Intimacies: Race, Homosexuality, and Globalization.* Minneapolis: University of Minnesota Press.

Korolczuk, Elzbieta, and Agnieszka Graff. 2018. "Gender as 'Ebola from Brussels': The Anticolonial Frame and the Rise of Illiberal Populism." *Signs* 43(4):797–821.

Kulpa, Robert. 2014. "Western *Leveraged Pedagogy* of Central and Eastern Europe: Discourses of Homophobia, Tolerance, and Nationhood." *Gender, Place & Culture* 21(4):431–448.

Leksikov, Roman. 2017. "Post-Soviet Queer as the Colonial Theory and Practice." *Actual Problems in Sociology, Psychology, and Pedagogy* 33(2):5–14.

Leksikov, Roman, and Dafna Rachok. 2020. "Beyond Western Theories: On the Use and Abuse of 'Homonationalism' in Eastern Europe." In *LGBTQ+ Activism in Central and Eastern Europe*, edited by Radzhana Buyantueva and Maryna Shevtsova, 25–49. London: Palgrave Macmillan.

Manalansan, Martin. 2003. *Global Divas: Filipino Gay Men in the Diaspora.* Durham, NC: Duke University Press.

Massad, Joseph. 2008. *Desiring Arabs.* Chicago: University of Chicago Press.

Mbembe, Achille. 1992. "The Banality of Power and the Aesthetics of Vulgarity in the Postcolony." *Public Culture* 4(2):1–30.

Mikdashi, Maya, and Jasbir K. Puar. 2016. "Queer Theory and Permanent War." *GLQ: A Journal of Lesbian and Gay Studies* 22(2):215–222.

Mizielinska, Joanna, and Robert Kulpa. 2011. "'Contemporary Peripheries': Queer Studies, Circulation of Knowledge and East/West Divide." In *De-Centering Western Sexualities: Central and Eastern European Perspectives*, edited by Joanna Mizielińska and Robert Kulpa. London: Routledge.

Moss, Kevin. 2014. "Split Europe: Homonationalism and Homophobia in Croatia." In *LGBT Activism and the Making of Europe: A Rainbow Europe*, edited by Philip M. Ayoub and David Paternotte. New York: Palgrave Macmillan.

Muñoz, Jose Esteban. 1999. *Disidentifications: Queers of Color and the Performance of Politics*. Minneapolis: University of Minnesota Press.

Puar, Jasbir. 2007. *Terrorist Assemblages: Homonationalism in Queer Times*. Durham, NC: Duke University Press.

Rivkin-Fish. 2013. "Conceptualizing Feminist Strategies for Russian Reproductive Politics: Abortion, Surrogate Motherhood, and Family Support after Socialism." *Signs* 38(3):569–593.

Rofel, Lisa. 2007. "Desiring China." In *Perverse Modernities*, edited by Judith Halberstam and Lisa Lowe. Durham, NC: Duke University Press.

Shirinian, Tamar. 2020. "The Illiberal East: The Gender and Sexuality of the Imagined Geography of Eurasia in Armenia." *Gender, Place & Culture*.

Valentine, David. 2004. "The Categories Themselves." *GLQ* 10(2):215–220.

Wedel, Janine. 2001. *Collision and Collusion: The Strange Case of Western Aid to Eastern Europe*. New York: St. Martin's Griffin.

Woodcock, Shannon. 2011. "A Short History of the Queer Time of 'Post-Socialist' Romania, or Are We There Yet? Let's Ask Madonna!" In *De-Centering Western Sexualities: Central and Eastern European Perspectives*, edited by Joanna Mizielińska and Robert Kulpa. London: Routledge.

Yurchak, Alexei. 2005. *Everything Was Forever, Until It Was No More: The Last Soviet Generation*. Princeton, NJ: Princeton University Press.

Section I

THE CATEGORIES THEMSELVES

Chapter 1

Body Politics, Trans* Imaginary, and Decoloniality

Tjaša Kancler

Concerning our work in Eurocentric academia, to rethink trans* politics and activism in relation to decoloniality, I focus this text on body politics, knowledge production, and trans* imaginary in the context of crisis. This asks also for an analysis of the post–Cold War reconfiguration and multiplication of European borders, as my intention here is to shift the geography of reason, point to counter-genealogies of thought and to decolonial practices of resistance. As a not quite white,[1] not quite trans*[2] former Eastern European (from former Yugoslavia, Slovenia), I understand my position through a constant state of transition, dwelling in the border, in a liminal space, which necessarily means taking an un-disciplinary approach in the search for decolonial lines of flight, modulations, interferences, and ruptures, that continuously morph the grid, its point system, coordinates, pre-established channels and threads, moving in new directions. Seeking to disrupt totalization and relativism, two sides of the same coin of "objectivity," I want to understand embodiment, partial perspective, and location through entangled connections as the possibility for dissident research, ways of envisioning transformation, and radical social change. This means engaging with decolonial critique in relation to the processes of colonial capitalist divisions and differentiation, when speaking about the coloniality of gender, as well as the global imposition of Western Eurocentric feminist, queer, and transgender knowledge.

BODY POLITICS

Let me begin with one critical aspect of Transgender Studies and trans* politics—characterized from the 1990s by debate and contestation over methods, theory, identity, and the very boundaries of the category itself and its meaning in different contexts—tracing the Western genealogy of "transgender" as a category (V. Prince, H. Boswell, L. Feinberg, S. Stone). Here we should recall the question posed by David Valentine: "How and to what effect is this concept deployed; and what does it do ?" (2007, 30). This might help us to reconsider the consequences of its rapid expansion in a wide range of contexts, to reflect on the ways in which it can function as a mechanism for surveillance and control, as a "neutrally" descriptive technical term, or on its potentials for resistance or liberation. To move into the sphere of the political where race, class, sexuality, ability, spirituality, geographical location, and so on figure into the naming of people as transgender or trans*, a strong interest lies in studying how this category is productive of the very experience it seems to describe, regulating and organizing bodies in a particular bio-necropolitical recognition framework, as well as decolonial potentialities for resistance.

From the 1990s on, in the emerging field of Transgender Studies, trans* scholars contribute from diverse theoretical backgrounds with a heterogeneous set of methodological positions, self-reflexive insights, and creative interpretations of the meaning of embodiment. Despite the significant enthusiasm that fuelled the making of Transgender Studies, as Howard Chiang writes in the introduction of his book *Transgender China* (2012), they have been confined mainly to North American and European (mainly Anglo-American) academic circles, oriented toward exploring and challenging categorizations, the gender binary system, the use of transgender people as objects within medicine, psychiatry, law, as well as the conflictive relations with feminism (Stone 1991).

Without negating the importance of these experiences along with their theoretical and political contributions, my aim is rather to question their application as a "universal" set of references with the development of Transgender Studies, without problematizing the ways in which they conceal or lack intersectional critical perspectives and practices. Furthermore, in their introduction to *The Transgender Studies Reader*, Susan Stryker and Stephen Whittle stress:

> We were struck by the overwhelming (and generally unmarked) whiteness of practitioners in the academic field of Transgender Studies. This is due, no doubt, to the many forms of discrimination that keep many people of color from working in the relatively privileged environment of academe, but also to the uneven distribution and reception of the term "transgender" across different racial, ethnic, linguistic, and socioeconomic communities. (2006, 15)

These concerns demand, as Mauro Cabral (2014) writes, that we examine the transnational circulation of Transgender as a *corpus*; a certain number of texts and theories, names and definitions, statistics, analysis, images, and interpretations. A circulation that also labors in the politics of archive and preserving/erasing of knowledge, which opens many challenges, as Stryker (2006) argues, of how to reread the immense body of clinical, juridical, and ethnographic work that documents European perspectives on cultures subjected around the world through exploration, trade, conquest, and colonization. According to Cabral, the production of trans* knowledge and imaginary is heavily determined by geopolitics in a violent capitalist colonial landscape, and many people still circulate across the transnational routes of the industrial-academic complex, reified as the objects of colonial knowledge. Thus, following Tlostanova, "we have to question the Western monopoly of knowledge, the very methodology of applying a ready-made travelling theories created in the West, even if by the ex colonial others and those who chose to wear this mask, to the rest of the world with its multiplicity of local histories and trajectories of relations" (2013).

Thinking about the processes of the construction of genealogies, the ways in which the "origin" is being instituted, the production of knowledge, our vocabulary (language) and imaginary, the analytical frames we draw in order to understand what "transgender" does, and how we can disrupt the capitalist colonial processes of differentiation, hierarchization, exclusion, and death, is crucial for our debate around articulation, organization, and embodiment of trans* politics.

Here I would like to stress four points:

transgender as a noun

1. Neoliberalism: We should not forget that in the very moment in which "transgender" is being institutionalized, there is a rise and expansion of neoliberalism on a global scale after the fall of the Berlin Wall in 1989—a reconfiguration and multiplication of borders. In the Western context, as Valentine claims, this means a broader change in understanding the body and embodied identities, which are being shaped "by shifts in neoliberal capitalist modes of production and consumption where 'difference' can be exploited as a market niche as much as enabling new forms of subjectivity" (2007, 36). In her book *On Being Included: Racism and Diversity in Institutional Life*, Sara Ahmed (2012) argues that feminists of color have already explored the relationship between diversity and power by showing how diversity is incorporated by institutions and becomes a way of managing or containing conflict or dissent. Hence, we should be deeply concerned by the circulation of "transgender" as a new commodity in both theory and practice, as well as with a question of the political economy of knowledge production that frames Euro-America as the center of discourse

about gender and sexual diversity, while capitalizing on racial and cultural difference. These transformations also point to the articulation of a set of new micro prosthesis devices for the control of subjectivity, as Paul B. Preciado (2013) writes, with molecular biological techniques and media networks. As he states, we are facing a new kind of capitalism that is hot, psychotropic, and punk, but we should add: in the "zones of being," while cold, bureaucratic, necrotoxic, and heavy metal in the "zones of non-being" (Fanon 1963).

2. Trans liberalism: While in the public discourse, as Nat Raha (2015) argues, the visibility of trans* issues is increasing with positive media representations and trans celebrities, intertwined with demands for depathologization and transgender legal rights (such as legal gender recognition, employment rights, rights for trans-related healthcare, marriage rights, etc.), the differentiation of livable trans* and gender non-conforming lives along the line of race/ethnicity, class, gender, dis/ability, and migration status remains firmly and increasingly in place. Thus, we have to pay attention to the ways in which transgender liberal politics or "trans liberalism" is inscribed within or fits into neoliberal globalization, and to its complicity with global colonial capitalist restructuring, continuous production of new methods of (border) control, shifting from one group to another in legitimizing liberal multiculturalism/processes of racialization and labor exploitation.

transgender as an adjective

In this context, we should return to Leslie Feinberg's text, "Transgender Liberation: A Movement Whose Time has Come," published in 1992, which, as Valentine points out, explicitly politicized transgender identification beyond individual radical acts and called for a political alliance between the oppressed by gender norms and a social movement organized around its terms. In Feinberg's usage, "transgender" came to mean an adjective rather than a noun, a term for an imagined community of transsexuals, drag queens, butches, crossdressers, masculine women, effeminate men, sissies, tomboys, or anybody who felt interpellated by this call for mobilization and banding together in a struggle for social, political, and economic justice. While Feinberg's call was not a liberal one (he said: "Remember me as a revolutionary communist!"), and the word "transgender" took on its meaning at that moment; what has happened? Why it has gradually moved toward a socially reformist trans rights agenda, reproducing inclusion/exclusion by dividing trans* and gender non-conforming populations along material hierarchies of race, class, dis/ability, spirituality, and migration status?

trans* as a verb—decoloniality as a verb, meaning doing, taking action

3. Transfeminism: Regarding Feinberg's and Stone's work, but also previously in relation to Sylvia Rivera and Marsha P. Johnson's activism from the 1960s on, we have to emphasize further that a progressively institutionalized and collective usage of the term "transgender" has important and conflicting relations with the history of feminist, gay, and lesbian movements, which in the 1990s brought about the term "transfeminism," introduced by Diana Couvant and Emy Koyama, first at Yale University and after in Koyama's "Transfeminist Manifesto." They spoke about transfeminism as a movement for and by trans women who understand their liberation entangled with women's liberation and beyond. These references and their introduction into the Russian context are being discussed at the present moment by trans* activist Yana Sitnikova in her texts, "Transgender activism in Russia" (2014) and "The Emergence of Transfeminism in Russia" (2016).

In the Spanish context, the term transfeminism first appeared in the text "Women or trans? The insertion of transsexuals into feminist movement" (2016), written by Kim Pérez F.-Figares, the former president of the Gender Identity Association of Andalusia. From 2006, the activist group Guerrilla Travolaka and other autonomous trans* and feminists pushed for a pro-depathologization movement as a political project based on transmarikabollo feminist radical critique and struggles. The activists challenged the problems in feminism in relation to trans issues, and the trans movement in relation to feminism, in order to make trans* demands for depathologization a common issue. Understanding sex and gender in the sense of technological interventions (technologies of gender), Preciado introduced the term "technogender," stating that "man" and "woman" exist as a social norm that is maintained by means of control: pharmacological and audiovisual techniques that constantly distort the reality that surrounds us. As he claims, "sex," "heterosexuality," and "race" are three violent somatic fictions, produced by the Western capitalist colonial system and which continue to persist nowadays (2008). During the State Feminist Conference in Granada in 2009, "Manifesto for a Transfeminist Insurrection" was written collectively to expose the problems of binary thinking and reduction of feminist struggle to abortion rights, sexism, violence, precarity, and access to the labor market. In order to broaden the scope of issues, as Miriam Solá (2013) writes, pornography, sex work, depathologization of transsexuality, HIV, critique of institutional feminism, mercantilization, and depoliticization of LGBT movement, immigration laws and regulations, transmigrations, and so on took place in further debates. Thus, transfeminism that arises after queer critique and activism, which was at that moment exposed to the accelerated process of mercantilization and recodification by dominant discourses and losing its political potential, became the position of those who experiment with multiplicity by deconstructing the political fiction of the binary categories man/woman, while stressing the fact that our common basis of oppression remains capitalism and heteropatriarchy.

In relation to coloniality, the potentials of "sudaca/euraca/norteca transfeminism," to use Sayak Valencia's expression, are being discussed in the Latin American context, pointing to another genealogy, where, as Valencia emphasizes, four lines cross: "US women of color third world feminism (by Black, Chicanas, Native American and Asian American feminists); sexual dissidence and its geopolitical displacement to South: from Queer to Cuir; movement for depathologization of trans identities (Stop Trans Pathologization) and pro-puta movement for de-stigmatization and legalization of sex work; minoritized becomings, migrations and economic precarity" (2014).

Throughout these years, transfeminism and trans* activism are questioned by decolonial critique, which places its focus of analysis on the coloniality of gender. Many theoreticians, artists, and activists articulate their interventions through historic relations with Black, indigenous, women of color feminisms as well as queer of color critique to continuously expose the reproduction of Eurocentrism and racism by marginalizing the concerns around racialization processes, which are actually central to the colonial capitalist gender system and its logics of oppression. Rethinking the potentials in relation to becoming a migrant and relational movements, in which many different practices, voices and discourses, embodiments and mobilities are inscribed, brings us to decolonial turn and positionality.

4. Decolonial (erotic) turn: After the fall of the Berlin Wall in 1989, Aníbal Quijano, one of the founding members of the research group Modernity/Coloniality/Decoloniality, formed in the 1990s in the Latin American context and beyond, introduced a new concept named coloniality, being the indispensable underside of modernity from the sixteenth century on. Quijano has defined it as a matrix of power, which operates through four interrelated domains: the control of economy, the control of authority, the control of gender and sexuality, and the control of subjectivity and knowledge (see Mignolo 2008). If the critique of capitalism from the Eurocentric point of view privileges economic relations over others, without negating the incessant accumulation of capital on global scale, Quijano conceptualized the intersectionality of multiple, heterogeneous, global hierarchies and forms of domination and exploitation: racial, sexual, political, economic, spiritual, and linguistic, where the racial/ethnic hierarchy reconfigures transversally all global structures of power. Emphasizing its structural, constitutive, and not derivative relations, by claiming intersectionality, these are analytical methods introduced previously by Black

feminists (Combahee River Collective, Kimberle Crenshaw, Audre Lorde, Patricia Hill Collins, among others) and developed further by and with feminists of color (Chela Sandoval, Chandra Mohanty, Gloria Anzaldúa, Cherrie Moraga, etc.) to point to their historical, theoretical, and practical exclusions, and take action.

From that moment on, the intersectional method is placed in relation to the concept of coloniality, which makes us understand, as Tlostanova argues, how the West determined one single norm of humanity, the legitimate knowledge of economic and social systems, spatial and temporal models, values, and cultural norms. Taking into the analysis the body-political aspects of control we see that coloniality has as its central element the idea of classifying humankind and the ontological marginalization of non-Western and not quite Western people. Therefore, a decolonial (erotic) turn with its ongoing attempt to push for a conceptual denaturalization, aims at undermining the fundamental logics of modernity and its disciplines, in need of an assertion of rights (also epistemic and visual) of the wretched (Fanon 1963). Based on continuous re-elaboration of counter-genealogies of dissident embodiments by minoritized positions, excluded from white, Western feminist and LGTBIQ+ movement, decoloniality as a political intervention—having in mind its performative potential, meaning doing or taking action—is thus a radical attempt to de-universalize, de-naturalize, and dismantle capitalist/colonial material and affective hierarchies, political, institutional, and border structures operating globally today. As the artistic-activist group Diásporas Críticas (2014) claim, we need to grasp it as tactics "that traverse materiality and writing, memory and archive, affect and body."

SITUATING POSTSOCIALISM

Pointing to the geopolitical and body-political aspects of the organization of European space, Kwame Nimako and Marina Gržinić expose the following thesis in their conversation, during the workshop "Education, Development, Freedom" at Duke University (Durham, United States), organized by the Centre for Global Studies in February 2010, and filmed for the video Naked Freedom (Image 1.1).

Kwame Nimako:

"We are here (in EU) because you were there (in Africa!)"

Marina Gržinić:

"We are here (in EU) because you want to go there (in Eastern Europe!)"

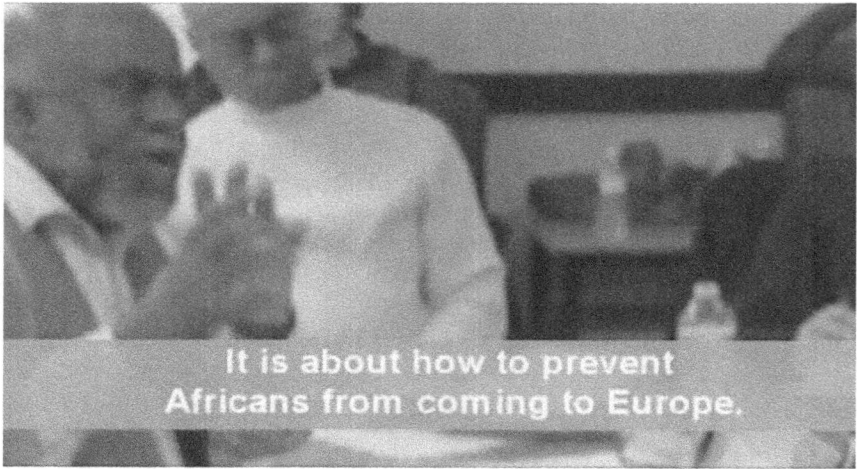

Image 1.1 Conversation between Kwame Nimako and Marina Gržinić. "Naked Freedom," Video by Marina Gržinić and Aina Šmid, 2010, Videoframe, http://grzinic-smid.si/?p=413.

This is developed further around two important questions to take into consideration. As Nimako emphasizes, after the fall of the Berlin Wall, the former Eastern Europe was subjected to the process of political reorganization, integration, and subordination to the Western model and servitude; this consisted of re-implementing directives and legislation already active in the EU. We can call such relations, following Gržinić (2009), the relation of repetition. It is a repetition of Western Europe's political and economic model, of its structures of government and governmentality, its modes of life and modes of death, the institutional and migration control, its system of knowledge (theory) and aesthetic regimes (art), activism, and so on. This specific process of coloniality through repetition is also functioning through a suppression of "local" histories, knowledge, and practices of resistance. Likewise, while Western Europe is also naming itself "former," it seems that it does not have to be conscious or responsible for its historic and contemporary colonial and fascist regimes of power. Moreover, by claiming the division West/East "obsolete" after the fall of the Berlin Wall, the division Occident/Orient is escalating. As Gayatri Spivak explains, "Terror in this guise is not a monopoly of some Muslim fundamentalists. It is the preserve of whatever entity—including our democracies—convinced that its enemy is by definition the enemy of 'humanity,' 'civilization,' even 'God' himself—a theological enemy" (2007, 169).

The second issue Nimako points out is the process of zonification. We can say that the European politics of apartheid transformed the former Eastern

Europe into a border-zone in the way that the territory of former socialist countries functions as a buffer zone to control and block migrations from Africa and Asia, while migrants from former Eastern countries are at the same time subjected to control, discrimination (employment), and processes of deportation from the "former" Western Europe.

In such a framework of analysis, if postsocialism is not at all postcolonial, this means that we have to modify the basis of our analysis and its paradigms, conceptualizing the entanglement of modernity, colonialism, and capitalism in order to understand the East in a condition of coloniality in relation to the West. As Neda Atanasoski argues, "What is crucial here is that if postsocialism is relegated to periodizing a particular moment of regional transition that at once affirms the death of socialism and consigns it to an ideological formation inferior to Western modernity and universality, it particularizes what is actually a global condition in which the West situates the universal claims of human rights, freedom, democracy, that underwrite its global violence" (2013, 26). This implies as well taking into account the imitation of Western modernity by the East, with racism in its core.

It is within these processes, where the colonial history of European colorblindness is inscribed, though the concept "race" has its geographic and intellectual origin in Europe. While racism is silenced or presented as a marginal problem we have to emphasize that racialization is the main logic of global capitalism/coloniality, which regulates and differentiates the social, political, and economic space (see Goldberg 2009; El-Tayeb 2011; Gržinić and Tatlić 2012). These brutal processes of selection of migrants, in terms of racial, class, gender, sexual, religious categories, construct us as differentiated subhuman(s) through different processes of dehumanization (see Gržinić 2015).

The countries of the former Eastern Europe, which became subsidiary States, perepherialized in their servile relation to EU politics, show on the one hand, contempt toward "those below them" in processes of constant hierarchization, and on the other, intensified servitude toward European colonial/imperial centers. Ethno-nationalism and differentiation with labor division on a global scale are today presented as "liberation" from what was suppressed during decades of communism/socialism. To ethno-national constructions, European abstract universalism as a form of "new cosmopolitanism" is being counterposed. Correspondingly, what we are witnessing in the current context of old-new forms of European migration politics and re-launching of Western hegemony (supremacy) is also, referring to Jin Haritaworn, how "the sign of diversity moves from the racialized body, (who becomes the 'migrant homophobe') to the sexualized one (who becomes the 'injured homosexual' in need of protection from the 'migrant homophobe')" (2012, 138). While the "former" Western Europe, its politics of racialization and discrimination now integrate within its borders those "Other(s)" who were discriminated in the past (women, LGTBIQ+ . . .), and who in many contexts continue living without the full recognition of their rights, as Gržinić (2015) argues, it produces at the same time its nonwhite population, migrants, refugees, LGTBIQ+ of color, as "Other(s)" (see also Dietze 2012).

To challenge the colonial formulation of gender classification, Maria Lugones's (2008, 2010) work is crucial here. On the one hand, she developed a critique of Quijano's understanding of sex as biological, of his failure to see that within the concept of gender the idea of sexual or biological dimorphism (man-woman dichotomy), heteronormativity and the patriarchal distribution of power are inscribed. On the other hand, her analysis of gender within coloniality poses important challenges for transfeminism and trans* activism by revealing that Eurocentrism and racism are embedded in the universal notions of the gender binary system. Along these lines she exposes how gender and sexual diversity are filtered through a colonizing binary gaze and presented as naturalized ideas of "sex" and "gender," both operating as Eurocentric categories. Lugones's main claim is that sexual difference, which is itself a colonial invention (fiction), is not socialized as such. The enslaved and racialized workers, as she states, were bestialized. The concept of gender does not pick them up as men and women in a Western sense, negating their humanity and gender, while erasing the fact that in many societies and locales, before Western colonization, such categorization did not exist, or categories of seniority, professional, and other principles were more important than biologized gender. Instead, as she writes, we must understand its meaning within the particular cosmology/metaphysics. These are important statements because the traces of those histories of removal and dispossession remain, as do their entanglements in global sexual and gender politics today. As Yuderkys Espinosa, Diana Gómez, and Karina Ochoa (2014) argue, through such analysis, the reach of her postulates is entangled with today's re-empowered critique and work already previously developed by counter-hegemonic, anti-racist feminisms, which at the same time have an important influence on the development of the decolonial option.

What we learn from all of the above-mentioned theoretical and activist contributions is that by shifting the geography of reason and disrupting the Western progressive narrative, we see that it is the European colonial expansion which started with conquest of America in fifteenth century, the one that progressively introduced the first regulations and punishment laws, prohibition of homosexuality and multiplicity of gender expressions, and deployed gender and sexuality as technologies to categorize colonized subjects, as well as organize their removal, re-education or genocides. Thus, in decolonial discourses, the coloniality of gender—the assumption that the whole world must operate according to modern/colonial gender binary model—is constantly being questioned and deconstructed.

If we situate the "postcolonial" and postsocialist dialogues within this context, we have to take into account the specific features of the coloniality of gender, as Tlostanova writes, due to the erasure of socialist gender trajectories and the pre-socialist "local" genealogies of women's and feminist struggles, as well as the multiplicity of gender expressions and dissident sexual experiences. This is related to the intensified imposition after 1989 of Western feminism and queer theory as a new kind of mind-colonization, to use Tlostanova's words, supported by grants and accompanied by particular ideological demands, but also to difficulties in the proper production of transfeminist knowledge and articulation of struggles from decolonial positionality, which would take into account a specific pre, post and socialist experiences. Relatively scarce or entirely missing from the analysis is a sustained critical engagement with gender dissident practices, embodiment, history, and culture in the former East, with the ability to capture the systems of knowledge and experiences that exceed the categorizations of gender, sexuality, and even transgender. While such discourse is yet poorly or not at all conceptualized, our condition should be regarded, as Tlostanova (2013) argues, in its complexity and dynamics with today's dispersion of former socialist subjects in different directions. Many of us are migrants, crossing multiple body-political and geopolitical borders while being displaced from our countries due to a number of factors—colonial/imperial wars, homotransphobia, poverty, and so on. Thus, it is necessary also to interrupt the existing conceptual frameworks from trans* migration experiences, becoming and movements, while interrogating the complicity of our feminist and LGTBIQ+ struggles in the very oppressions they claim to oppose. This means asking at the same time how we might better engage materially with dismantling white supremacy, colonization, and capitalism in all their forms. In reference to Chiang (2012), this also implies insisting on a radical approach to developing analysis by leaving behind Western-derived meanings of sex-gender altogether or at least problematizing them.

By creating new codes in the act of re-existence, decolonial subjects question and intervene continuously into modern/colonial logics of naming and categorization, resisting, creatively appropriating, translating, transforming, and critically redeploying the concepts by making a cut in the knowledge production flow and fight against colonial violence.

TRANS* IMAGINARY AS DECOLONIAL POLITICS

To the extent to which the body as a culturally intelligible construct, and the modern/colonial techniques in and through which bodies are positioned and transformed are in fact inextricably related, we have to discuss as well its relations with the visual—with the production of images and trans* imaginary.

Entangled in the colonial/capitalist system in order to stimulate desire and reconfigure the everyday, physical, political, and sensible conditions of embodiment, they shape subjectivities for the hypermachine of capitalist production. Achille Mbembe defines this phenomenon "image capitalism" (2013), and we can also call it, referring to Joaquín Barriendos, "the coloniality of seeing" (2010). In this sense, the production of trans*imaginary in opposition to the mainstream (also transgender) visual codes has to challenge the colonial binary gender system, conceptualizing political interventions from multiple local interrelated positionalities, with the aim of disrupting the logics of colonial visual orders, to make visible beyond what we already see. Directing critical attention toward the questions of embodiment, positionality, and the visual means taking into consideration a much more complex system of colonial power relations that also point to the need to break down the body politics in a molar sense (a whole, integrated body with one identity), in the name of multiplicity, affect and sensibility, its resistant and transformative political potentials.

To think about (post)socialist Eastern Europe, and more specifically former Yugoslavia, and the Balkans today, by taking into account a decolonial history and present critique and struggles, I want to recall the "Transvestite Museum of Peru" (2003–2013), a project developed by philosopher and drag activist Giuseppe Campuzano, on the one hand, and "East Art Map" (1999-2005), a project and a book edited by the group IRWIN to (re)construct the history of contemporary art in Eastern Europe, on the other. These references are important to think about gaps and the potentials for re-reading postsocialist space by making gender and sexual dissident practices interrelated with processes of racialization a central political question for any construction of history and articulation of our struggles against the logics of coloniality.

Given the context described above, I turn my attention to the theoretical, artistic, and activist work done during the last three decades in the context of former Yugoslavia, by Marina Gržinić and Aina Šmid, first as a members of the group Borders of Control N.4. The artists produced one of the first videos in the former East during socialism, entitled "Icons of Glamour, Echoes of Death" (1982) (Image 1.2) and "The Threat of the Future" (1983), in which they present and dramatize conceptually and politically the institution of masculinity, through lesbian politics, feminist relations, and drag practice. Staging a performance in front of the camera, they speak about sexual and gender politics, pleasure, sadomasochism and pornography. Gržinić further developed theoretical research on dissident feminist practices, artistic performances and spaces in her texts, "Former Yugoslavia, Queer and Class Struggle" (2008), "Europe: Gender, Class, Race" (2012) and "Dissident feminisms, anti-racist politics and artistic interventionist practices" (2014). With her work, she continuously questions the processes of racialization, class divisions, and labor conditions, as well as the construction of feminist genealogy, by articulating a different history of feminism seen from the former Eastern Europe.

Image 1.2 "Icons of Glamour, Echoes of Death," Borders of Control N.4, 1982, Videoframe, http://grzinic-smid.si/?p=170.

In their video "Relations: 25 Years of the Lesbian Group ŠKUC-LL" (2012) (Image 1.3), Gržinić and Šmid elaborate a testimony of the counter-power of lesbian movement and its struggles for visibility and emancipation. From the dissolution of socialism at the end of the 1980s, through war and transition in the 1990s, up to the present time of global capitalism, the video brings together critical discourses, artistic potentialities and interventions in relation to politics, economy, law, culture, arts, and institutions. Since the 1980s, ŠKUC-LL and its founding members Nataša Sukič, Susana Tratnik, Tatjana Greif, and Nataša Velikonja (2012) produced the most important analysis and political interventions in the form of texts, books, performances, events, actions, and manifestations, redefining the very point of struggle(s) against discrimination in Slovenia, as well as locating the memory for our future. The need for a persistent redefinition of the subject of the feminist movement in Slovenia expressed itself first as a political lesbian stance. As stated by Gržinić in the radio program "Lezbomanija" (September 2011), which was hosted by Nataša Sukič and recently passed over to Urška Sterle on Radio Študent Ljubljana: "Before being feminist, we were lesbians." Lesbians that took the position through a rereading of history, language, and performativity developed a sharp critique of Western activism, as well as established alliances across (post-)Yugoslav space, not only among lesbian activists but also with other minoritarized groups.

Image 1.3 "Relations: 25 Years of the Lesbian Group ŠKUC-LL," by Marina Gržinić, Aina Šmid, and Zvonka T. Simčič, 2012, videoframe, http://grzinic-smid.si/?p=276.

Image 1.4 "The Caravan of the Erased," a Documentary Film by Dražena Perić, 2007, Videoframe, https://archive.org/details/Karavana_izbrisanih_-_The_Caravan_of_the_Erased.

In 2007, Dražena Perić's documentary "The Caravan of the Erased" (Image 1.4), among other publications, documents, and an ongoing self-organized struggle by the Erased since the 1990s, is showing that the most illegal is the State itself, its repressive apparatuses and collaborationists, which is exposed in Slovenia paradigmatically through the erasure, the continuity of expulsion and discrimination of migrants, refugees, LGBTQI+ and sex workers. Slovenia was constituted as a sovereign racist State on the basis of the erasure of more than 20,000 Yugoslav citizens, who were erased from the register of permanent residency on February 26, 1992. The question of erasure, and as committed in the Republic of Slovenia, still remains unsolved. Therefore, we need to put in the center of analysis the process of the constitution of a new State on the basis of organized administrative genocide, the need for transformation of citizenship concept, and to stand in opposition to EU's criminal migration politics and control as well as precarious conditions of labor, related to history and present colonial capitalism.

Among this critical audiovisual production that goes back to the Yugoslav Black Wave, it is necessary to mention and develop further the analysis of Želimir Žilnik's film "Marble Ass" (1995) (Image 1.5), which is the only fiction film depicting trans* practice, showing the subversive power of the transvestite and sex work to challenge nationalism at its core, by disrupting the very idea of natural, essential and identity (Moss 2005, 91).

Image 1.5   "Marble Ass," a Film by Želimir Žilnik, 1995, Filmframe, https://www.zilnikzelimir.net/marble-ass.

Furthermore, recently developed critique coming from a younger generation of theoreticians and activists is put forward in the book published in 2016, entitled *LGBT Activism and Europeanisation in Post-Yugoslav Space*, edited by Bojan Bilić, in which they interrogate a linkage between "Europeanization" and "gay emancipation" which elevates certain forms of gay activist engagement to a measure of democracy, progress and modernity while at the same time relegates homo-transphobic attacks to the status of non-European "Other(s)," who are inevitably positioned in the patriarchal past that should be left behind. As Piro Rexhepi (2016) writes in his text, this separation serves the purpose of creating and strengthening a local liberal European-oriented elite, which then acts as local interlocutors that, in advocating Europeanization as the solution to violence directed toward queer communities, become vehicles of EU expansionism. In this sense, inviting-in, disidentifications, imperceptibility and invisibility, as he argues, may be just some of the living strategies "queers" are also using to confront the normative liberal politics of coming-out and visibility, to avoid being absorbed into neoliberal governmental technologies.

Another crucial book for further debates is entitled *Džuvljarke. Roma Lesbian Existence*, written by Vera Kurtić and published in 2013. *Džuvljarke* is a term used among Roma living in Serbia, and together with its Serbian-influenced suffix, refers to lesbians, implying a negative connotation within the heteronormative patriarchal social matrix. Kurtić's research work shows that Romani lesbian existence and its visibility cannot remain as separate issues from the challenges that are encountered by non-Romani LGBTQI+ community in Serbia and beyond, nor from those once within the Roma community. As she writes, "Romani lesbian existence needs to be on the shared agenda, just as yesterday's impossible is tomorrow's inevitable" (2013, 17). Kurtić's analysis points to whiteness and racism being reproduced within former Eastern European space, feminist and LGBTQI+ theory and activism, which is not an outcome of postsocialism but has much deeper historical roots. And, as Rexhepi asks,

What does it mean, that while Roma, Black and Muslim people were (in socialism) and are racialized in Eastern Europe—their racialization is subsumed and leveled out under broader critique of coloniality or Orientalization of former socialist subjects? What does this erasure through leveling achieve? More importantly, who speaks in the name of the post-socialist subject? These questions are very important because they also highlight frequently ignored racialized hierarchies during socialism (as a result of the imitation of Western modernity) by anchoring the contemporary rise of racism as a simple outcome of post-socialist Europeanization (2018, 13).

All this material, among many others that we should search for in the context of the former Eastern Europe, is crucial to elaborate a politically dis/continuous narrative that would allow us to imagine new forms of community and commons, as well as to undo the foundational myths and ideological fantasies that lay hidden under the colonial/capitalist, socialist and postsocialist nation-state binary gender system. Such a map would fill the gap through its attempt at a decolonial erotic counter-reading and intersectional thinking of history, bringing together objects, images, texts, documents, press clippings, artistic and activist practices related to gender/sexual dissidence, feminist, anticolonial, and antifascist struggles, in order to render visible its own contingency and the social processes that led to its constructions. It is not about uncovering the lost truth from the past, but instead it becomes a creative process of inventing a new truth, which is coming from the past. Learning to read the material as it is, in its fragmented and shattered form, not to search for the way back to some original unity, not by restoring their original meaning. but by elaborating a performative archive in order to expose the forms in which colonial/imperial capitalist discourses around body, race, ethnicity, class, ability, gender, and sexuality were initially imposed in former Eastern European space, how they were modifying and updating through time, to our present state of fragmentation.

To use Somerville's (2000) and Puar's (2017) expression, we should engage in "reading sideways." As they write, this means the linking together of seemingly unrelated and often disjunctively situated moments and their effects in ways that attend to the interconnected histories of racial, gender, sexual and other bio-necro-political formations and regulations. By challenging the colonial epistemology of binary gender, we can begin to unleash the binds, which produce the modern/colonial terms of recognition and continue to create our resistance from different envisioning that gender and sexually disobedient pre/post/socialist subjects have to subvert the regulation of bodies, labor, and space.

NOTES

1. To quote Marina Gržinić: "In relation to 'former' Western Europe, its hegemony (supremacy) and construction of deficient 'other,' someone coming from former Eastern Europe is always part of process of discrimination; because there is always implemented the so-called principle of the 'deficiency' of a certain geographical region called former Eastern Europe, where it is seen as such by its Western counterpart. (. . .) But when the color of the skin is a border, then within the discrimination processes, we have to recontextualize ourselves, so to speak, every moment, both while entering the public and in the private context, because it is not the same,—we can still hide ourselves within a system of mimicry." From "The System

of Racism/White Supremacy." A conversation between Jude Sentongo Kafeero and Sheri Avraham, Marina Gržinić, Marissa Lôbo, and Ivana Marjanović, in *Utopia of Alliances, Conditions of Impossibilities and the Vocabulary of Decoloniality*, 117.

2. The term "trans*" with an asterisk is being used recently as an umbrella concept to include many different gender expressions and identities, such as trans, transsexual, transgender, gender queer, and so on. The asterisk emphasizes the heterogeneity of bodies, identities, and experiences, which goes beyond the imposed gender binary social norms. Trans* is a concept introduced by its protagonists out of rejection of the terms coming from the pathologizing medical discourse. The asterisk also points out that while our struggle is common we recognize that there is not just one interpretation of what it means to be trans, transsexual, or transgender. Both terms, queer and trans*, have to be re-thought from decolonial positionality.

REFERENCES

Ahmed, Sara. 2012. *On Being Included: Racism and Diversity in Institutional Life.* Durham, NC: Duke University Press.

Atanasoski, Neda. 2013. *Humanitarian Violence: The U.S. Deployment of Diversity.* Minneapolis: University of Minnesota Press.

Barriendos, Joaquín. 2010. "La colonialidad del ver. Visualidad, capitalismo y racismo epistemológico." In *Desenganche. Visualidades y sonoridades otras.* Quito: La Tronkal.

Bilić, Bojan, ed. 2016. *LGBT Activism and Europeanisation in Post-Yugoslav Space.* London: Palgrave Macmillan.

Cabral, Mauro. 2014. "Decolonizing the Transgender Imaginary." *Transgender Studies Quarterly* 1(3):419–439.

Chiang, Howard. 2012. *Transgender China.* New York: Palgrave Macmillan.

Cisneros Anyely, Rebecca Close (Diasporas Críticas). 2014. "Decolonize. Glossary of Common Knowledge, MG+MSUM Ljubljana." http://glossary.mg-lj.si/referential-fields/subjectivization/decolonize.

Dietze, Gabriele. 2012. "Analysis of Gender." *Journal Deartikulacija*, part 2. http://www.damne.net/wpcontent/uploads/pdfs/De-Artikulacija2.pdf.

El-Tayeb, Fatima. 2011. *European Others: Queering Ethnicity in Postnational Europe.* Minneapolis: University of Minnesota Press.

Espinosa Miñoso, Yuderkys, Diana Gómez Correal, and Karina Ochoa Muñoz, eds. 2014. *Tejiendo de otro modo: Feminismo, epistemología y apuestas descoloniales en Abya Yala* [Weaving from Another World: "Feminism, Epistemology and De-colonial Stakes in Abya Yala]. Popayán: Universidad del Cauca.

Fanon, Frantz. 1963. *The Wretched of the Earth.* New York: Grove Press.

Feinberg, Leslie. 1992. *Transgender Liberation: A Movement Whose Time Has Come.* Women's International Network News Quarterly.

Goldberg, David T. 2009. *The Threat of Race: Reflections on Racial Neoliberalism.* Singapore: Utopia Press.

Gržinić, Marina. 2009. "Capital Repetition." *Journal Reartikulacija* 8. http://grzinic
-smid.si/?p=907.

———. 2015. "100 Years of Now." *German Pavillion La Biennale di Venezia*. http:
//www.deutscherpavillon.org/2015/en/.

Gržinić, Marina, and Šefik Tatlić. 2012. "Global Capitalism's Racializations."
Journal Deartikulacija, part 2. www.academia.edu/2096960/Global_Capitalisms
_Racialization_s.

Haritaworn, Jin. 2012. "Wounded Subjects: Sexual Exceptionalism and the Moral
Panic on 'Migrant Homophobia' in Germany." In *Decolonizing European
Sociology: Transdisciplinary Approaches*, edited by Encarnación Gutiérrez
Rodríguez, Manuela Boatcă, and Sérgio Costa, 136–151. Surrey: Ashgate.

Kurtić, Vera. 2013. *Džuvljarke. Roma Lesbian Existence*. Niš: European Roma Rights
Centre.

Lugones, María. 2008. "The Coloniality of Gender." In *Worlds & Knowledges
Otherwise*, 1–7.

———. 2010. "Toward a Decolonial Feminism." *Hypatia* 25(4):742–759.

Mbembe, Achille. 2013. "Lectures to African Future Cities." Presented at Harvard
University, Cambridge, Massachusetts, September–December 2013.

Mignolo, Walter, ed. 2008. *Género y descolonialidad* [Gender and Decoloniality].
Buenos Aires: Ediciones del Signo.

Moss, Kevin. 2005. "From Sworn Virgins to Transvestite Prostitutes: Performing
Gender and Sexuality in Two Films from Yugoslavia." In *Sexuality and Gender
in Postcommunist Eastern Europe and Russia*, edited by Aleksandar Stulhofer and
Theo Sandfort. New York: Haworth Press.

Pérez F.-Figares, Kim. 2006. "¿Mujer o Trans?La inserción de las transexuales en
el movimiento feminista" [Women or Trans?The Insertion of Transsexuals into
Feminist Movement]. *Feminist Summit in Cordoba*. http://pendientedemigracion
.ucm.es/info/rqtr/biblioteca/Transexualidad/MUJER%20O%20TRANS.pdf.

Preciado, Beatriz. 2008. *Testo Yonqui*. Madrid: Espasa.

Preciado, Paul B. 2013. "Pharmaco-Pornographic Capitalism Postporn Politics and
the Decolonization of Sexual Representations." In *Utopia of Alliances, Conditions
of Impossibilities and the Vocabulary of Decoloniality*, edited by The Editorial
Group for Writing Insurgent Genealogies. Vienna: Löcker.

Puar, Jasbir. 2017. *Terrorist Assemblages: Homonationalism in Queer Times*.
Durham, NC: Duke University Press.

Raha, Nat. 2015. "The Limits of Trans Liberalism." *Verso Blog*, September 21,
2015. www.versobooks.com/blogs/2245-the-limitsof-trans-liberalism-by-nat-
raha.

Rexhepi, Piro. 2016. "From Orientalism to Homonationalism: Queer Politics,
Islamophobia and Europeanization in Kosovo." In *LGBT Activism and
Europeanisation in Post-Yugoslav Space*, edited by Bojan Bilić. London: Palgrave
Macmillan.

———. 2018. "Prologue." In *Arte-Política-Resistencia* [Art-Politics-Resistance],
Tjaša Kancler. Barcelona: Ediciones t.i.c.t.a.c.

Sitnikova, Jana. 2014. "Transgender Activism in Russia." *Freedom Requires Wings*, January 28, 2014. www.freedomrequireswings.com/2014/01/report-transgender -activism-in-russia.html.

———. 2016. "The Emergence of Transfeminism in Russia." *Transgender Studies Quarterly* 3(1–2):165–174.

Solá, Miriam, and Elena Urko, eds. 2013. *Transfeminismos. Espistemes, fricciones y flujos* [Transfeminisms. Epistemes, Frictions and Flows]. Bilbao: Txalaparta.

Somerville, Siobhan. 2000. *Queering the Color Line: Race and the Invention of Homosexuality in American Culture*. Durham, NC: Duke University Press.

Spivak, Gayatri C. 2007. "Religion, Politics, Theology: A Conversation with Achille Mbembe." *Boundary 2* 34(2):149–170.

Stone, Sandy. 1991. "The Empire Strikes Back: A Posttranssexual Manifesto." In *Body Guards: The Cultural Politics of Gender Ambiguity*, edited by Kristina Straub and Julia Epstein. New York: Routledge.

Stryker, Susan, and Stephen Whittle, eds. 2006. *The Transgender Studies Reader*. New York: Routledge.

Tlostanova, Madina. 2013. "Post-Soviet Imaginary and Global Coloniality: A Gendered Perspective." Interview with Madina Tlostanova. *Kronotop.org*. www.k ronotop.org/folders/post-soviet-imaginary-and-globalcoloniality-a-gendered-persp ective-madina-tlostanova/.

Valencia, Sayak. 2014. "Interferencias transfeministas y pospornográficas a la colonialidad del ver" [Transfeminist and Postpornographic Interferences in the Coloniality of Seeing], *Gesto Decolonial* 11(1). http://hemisphericinstitute.org/ hemi/es/e-misferica-111-gesto-decolonial/valencia.

Valentine, David. 2007. *Imagining Transgender: An Ethnography of a Category*. Durham, NC: Duke University Press.

Velikonja, Nataša, and Tatjana Greif. 2012. *Lezbična sekcija LL: kronologija 1987–2012 s predzgodovino* [Lesbian Section LL: Chronology 1987–2012 with Pre-History]. Ljubljana: Škuc-Vizibilija.

Chapter 2

Querying Identity

Misrecognition as Performative Refusal in Armenian LGBT Advocacy

Tamar Shirinian

Since the 1990s, Euro-American queer theorists and activists have established that gender, sex, and sexuality are fluid and open. Gender and sexuality are no longer stable "things" that can be identified or located, but dependent on social meaning, language, and the workings of power. At the same time, state socialisms in Central and Eastern Europe and the Soviet Union came to an end, entirely changing the political, economic, and social landscapes of space and time. The repercussions of these political-economic transformations on gender, sex, and sexuality were immense. By the late 1990s and early 2000s, most of the now-independent Republics in this region, because of the work of activists, had decriminalized homosexuality and various gay and lesbian organizations were emerging. New public discourses of non-normative genders and sexualities began to develop, becoming more visible in time. Eventually, sexual orientation and gender identity (SOGI) as "things" made their way into postsocialist spaces.

The new forms of understanding gender and sexual difference—especially the emergence of categories to express one's identification with these differences and a set of politics that insisted on their social and political inclusions in varying scales—have, as would be expected, not gone unchallenged. Along with these new words for ways of being (*gay, lesbian, bisexual, transgender*, and more recently *queer*) came new forms of nationalisms (Shirinian 2017), illiberal populisms (Korolczuk and Graff 2018), and religious right-wing movements (Renkin 2009)—often aided by state power (Woodcock 2009)—aimed to purify the space of the nation and often articulated these new formations of identity and politics as products of Western imperialism. While the problem of identity and identification was central to debates in queer anthropology in the mid-2000s and has more recently fallen out of style, this is not because we have arrived at some resolution. The question of what to make of gender and sexual identification processes and how they are entangled in multivalent forms of power as they travel through various borders remains. And, importantly, staying with this trouble does not necessarily mean falling prey to assumptions of national or cultural purity. The discomfort with which I approached LGBT identification in Armenia—a discomfort that was in many ways, although not explicitly stated, shared by my interlocutors—was tied to other feelings and oppositional sensibilities as I hope to make clear in this chapter.

The identity and identification questions within the queer (geo)political were brought into full focus for me when, as I was conducting fieldwork on LGBT activism in Yerevan, the capital city of Armenia, from 2012 to 2013, I witnessed a moment of intense focus on identity that also interrogated structures of power that challenged many assumptions about the political work of identity. In this chapter, I investigate the process that PINK (Public Information and Need for Knowledge)—an LGBT advocacy organization in Yerevan, Armenia—underwent in the construction of a survey instrument that was meant to measure the human rights violations of lesbians, gays, bisexuals, and transgender persons in the country. As a survey—meant not only to measure norms, marking it a process of normalization itself (Foucault 1978; Wiegman and Wilson 2015), but also to prop up notions of Armenia as a space that required work to move the country into a tolerant civilization— its purpose might be regarded as entirely a project of what Joseph Massad has called the Gay International (2008). However, the discussions to which the preparation of the survey gave rise simultaneously opened up possibilities that challenged the very desires of a global gay identity, placing pressure on those forms that these organizations were to use as normalizing tools. It is through this practice of *query,* I argue, that we locate the tensions and performative resistances to a global Gay International. In Armenia, the time of my fieldwork (2010–2013) might be regarded as the early years of LGBT identification and LGBT politics-making. While Euro-American identity categories were being assumed—taken on, becoming the objects that oriented selves (Ahmed 2006) in Armenia—these identity categories were still sites where normalization, as well as geopolitical power, was being contested. While these categories are now becoming more solidified and less and less objects of query, it is important to note the tensions with which they emerged into Armenia's queer political. As a performative practice, querying—as I will discuss below—opens up the gaps and fissures in processes of identification with a Gay International. While the vocabulary of the Gay International was eventually adopted, the political and ethical conditions behind its adoption were also challenged.

THE GIFT OF IDENTITY: BETWEEN
IMPERIALISM AND OPPOSITION

Queer scholars of postsocialist spaces have problematized the ways in which gay and lesbian politics—now LGBT(IQA+) politics—came to be normalized in the region. While many of these initial projects emerged from the local grassroots—making sense of what was going on in the social, political, and economic contexts of real lives and worlds—external funding, most often by European governmental and nongovernmental organizations, would eventually set the stage for what politics would come. Western funding for nongovernmental organizations in the postsocialist world, especially organizations working on "women's issues" and gender, often came with normalizing discourses of how those societies should function, like the rest of the proper Western and European World, through free markets, individualism, and entrepreneurship (Ghodsee 2004; Rivkin-Fish 2013). In this regard, there has been overlap with lesbian and gay or LGBT organizations, where similar market logics and activisms based on individualism have played out. The need for funding often turned local concerns into Western concerns. Thus, while grassroots activists originally worked to form communities and senses of solidarity with other sexually non-normative persons, funding has meant that more and more activists and organizations are working within frameworks of visibility, tolerance, child adoption, disease containment (especially HIV/AIDS), civil unions, and marriage rights even when these were not or are not local needs (Woodcock 2011). Indeed, as some scholars have pointed out, many of the frameworks for understanding, figuring, and measuring "tolerance" and "acceptance" in the West—especially those tied to visibility—are inappropriate for the particular forms of cultural, social, and political realities of postsocialist worlds (Neufeld and Wiedlack 2020). Nonetheless, these measurements and methods of activism produce a narrative of postsocialist actors as needing constant support and pedagogy by Western actors. Western-funded projects in the postsocialist world became, in Shannon Woodcock's terms, "pinned to quantifiable identity groups and social changes," in which same-sex sexual practices and underground communities were not only being actively transformed into identifiable (and visible) identities, but those identities were ones deemed "correct" by European standards (2011). As Nicole Butterfield argues, Europe presents itself as a civilizing entity, to teach the once-socialist world about homosexuality, how to properly name it, and how to properly practice it (2013). In other words—Euro-America's "others" are illiberal and intolerant, while Europe and America are civilized and free. The spread of LGBT identity to non-Euro-American sites, including postsocialist sites, thus, has been seen as a normalizing as well as colonizing project.

Others, however, have disagreed with these assessments. Scholars of queerness point out that global gay identity does not necessarily look the same everywhere—for instance, the particular meanings of "gay" or "trans" might be different in different places, affected by differing social, political, and economic realities (Manalansan 2003; Boellstorff 2005; Rofel 2007; Valentine 2007). These assessments provide critique of other scholarly contributions that tended to see global gay identity as a product of imperialism (Altman 1997) with an assimilationist agenda that aimed to "produce homosexuals, as well as gays and lesbians, where they do not exist, and repress same-sex desires and practices that refuse to be assimilated into its sexual epistemology" (Massad 2008, 163).

Debates in queer studies have also taken up the process of identity and identification as a critical category of analysis. Lawrence Cohen, in a discussion of the gendered understandings of *hijra* and *jankha* in India, for instance, argues that academics have reified these notions into particularly Indian "systems," ignoring the very real on-the-ground uses that often trouble boundaries between them as well as offer up other possible ways of making sense of gendered possibilities (including violence inflicted on bodies). Hijra and jankha (or zenana) are neither categories that belong entirely to properly defined traditional systems nor are they wholly ways in which subjects themselves assume a body; they are contested and negotiated positions contingent on other political, social, geographical, and economic markers (Cohen 1997). Deborah Elliston questions the assumptions at the center of sex and sexuality as identity, maintaining that notions of desire and the erotic might themselves be marked by Western ideas of interiority (1995).

Is identity useful? Is it necessary for social justice? Tom Boellstorff has shown how identities might provide possibilities of mobilization—producing senses of community and groups that can speak around affectedness by political and social problems—but can also be highly depoliticizing, as in the case of MSM (men who have sex with men), which disentangles political and social realities from sexual behaviors (2011). As Cathy Cohen has argued, a radical queer politics that challenges the status quo of racialized, classed, gendered, and sexual oppression has been obfuscated by a queer politics dependent on identity. She points out that "in many instances, instead of destabilizing the assumed categories and binaries of sexual identity, queer politics has served to reinforce simple dichotomies between heterosexual and everything 'queer'" (1997, 438). Rather than gay identity categories as the basis of politics, thus, Cohen argues for queer politics to be established on the "radical potential of queerness to challenge and bring together all those deemed marginal and all those committed to liberatory politics" (1997, 440). Queers of color in the West have challenged identity categories as applicable to their own lives and bodies (Manalansan 2003), sometimes taking up a politics of disidentification that allows new performances of self to emerge (Muñoz 2009). At the heart of it, identity is a process of normalizing subjection—a constricting or narrowing of possibilities—and thus an act of power (Butler 1997). But, as Naisargi Dave has argued, it is through these processes of normalization that ethics and politics assert themselves, and it is through existing norms and the production of new norms that radical possibilities make themselves real in the world (2012).

I hold the tensions in these debates regarding imperialism, identity, and activism as a way of embracing the critical interventions that emerge and the scopes of analysis they make possible. I, however, place in question some of the premises on which these positions have been put forward. While Boellstorff, for instance, has argued that "*gay*" in Indonesia is dubbed so as to be in a slight difference to the beat of our understanding of "gay" in the West, the decolonizing impulse in my approach still wants to ask, *But, why is the term "gay" being used? Why are terms and notions of sexual and gendered beingness indigenous to spaces and places outside of Euro-America not being used in Europe or the United States?* As such, what Boellstorff and others who have argued for a less reproachful relationship to global gay identity have set aside is how the flow of cultural knowledge and practice seems to be one way: from the West to the rest. And yet, those who have spoken these trends in the language of colonization have also set aside the possible oppositional impetus of knowledge and practices of identity. After all, while identity practices are borrowed from Euro-American contexts and are normalizing, they might in themselves open up different ways of understanding anti-imperialist impulses. Furthermore, as the political-economic transition from socialism to something else (Verdery 1996) produced new aggressive forms of nationalism seeking to roll back many of the more progressive gendered and sexual ideologies of state socialisms (Ghodsee 2018), sexual and gendered differences from the "proper" defined by these nationalisms (Shirinian 2017) might in themselves be seen as oppositional as well as radical. As a result of these claims to radical alterity from and an insistence on intervention within proper national forms, there have been many coalitions between feminists and queer organizers in Armenia.

It is these *other* ways of understanding the resistance against a properly operating Euro-American field of queer politics and identity categories that I unfold here. LGBT (+) activists in Yerevan—and especially those who were staffed at PINK in 2012–2013—did not outright reject identity categories that came with membership in transnational LGBT organizations like the International Lesbian and Gay Association (ILGA). On the face of it, they wholeheartedly accepted these categories and the politics with which they were gifted. At a deeper look, however—especially at the process of translating and making these categories relevant to an Armenian world—it becomes clear that they were being questioned performatively, complicating the assumptions they contained as well as the geopolitics that undergirded them.

SEARCHING FOR IDENTITY

While homosexuality was decriminalized in Armenia in 2003, there are little to no legal protections for LGBT people in Armenia. This was precisely what PINK—an LGBT advocacy organization and the only one of its kind for many years in Armenia—was concerned with when I interned there as a part of a larger ethnographic research project on sexuality, nationalism, and activism in Armenia.

In May 2012, two major events occurred that would come to shape many of the debates within and about queer politics, identity, and visibility in Armenia. On May 8, two young right-wing nationalists (one of them eighteen years old and the other twenty-one years old) firebombed DIY Pub, a bar in central Yerevan, claiming that it was a gay bar. This began endless public debate—not about terrorism, but about the existence of homosexuals in Armenia. A few weeks following the firebombing, right-wing nationalists attacked a Diversity March, an event organized by some local nonprofits to emphasize Yerevan as a diverse city. The right-wing nationalists, forming a counterprotest that outnumbered the participants in the original event, claimed that the Diversity March was a gay parade. This continued the public discussions of homosexuality in Armenia and what it meant for the future and the survival of the nation.

Prior to these two events, there had been little to no discussion about homosexuality within the public sphere. Importantly, it was not just that sexuality was taboo for public discussion, but that the notions of sexual and gender identity were new discussions writ large, including among queer people themselves. In 2010, during my first research trip to Armenia, I found through various interviews with people who had been identifying as gay, lesbian, bisexual, or transgender, that their entry into their sexual or gender identity most often came about through clunky Google searches or through happenstance meeting with someone who happened to be in the know about such categories. As Manvel, a transgender man, explained to me, he had a feeling that he was different and that he had always been different, but never really understood why. All of his friends were boys, he dressed like a boy and always had. Even his mom treated him like a son, once telling him that since his father had passed away he was like the "man of the house" even though he was a girl. When he was sixteen, he had his first kiss with a girl who lived in his building and the girl, much like his mom, told him that she felt like he was a boy. He started googling such a possibility—that he was actually a boy. He didn't speak English at the time, so his searches were in Russian and brought up some Russian sources and stories of people whose lives and experiences sounded much like his and it was through these stories that he discovered the term "transgender" and eventually began identifying with it. Manvel at first, even if he was starting to put together a notion that there were a "community" of people in the world that were like him, didn't think about how there might be such a community in Armenia. He had never met anyone else like himself in Armenia. He also never thought about how his identity and his experience had something in common with "gays," people who he had heard about but never met and about whom he largely had a disparaging sense. Eventually Manvel, through his transnational online networks, would realize that his identity and experience of transgender were being linked to others who were lesbian, gay, and bisexual, and he would meet others in Armenia who had these things in common. "Now it feels very natural to me that we have an *LGBT hamayq* [LGBT community] in Armenia, but I know that it was not always like that. I felt very alone for many years," he told me.

PINK saw the formation of a community as essential to combating feelings of loneliness and to forming visibility through space so that others would be able to know that there were others like them out there. Critical to this formation of community and eventual visibility was identity. People needed to know that there was a name for their desires and experiences and that others also belonged to that name. But these very names were new not only to those like Manvel who eventually came to join the community that PINK was establishing, but new to staff at PINK as well. They themselves were learning about identity categories and their meanings through international forums. It wasn't just Manvel, in other words, who was googling his experience and finding that there was a term in the English language that others were using to describe themselves and their experience. Most staff members of PINK came to the organization knowing something or another about SOGI, but were constantly adding to this knowledge and their repertoire of names and practices—many of which were borrowed from colleagues in Europe who they met at international conferences and workshops. The newness of these categories—as well their foreignness to the context of Armenia where they were not only being discovered but negotiated and redefined—meant that the very categories of identity that queer scholars point to as part and parcel of processes of normalization were actively being queered within Armenia's activist and advocate worlds. This queering, while often stemming from confusion and the position of not knowing, was not passive.

THE QUEER PREPARATION OF AN INSTRUMENT

In September 2012, many of the staff at PINK had been spending their time in the office translating a survey that had been distributed through the South Caucasus Network as a part of a project to monitor the human rights violations of LGBT people across the region. The research was to lead to published reports for each country. PINK published its report on Armenia in August 2013 (see PINK 2013). The original distributed questions were in English, which needed to be translated into Armenian before the survey research could be done in Armenia. The translation process from English into Armenian was not only one of language but of cultural meaning. Arsineh, a staff member at PINK, who was eventually to do the quantitative analysis of the survey answers after it was conducted, had called a meeting one afternoon in which we would all agree on the ways in which the questions had been translated. This meeting, for which we had planned one hour, took two weeks—a total of about twenty hours of discussion—before we agreed on a version. And even then, there remained heavy contestations.

The survey originally had fifty-five questions (that would become sixty questions), organized into nine sections. The survey questions began with seemingly basic personal information before they went into more complicated solicitations to identify levels of being "out" and explain incidences of harassment, abuse, assault, and discrimination. As we grappled and debated with the questions, I thought about how politically incorrect these discussions were within the context of the United States. But I also thought about what it meant to negotiate and figure out categories and their separations and what it tells us about identity itself, especially in a context where these identities had not become—to borrow a term from Dominic Boyer and Alexei Yurchak— "hypernormalized," or cemented ideologically within rigid forms that limited the thematic modes and styles of political performance (2010). Every single one of these questions (beginning with the most seemingly mundane, such as age) became a contentious site of negotiation, reflection, and interrogation. Here, I will focus on one very small portion of these debates, that regarding SOGI, which was probably the most contentious moment.

3. You are . . . (choose only one answer)

1. Gay/lesbian
2. Bisexual
3. Heterosexual
4. Transgender

At first glance, we can probably see the most immediate problem with the question. The first issue that was brought up by Arthur was that only choosing one answer left out the possibility that one was transgender and heterosexual, bisexual, gay, or lesbian. This problem was resolved fairly quickly. Arsineh agreed that the restriction of choosing only one answer could be taken out. The grievances around the question, however, went in multiple other directions. Some objected that there were categories not mentioned in the options, such as asexual, autosexual, transsexual, or intersex. Others interrogated the topicality of the question—if this question is about sexual orientation, then "Transgender" does not belong as it is about gender identity. We needed to separate gender identity from sexual orientation because they relate to different parts of a person's identity, they claimed. But Arsineh, who was going to be the one who would eventually do the survey analysis for the report that would come out of this, argued that the most important measure of the survey here was SOGI, which was the unit by which the other questions about harassment, abuse, and violation would be measured. The point of the survey, she wanted to remind us, was not to count how many transgender or how many gays or how many lesbians there were in Armenia, but to get a general sense of how these experiences and identities were the cause of stigma and, thus, violence. Arsineh also responded that while we could list hundreds of different identities, the ones that Armenians were using were the four (gay, lesbian, bisexual, and transgender).

Arsineh also added that if a person identifies as asexual or as autosexual, then this would not necessarily cause any violations or discriminations. Some had an issue with this—arguing that it does cause discrimination—for example, if a person does not get married because they are asexual. Marriage, after all, was tied to various social positions, without which people often had no access to certain social rights in Armenia. PINK staff members were aware of a few gay- and lesbian-identified persons who had married friends of the opposite sex just to be able to do things like have freedom from prying family members, live on their own, and so on.

Here, some other comments were made. First, marriage doesn't say anything about sexual orientation. There are a lot of people who are in heterosexual marriages, but are gay or lesbian. This claim was mostly evidenced by the large number of clients of transgender sex workers (many who are rumored to be well-known politicians) as well as the heterosexual (and often married) men who frequented the *dzor*, a small canyon formed by a river that passes through the city of Yerevan and that has become a site commonly used for cruising other men. Second, marriage discriminates not only against gays and lesbians but against anyone who does not want to be sexual with another person. Considering also that this expectation and access to rights through marriage were larger burdens on women than on men, here gender also became important—returning us to the question of gender and sex, which we thought we had already resolved two hours earlier. These questions about gender, sex, and marriage also raised the problem of identity as a measure of experience and oppression. Someone pointed out that if a person is in a heterosexual marriage and yet has sexual relationships with same-sex partners, they might not identify as gay so we cannot identify them that way. While we were trying to understand whose rights were being violated in Armenia, doing so through identity categories might miss important experiences of violence. What about women who were married but did not want to be? What about domestic violence as a form of oppression and violence that was linked to gender, but not necessarily encapsulated within notions of SOGI?

This line of questioning opened up some anxious terrain regarding the problem of categorizing what pertains to sex, what pertains to gender, and what pertains to sexuality. We had already discussed whether the survey should ask for sex, gender, or both separately—a discussion that unnerved many of us. If we included sex, then we would be placing importance on a category that we all knew was a false one, at least to the extent that it didn't mark real social experience. But, some objected, asking only about gender might miss some important points. Considering that, because of fear of violence and harassment, most transgender women in Armenia—at least to the best of our knowledge—lived their everyday lives as men, asking only about gender would not get at the importance of the gendered differences between men and women in Armenia. "Being a transgender woman is not the same experience as living as a woman. We know how men treat women in our country," Hakob explained. He was referring largely to the ways in which public space in Armenia is often seen as the space of men. Thus, women were given much less freedom of movement without harassment than men. Others argued that if a person who passed as a man was a transgender woman, then he was probably perceived as gay anyway, which would not make him a man in the way that men see men in public space. The questioning of this line between sex and gender and reflection on experience was uncomfortable as it called into question many of the dictums of what we, as an organization, were teaching and attempting to educate the public about. Tom Boellstorff has argued that sexuality and gender are in a prosthetic relation to one another in that "each helps constitute the other even while remaining distinct" (2007, 27). These questions were being raised precisely because it was becoming hard to distinguish between sexual oppression and gendered oppression, practice, and identity, how identities merged and separated, and how to properly name and categorize them among multiple axes.

It was not just during the survey that these tensions emerged. Quotidian conversations in the PINK office, sometimes including gossip, would raise questions of who was "really" trans, who was "really" gay, or how to name certain practices. Hripsime and Aram sat at Hripsime's desk one day looking at the photos of a woman on her Facebook page and wondered if she was really trans—"She doesn't really look like a woman" and "She's wearing too much makeup" being the motivators of suspicion. Discussions such as these brought into focus the anxieties of drag on gender: who is a woman and who dresses like a woman? Who is trans and who is effeminate? How do we know? Should we know? Why do we want to know? On another occasion, Rita, a transwoman who was receiving legal counsel from PINK's attorney, had come into the office and was being hosted with coffee in the kitchen as Raffi came to the work station at which I was working on a document to ask me if I wanted to meet a "real transwoman." "Right now they are a man because it's daytime, but they are usually trans," he said, letting me know that this was an important opportunity for my research. Because of the Armenian gender-neutral pronoun *na* and the possibility of leaving out pronouns altogether in vernacular sentence construction, Raffi did not (mis) gender Rita linguistically, but—at least according to Euro-American norms of propriety—he misgendered her in meaning by describing her as a man now. It is also important to note that within the context of the PINK office, these forms of talk would not be taken as offensive necessarily. Indeed, when I walked into the kitchen to meet Rita, she exclaimed, "Oh! I feel sorry for this girl! Don't worry, my sweet, I am an ugly man right now but I'm usually not so ugly." This was partly Rita's way of moving attention away from the fact that she had been crying. She was receiving legal aid concerning a recent event of police brutality. But it was also her way of explaining her gender presentation.

These discussions, of course, also come dangerously close to the schism within Euro-American queer and feminist activism now called the TERF wars, or the contentious debates about transexclusionary radical feminism, a brand of feminism that denies the place and role of trans persons within the feminist project. But, in the context of Armenia, where SOGI were first emerging in the early 2000s and 2010s, these sorts of "sides," or hypernormalized debates (Boyer and Yurchak 2010; Boyer 2013), had not yet pitted activists against one another. Furthermore, claims of oppression made through properly articulated identity positions—what we might term identitarian politics—also did not quite exist. The field of the political was a wide and open one in Armenia when I was conducting fieldwork from 2012 to 2013. While debates concerning liberal and radical agendas were certainly emerging, which sometimes pitted radical queer and feminist activists against liberal LGBT activists (who were seen as contributing only to the potential granting of rights to gay men through a project of normalization—see Shirinian forthcoming), the political was largely oriented around Armenia's political-economic conditions: resisting the oligarchy was something in which all were invested. The misrecognition of identities and their categorizations were genuine forms of query.

QUESTIONS, QUESTIONS, QUESTIONS

The *Oxford English Dictionary* defines "query" as "A question, *esp.* one expressing some doubt or objection ("Query," n.2), "with interrogative clause or direct speech as object: to ask, enquire, put a question (*whether, if, what*, etc.)" ("Query," v.). The obsolete definition of the term, traced in etiology to a borrowing from Latin and combined with an English element, is "Perhaps: a complaint" ("Query," n.1). To query, then, is to actively and performatively place doubt and objection on something, to question something's validity. When it comes to questions of gender and sexuality, we often see this process of query come up in its more sinister possibilities of misrecognition. We see misrecognition all the time—something we might call misgendering, especially in regard to transgender identification, or denial of someone's sexual identity. Misrecognition is a form of violence—sometimes outright, sometimes as microaggression. Misrecognition is not just a discursive failure (to be recognized), but is also productive in its materialization as an enactment of violence (Butler 2011; Plemmons 2017). It can have grave consequences— quite literally, as when funerary rights become a site to reproduce the transgressive body as a normalized body, a form of necropolitical violence (Zengin 2019). As Nancy Fraser reminds us, misrecognition is

> not simply to be thought ill of, looked down on, or devalued in others' con- scious attitudes or mental beliefs. It is rather to be denied the status of a full partner in social interaction and prevented from participating as a peer in social life— not as a consequence of a distributive inequity (such as failing to receive one's fair share of resources or "primary goods"), but rather as a consequence of institutionalized patterns of interpretation and evaluation that constitute one as comparatively unworthy of respect or esteem. (1997, 141)

Fraser's point is that misrecognition is not just a problem of and in the per- sonal, the psychological, or the "merely cultural," but that it is a political and economic problem. It is a process imbued with institutional power.

I want to suggest here that when LGBT activists in Armenia misrecognize categories like transgender, or complicate the separations of gender, sex, and sexuality, they are participating in another form of misrecognition—one that does not necessarily work to constitute subjects as unworthy, but that queries the geopolitical and economic power through which these categories have become fixed and hypernormalized. Here, we might understand the querying of SOGI as a process of misrecognition that *resists* the geopolitical power of Europe over Armenian ways of life, everyday practice, and meaning. These forms of query, of misrecognition, are performative acts that push back against the normalization of what has constituted gender and sexual practices in Euro-America, the politically correct forms and formats in which this normalization has occurred, and the insistence that these processes are the only possible ones for other—non-Euro-American—sites. While my interlocutors at PINK did not necessarily represent themselves or their work as anticolonial or as decolonizing—and indeed, they are often embroiled in conflict with leftists in Armenia who see them as colonizing in their approach to politics—they still carry a sense of disquietude within questions of correctness defined by their European colleagues.

Coming back from conferences and workshops in Europe, or where there were European or American activists present. PINK staff were often discontented by how they were consistently placed within a pedagogical relation to European colleagues who, in their views, often came off as condescending. Hripsime and Armen, for example, PINK staff members, attended a conference in Prague in the spring of 2013, during which they had developed an inside joke about European political correctness. Every time they heard the word "gay" they would look at each other, and in a mocking British accent, say "I'm not gay, I'm queer." The joke had emerged when, upon meeting an activist from the UK at the conference, they had been told that it was incorrect to refer to Armenian queers as "gay" as that term did not encompass all experiences. Importantly, not only are both of these terms literally linguistically foreign to the Armenian language, but as the Armenian alphabet does not have a form of expressing the sound "we" in "queer," it comes off as even more foreign-sounding—often pronounced as *qvir*. Hrispsime and Armen, thus, were mocking not only the materiality of the language itself but the attitude and behavior of a European activist who dared to educate them about their own local reality.

It would be important here to note the ways in which terms that circulate within Euro-America as critical toward processes of normalization, discipline, and power, become the circulating forms of that power itself when they are transplanted beyond their original territories. As Roman Leksikov has argued, the entry of "queer" into the vernacular of postsocialist spaces that have only experienced that term as a command of politically correct propriety signals its colonial reverberations (Leksikov 2017). In this context, while we might be critical of the use of "gay" or "lesbian" or other foreign identity categories as descriptors of local experience and desire, we must be also be attuned to the specific migration patterns of these vocabularies. While my interlocutors often found "gay," "lesbian," and "transgender" through their own searches for self—and made use of what they found based on their own feelings and experiences of commensurability with those vocabularies—"queer" is one that has largely entered the landscape of Armenia and other postsocialist worlds through the prescriptions and proscriptions of international actors or local activists who have taken on global critiques embedded in Euro-American political and social histories. As Boellstorff (2011) has discussed, the category of MSM ("men who have sex with men")—which began as a medicalized term for behavior devoid of social and collective underpinnings and taken up as a way to avoid attaching "gay identity" to those who might not identify as gay—has now become a form of identification itself even if far more tied to uneven global forms of institutional power than "gay" identity. Local feelings—whether in postsocialist contexts or otherwise—about the origins of terms that describe desire and experience might disregard the critiques attached to those terms and instead take up their conditions and processes of circulation as sites of critique.

Bogdan Popa has urged us to think about feeling bad—such as the feeling of shame—as having the capacity to surprise or as "postponing a demand to appear normal and in order" with the potential to rethink the political and the ethical. For Popa, shame "interrupts a given order that is perceived as natural," and can possibly suspend "the liberal regime of business-as-usual" (2017, viii). Misrecognition as a form of query might also constitute such a bad feeling, a sense that one is being inappropriate but wanting still to understand—pushing at the boundaries of the appropriate. For those attuned to queer politics—whether within a local or a global scope—these moments of misrecognition are not intended to violate an other's sense of self and esteem but to question the institutional relations, imbued with (geo)political power, through which the appropriate has been constituted.

Misrecognizing might make one feel bad, knowing the strange alliance one forms with right-wing forces in the performative of such an act. While the constative meanings of this misrecognition might be radically different, queer activists and advocates are aware of the ways in which the discourses of questioning the grounds of sexual and gender identity merge performatively with other, violent, acts. They are aware of the proper forms of address and discussion regarding categories of gender and sexual identity and perform these properly in the company of others, such as European and American visitors and others whom they understand as those who might be offended by the ways in which they sometimes veer away from the paths of the proper.

But to misrecognize anyway, even if within the intimate space of the office and among friends, is an act of refusal: not a refusal of queerness per se, but one of the political grounds on which particular forms of queerness become things, words, forms, and practices that constitute the proper. Audra Simpson describes a politics of refusal as

> a political and ethical stance that stands in stark contrast to the desire to have one's distinctiveness as a culture, as a people, recognized. Refusal comes with the requirement of having one's *political* sovereignty acknowledged and upheld, and raises the question of legitimacy for those who are usually in the position of

recognizing: What is their authority to do so? Where does it come from? Who are they to do so? (Simpson 2014, 11, emphasis in the original)

While Simpson is writing on the multicultural forms of recognition bestowed upon indigenous nations in the context of settler colonialism, here we might think of Armenian LGBT activists' and advocates' claims to sovereignty regarding the conditions of how knowing and doing gender and sexuality might emerge within their own particular contexts. Acts of querying gender and sexuality categories, which might often be understood as misrecognition, work to refuse the Euro-American proper and assert a claim to understand that which is emerging in Armenia on its own sovereign terms.

CONCLUSION: THE STAKES OF ANALYSIS

The early 2000s were rife with Euro-American anthropologists debating identity and power. Although these debates have now simmered down, this chapter has shown the ways in which some of the problems being discussed then remain unresolved. What are the stakes of an analysis that harken back to earlier modes of queer thought? We may find that in places where Euro-American categories of identity are being used wholeheartedly along with the forms of the political that those identities often entail are also sites in which queer folks undermine those politics through their own bad feelings. These might include misrecognition, shame, or backroom critiques of propriety, as I have described here. Or they might also include other bad feelings—sensibilities that reproduce notions of the L, G, B, and T while also affectively remaining in opposition to those ways of being, knowing, and living.

When I returned to the United States from twelve months of fieldwork in Armenia and began examining my research materials, I first thought about these survey debates as an obsessive attachment—a cruel attachment, to use Lauren Berlant's phrasing (2011)—to something that was impossible. Identity could never be precise to experienced reality; sex, gender, and sexuality could never be accurately and entirely separated. But upon reflecting on these debates within the wider context and reality of LGBT activism in Armenia, it became more clear that this was a politics of refusal—a refusal to accommodate to the correct without challenging what that meant—what it *really* meant. These queries were processes of performatively enacting what Gayatri Gopinath has discussed as the impossibilities inherent in queer transnational desire (2005). They expressed the dreadfulness of translating oneself into the Other's language. Thus, even while LGBT activists in Armenia worked with the L, G, B, T, and now more and more the Q, they were also actively invested not only in redefining the meanings of these terms and concepts but making new meanings about their own relationship to the (geo)political forces that made them. In other words, these queries were queer—they challenged the present structure based on various levels of political, economic, and social status quo in order to get at something else. In challenging the articulation of categories and boundaries, these questions made us uncomfortable. They were asked even if with discomfort. They were meant to make us uncomfortable.

REFERENCES

Ahmed, Sara. 2006. *Queer Phenomenology: Orientations, Objects, Others*. Durham, NC: Duke University Press.

Altman, Dennis. 1997. "Global Gaze/Global Gays." *GLQ: A Journal of Lesbian and Gay Studies* 3(4):417–436.

Berlant, Lauren. 2011. *Cruel Optimism*. Durham, NC: Duke University Press.

Boellstorff, Tom. 2005. "Dubbing Culture." In *The Gay Archipelago: Sexuality and Nation in Indonesia*, 58–88. Princeton, NJ: Princeton University Press.

———. 2007. "Queer Studies in the House of Anthropology." *Annual Review of Anthropology* 36:1–19.

———. 2011. "But Do Not Identify As Gay: A Proleptic Genealogy of the MSM Category." *Cultural Anthropology* 26(2):287–312.

Boyer, Dominic. 2013. "Simply the Best: Parody and Political Sincerity in Iceland." *American Ethnologist* 40(2):276–287.

Boyer, Dominic, and Alexei Yurchak. 2010. "American Stiob: Or, What Late-Socialist Aesthetics of Parody Reveal About Contemporary Political Culture in the West." *Cultural Anthropology* 25(2):179–221.

Butler, Judith. 1997. *The Psychic Life of Power: Theories in Subjection*. Stanford, CA: Stanford University Press.

———. 2011. *Bodies That Matter: On the Discursive Limits of Sex*. New York: Routledge.

Butterfield, Nicole. 2013. "Sexual Rights as a Tool for Mapping Europe: Discourses of Human Rights and European Identity in Activists' Struggles in Croatia." In *Queer Visibility in Post-Socialist Cultures*, edited by Narcisz Fejes and Andrea P. Balogh Fejes, 12–33. Chicago: Intellect.

Cohen, Cathy. 1997. "Punks, Bulldaggers, and Welfare Queens: The Radical Potential of Queer Politics?" *GLQ: A Journal of Lesbian and Gay Studies* 3:437–465.

Dave, Naisargi. 2012. *Queer Activism in India: A Story in the Anthropology of Ethics*. Durham, NC: Duke University Press.

Elliston, Deborah A. 1995. "Erotic Anthropology: 'Ritualized Homosexuality' in Melanesia and Beyond." *American Ethnologist* 22(4):848–867.

Foucault, Michel. 1978. *The History of Sexuality*, Vol. 1. New York: Vintage Books.

Fraser, Nancy. 1997. "Heterosexism, Misrecognition, and Capitalism: A Response to Judith Butler." *New Left Review* 52/53:279–289.

Ghodsee, Kristen. 2004. "Feminism-by-Design: Emerging Capitalisms, Cultural Feminism, and Women's Nongovernmental Organizations in Postsocialist Eastern Europe." *Signs* 29(3):727–753.

———. 2018. *Why Women Have Better Sex Under Socialism: And Other Arguments for Economic Independence.* New York: Nation Books.

Gopinath, Gayatri. 2005. *Impossible Desires: Queer Diasporas and South Asian Public Culture.* Durham, NC: Duke University Press.

Korolczuk, Elzbieta, and Agnieszka Graff. 2018. "Gender as 'Ebola from Brussels': The Anticolonial Frame and the Rise of Illiberal Populism." *Signs* 43(4):797–821.

Leksikov, Roman. 2017. "Post-Soviet Queer as the Colonial Theory and Practice." *Actual Problems in Sociology, Psychology, and Pedagogy* 33(2):5–14.

Manalansan, Martin. 2003. *Global Divas: Filipino Gay Men in the Diaspora.* Durham, NC: Duke University Press.

Massad, Joseph. 2008. *Desiring Arabs.* Chicago: University of Chicago Press.

Muñoz, Jose Esteban. 2009. *Cruising Utopia: The Then and There of Queer Futurity.* New York: New York University Press.

Neufeld, Masha, and Katharina Wiedlack. 2020. "Visibility, Violence, and Vulnerability: Lesbians Stuck Between the Post-Soviet Closet and the Western Media Scape." In *LGBTQ+ Activism in Central and Eastern Europe*, edited by Radzhana Buyantueva and Maryna Shevtsova, 51–76. London: Palgrave Macmillan.

PINK. 2013. "Monitoring of Human Rights Violations of LGBT People in Armenia."

Plemmons, Eric. 2017. *The Look of a Woman: Facial Feminization Surgery and the Aims of Trans-Medicine.* Durham, NC: Duke University Press.

Popa, Bogdan. 2017. *Shame: A Genealogy of Queer Practices in the 19th Century.* Edinburgh: Edinburgh University Press.

"Query." December, 2007. *Oxford English Dictionary Online*, Third Edition. Available from oed.com.

Renkin, Hadley Z. 2009. "Homophobia and Queer Belonging in Hungary." *Focaal* 53(Spring):20–37.

Rivkin-Fish. 2013. "Conceptualizing Feminist Strategies for Russian Reproductive Politics: Abortion, Surrogate Motherhood, and Family Support After Socialism." *Signs* 38(3):569–593.

Rofel, Lisa. 2007. "Desiring China." In *Perverse Modernities*, edited by Judith Halberstam and Lisa Lowe. Durham, NC: Duke University Press.

Shirinian, Tamar. 2017. "Sovereignty as a Structure of Feeling: The Homosexual Within Post-Cold War Armenian Geopolitics." *lamda nordica* 2–3:93–124.

———. Forthcoming. "To Foresee the Unforeseeable: LGBT and Feminist Civil Society and the Question of Feminine Desire." In *Is Female to Male as NGO Is to State? Gendered Analyses of Nongovernmentality*, edited by Andria D. Timmer and Elizabeth Wirtz. Tuscaloosa: University of Alabama Press.

Simpson, Audra. 2014. *Mohawk Interruptus: Political Life Across the Borders of Settler States.* Durham, NC: Duke University Press.

Valentine, David. 2007. *Imagining Transgender: An Ethnography of a Category.* Durham, NC: Duke University Press.

Verdery, Katherine. 1996. *What Was Socialism, and What Comes Next?* Princeton, NJ: Princeton University Press.

Wiegman, Robyn, and Elizabeth A. Wilson. 2015. "Introduction: Antinormativity's Queer Conventions." *Differences: A Journal of Feminist Cultural Studies* 26(1):1–25.

Woodcock, Shannon. 2009. "Gay Pride as Violent Containment in Romania: A Brave New Europe." *Sextures* 1(1):7–23.

———. 2011. "A Short History of the Queer Time of 'Post-Socialist' Romania, or Are We There Yet? Let's Ask Madonna!" In *De-Centering Western Sexualities: Central and Eastern European Perspectives*, edited by Joanna Mizielinska and Robert Kulpa. London: Routledge.

Zengin, Asli. 2019. "The Afterlife of Gender: Sovereignty, Intimacy, and Muslim Funerals of Transgender People in Turkey." *Cultural Anthropology* 34(1):78–102.

Chapter 3

Escaping the Dichotomies of "Good" and "Bad"

Chronotopes of Queerness in Kyrgyzstan

Syinat Sultanalieva

Being queer—lesbian, bisexual, or transgender—in Kyrgyzstani public discourse is the ultimate expression of a "bad girl" (*jaman kyz* in Kyrgyz). The main reason for this is that she is not interested in men (or at least not exclusively), and so she is not interested in marrying them and providing them with all the accompanying services expected of a wife. In the contemporary setting, this definition of a "bad girl" seems to have expanded to include feminists as well, who question the hegemonic role of males in Kyrgyzstan, re-established after the fall of the Soviet Union as the country grappled with its unwanted sovereignty (Kandiyoti 2007).

The definitions of "good/bad girls" are heavily dependent on the temporal and spatial contexts of the analysis. The same set of qualifiers that today generalizes feminists and lesbians into bad girls and women would be different thirty years ago, when a girl possessing these qualities would have been described as a good Soviet girl. The relationship is further complicated when taken out of macro and micro contexts, as a "bad girl" may be considered a "good girl" (*jakshy kyz*) in a different place at the same time. These nuances allow for the introduction of Bakhtinian "chronotopes" into the analysis, which help in understanding how "specific timespace configurations enable, allow and sanction specific modes of behavior as positive, desired or compulsory (and disqualify deviations from that order in negative terms)" (Bloemmaert and De Fina 2017, 5).

This chapter attempts to understand the chronotopic representation of queer women in Kyrgyzstan through their self-narratives of living under the pressure of the "good/bad girl" dichotomy, while localizing these narratives within the greater context of the country's recent history as a transitional democracy that is catering to both liberal and conservative global and regional agendas of religion and tradition. In order to do so the chapter is organized along four major themes—the history of the women's movement in Kyrgyzstan, the influence of religion on gender and sexuality issues in Kyrgyzstan, the disciplinary power of local concepts of *jakshy kyz* (good girl) and *el emne deit* (what will people say), and an insight into chronotopes of being a queer woman in Kyrgyzstan. Together these themes help reconstruct the context within which the chronotopic narrative identities of women come to be.

The methodology of this chapter was based on self-ethnography of queer women in Kyrgyzstan, with two focus group of five and eight people, respectively, and twelve individual interviews. All of the respondents were activist queer women, so in their responses they mentioned quite a few times that their experience may be different from that of non-activist queer women. In the majority of the cases, my respondents were able to relate the experiences of non-activist queer women, who happened to be either their former or current partners, or friends and acquaintances. Elements of auto-ethnography were also incorporated in the research to reflect my own positionality as the author, who self-identifies as a queer woman, feminist, activist, and scholar from a traditionally Kyrgyz background, which provided a good entry point to the field, as well as a useful angle from which to analyze the findings.

Theoretically, this chapter relies partially on the concept of chronotopes developed by Mikhail Bakhtin in Soviet Russia in the 1960s–1970s and rediscovered by Western academia in the 1980s after his death (Pushkin 2017). Bakhtin defines the concepts as such:

> We will give the name chronotope [literally, "time space"] to the intrinsic connectedness of temporal and spatial relationships that are artistically expressed in literature. (Bakhtin 1988, 252–253)

Although intended for literary theory and semiotics, the concept of chronotopes has recently been applied outside the main literary genre, ranging from critical geographies (Lawson 2011), strategy studies (Vaara and Reff Pedersen 2013) to sociolinguistics (Bloemmaert and De Fina 2017) when understanding narratives and discourses as they may appear in history, in reality, not just in fiction. The usefulness of the concept outside its genre limits seems to have been intuited by Bakhtin himself, as he writes about meanings:

> in order to enter our experience (which is social experience) they must take on the form of a sign that is audible and visible for us (a hieroglyph, a mathematical formula [. . .]). Without such temporal-spatial expression, even abstract thought

is impossible. Consequently, every entry into the sphere of meanings is accomplished only through the gates of the chronotope. (Bakhtin 1988, 256)

For Bakhtin, this term indicates the inseparability of time and space in human socialization, best represented in the literary genre for which the theory was initially intended, where "spatial and temporal indicators are fused into one carefully thought-out, concrete whole" (Bakhtin 1988, 252). The novel, for Bakhtin, was an interplay of different chronotopes, which were in dialogue with each other, as every chronotope was related to shared and differential, external values relevant to specific identities as perceived and described through appearance, actions, speech of characters representing certain social groups in specific time-space settings. In this sense the chronotopes necessarily involve specific forms of agency and identity as adopted within each such time-space configuration, producing a sense of "belonging" to this social group or setting, and of "transgression" when the expressions of agency and identity do not fit the existing frames of identities related to specific time-space configurations (see, e.g., Bloemmaert and De Fina 2016).

Bakhtin indicates the importance of focusing on the time-space configurations of any narrative or discourse, in other words, on their chronotopes, in order to understand them—which in our case is applicable to narrative identities. There are quite a few studies that have focused on the complex relationships between narratives and identities (Schiffrin 1996; Johnston 1997; Razfar 2012), which seems to indicate that there may be numerous narrative identities depending on context. Schiffrin writes that "our identities as social beings emerge as we construct our own individual experiences as a way to position ourselves in relation to social and cultural expectations" (1996, 170). This relates closely to the experience of queer women in Kyrgyzstan in partitioning their lives and divulging certain narratives in certain spaces and certain times to certain people or groups of people. When applied to the narratives of queerness and their queer life experiences, the women refer to specific time-space settings within which their self-assessments, as well as external assessments as that of a "good" or a "bad" girl shift and take on diametrically opposite meanings. These configurations may exist geographically in the same space, but temporally—in two different mini-eras, or at the same time, but in distinct spatial configurations. Here the concept/image of a "queer woman" itself is a material symbol, which contains within it numerous signifiers that are completely different from one chronotope to another, almost endlessly.

In understanding the chronotopic representation of queer women in Kyrgyzstan it is also helpful to investigate the relationship between chronotopes and various discourse-formulating institutions. While strongly influenced by religion (mainly Islam and Orthodox Christianity to a lesser degree), the Kyrgyz population heavily relies in its judgments of ab/normality on the notion of *el emne deit* or "what will people say," based on the concepts of *namys* and *uyat*—honor and shame, respectively (Satayeva 2017). Theoretically, these concepts most closely relate to Foucauldian "disciplinary power," which seeks to control the individual and centers "on the body, produces individualizing effects, and manipulates the body as a source of forces that have to be rendered both useful and docile" (Foucault 2003/1976, 249). Here disciplinary power "makes possible the operation of a relational power that sustains itself by its own mechanism and which . . . substitutes the uninterrupted play of calculated gazes" (Foucault 1995, 177), entrenching norms for an individual through comparison and judgment, disciplining anyone who falls beyond the normal range. *El emne deit*, *uyat*, and *jakshy kyz* are such tools in the Kyrgyz culture that discipline the bodies and identities of women to be reproductive and docile, drawing boundaries that are dangerous to cross.

HISTORY OF THE WOMEN'S
MOVEMENT IN KYRGYZSTAN

While it is possible to say that women's rights issues in Kyrgyzstan have been among the most salient social issues in the country's relatively recent history, the same cannot be said of queer women's rights in Kyrgyzstan, which until 2004 were not organized in the slightest. Still, understanding the context of being a queer woman in Kyrgyzstan necessarily involves understanding the history of women's emancipation in the country, which was the biggest impact of Soviet Union on the region, resulting in initial extreme pushback from the aggrieved male contingent of the region.

Ostensibly one of the most contested projects undertaken by the Soviet Union in Central Asia in the early years was *hujum* (assault), a large scale attack on the widely practiced social customs of women's religious veiling, seclusion, child marriage, bride price, bride abduction (Suyarkulova 2016). The veil symbolized the region's "backwardness" that needed to be cured by Soviet modernity, so women's emancipation in Soviet Central Asia became one of the key objectives of the Bolsheviks, who saw women as "surrogate proletariat" (Massell 1974) in the absence of a local working class that could be enlisted as the most exploited and humiliated in pre-Soviet Central Asia.

At the same time, although Central Asian societies responded negatively to Soviet meddling with the age-old gender order, they were able to adapt the newly offered/forced economic, social, political, and cultural codes to this same order. For example, owing to the specifics of the Soviet planned economy, which categorized Central Asia as primary commodity producers, as well as Soviet nationalities policy, the region was able to incorporate the old customary ways of social organizing into new conditions, such as *mahallas* (neighborhood) or *uruu* (nomad lineages) becoming the basis for *kolkhoz* (collective farm) formation. This ensured that the conditions were created to allow for practices of custom and tradition to remain and be reinforced, resulting in the "Soviet Paradox" of "high literacy and labor force participation rates against the background of high fertility rates, large families and relatively untransformed domestic divisions of labor" (Kandiyoti 2007, 607).

While many other post-Soviet countries had a history of modern statehood before the Soviet Union to which they could turn in search of a new ideology, Kyrgyzstan did not have such a luxury (Huskey 2003) and had to reinvent itself; however, it was not simply a return to the "pristine national traditions, interrupted by a Soviet regime now recast as 'colonial,' but [. . .] a strategic redeployment of notions of cultural authenticity in the service of new ideological goals" (Kandiyoti 2007, 602–603). The continuity of Soviet tradition was ensured by current nationalist policies that were created from the blueprint of Soviet nationalism (Fragner 2001). Elites openly exploited the familiar structures and toolbox. They praised history and invented the past by awakening old names and giving them a new birth, and then imposing them on people. To contemporary political leaders and elites, Soviet nationalism offered the possibility of continuing to use the familiar ideological tool of public mobilization without maintaining any debt to Marxism-Leninism and to the vanished Soviet ethical standards.

And so the country saw—with each of its new Presidents (Akaev 1991–2005; Bakiyev 2005–2010; Otunbayeva 2010–2011; Atambayev 2011–2017)—a parade of mostly male national heroes making their way into history books, community classes in school, all the way to becoming symbolic capital of state holidays and awards. These heroes were to symbolize the reinstatement of male privilege, previously unceremoniously interrupted by the Soviet regime in its quest to emancipate women of Central Asia. Now women's place was to retreat to the domain of the "private" and out of the "political," being central only to the biological reproduction of the nation. As Shirin Akiner argues, "The concept of male guardianship has now been re-established as a parameter of private as well as of public life" (1997, 287). Societally this was justified as the final reclaiming of national identity, traditions, and customs. Socialism was over, and it was time for women to

> return to their "natural" roles as mothers and housewives (conveniently assuming many of the caring responsibilities that the state could, or would, no longer provide), allowing men to reassert their "natural" position as head of the family and breadwinner after years of "unnatural," damaging, state-enforced gender equality. (Hoare 2009, 8)

INFLUENCE OF RELIGION ON GENDER AND
SEXUALITY ISSUES IN KYRGYZSTAN

Kyrgyzstan is a multiethnic and religiously diverse country with over twenty different denominations registered, of which a large majority are Islamic or related to Islam—about 85 percent of the population is Sunni Muslim, about 5 percent are Russian Orthodox, and the remaining 10 percent are spread across other Christian communities, as well as some Jewish, Buddhist and Baha'i.[1] After the fall of the Soviet Union, which prohibited any religion in its territories, Kyrgyzstan, like many other post-Soviet countries, was overtaken by various missionary movements of Christian and Islamic origin. Sunni Islam and the Russian Orthodox Church, however, are the only two religious institutions that the Kyrgyz State officially recognizes, considering these are the religions that were established in the country prior to the Soviet Union.

Homosexuality is legal in Kyrgyzstan, having been decriminalized in 1998. However, society as a whole, including religious communities, continues to be homophobic and transphobic. At the same time, respondents in this research, queer women-activists from the LGBT organization "Labrys" in Kyrgyzstan, noted that throughout their monitoring of the situation of LGBT people in the country from 2004 to 2019, they would not be able to say that the religious authorities have a structured approach to the issue of homosexuality or transsexuality:

> The attitude is definitely negative, there was even a fatwa issued [in 2014, see below for more details] which called for every Muslim to kill LGBT people. But I don't think they have a special anti-LGBT program—what I mean is they do not have a whole plan of eradicating us, which they would execute every Friday during *Juma namaz* [Friday prayer]. They usually just respond to some kind of news from the society. (Respondent A)

The fatwa that Respondent A is referring to was issued at the end of January 2014 by the SAMK (Spiritual Administration of Muslims of Kyrgyzstan—the official Muftiyat) and head Mufti, Maksat Haji Toktomushev, in response to a press conference organized by Human Rights Watch with the participation of a gay activist as a result of their research into the situation of gay and bisexual men in the country. The report stated that gay and bisexual men are regularly blackmailed and threatened, arbitrarily arrested, battered and sexually abused by the Kyrgyz police.[2] This press conference triggered a host of negative and extremely homophobic reactions from the public and religious authorities alike, resulting in the fatwa, which read:

If you see a community of luts [note: a reference to the Lut tribe (also Lot), described in the Koran as practicing sodomy] doing their deeds, you should kill the one who is doing it and the one to whom it is being done.[3]

Although later the SAMK revoked the fatwa, in fear that people might understand the call literally, whereas it is claimed it was only a reminder of the gravity of the sin of homosexuality, the fatwa itself, as well as the public outcry against the Human Rights Watch (HRW) press conference and the public coming out of a gay activist at that conference have directly predated the introduction of a homophobic "anti-LGBT propaganda" draft law in March 2014 (Bonheur 2016). Following these events, it has become much harder for LGBT people to be open about their identities, forcing them and their organizations to go underground:

Compared to early 2010s that I think of—it is like a golden era, when we could organize rainbow flashmobs in the city center, or hold candlelight vigils for Transgender Day of Remembrance in the central square, or do "hug me, I have HIV"/"hug me, I am a lesbian" etc., campaign right next to ZUM [central shopping mall]. We had three thematic clubs, and we could choose which one we feel like going to. Today? It's just meager bits, here and there—no longer public flash mobs or public actions. How could we? With that draft law still not going anywhere, even though it's 2019 already. (Respondent S)

Together with the draft law, which, although it had not passed beyond two parliamentary readings, still has not been struck down officially (Jacques 2018), respondents indicate the tightening of social control on their bodies and the expression of girls and women, especially if they are unmarried. This disciplining power is exercised by people and religious authorities alike by referring to the traditionalist norms of Kyrgyz society, which while not codified textually anywhere, are transferred from generation to generation— modified according to each different chronotope in which they are referred to, but always with the same absolute confidence that "this is how it used to be and this is how it should be."

THE DISCIPLINARY POWER OF *JAKSHY KYZ* AND *EL EMNE DEIT*

One of the main narratives of societal expectations and the role of women that the queer-feminist respondents of the research identified as having intensified in recent years was the patriarchal image of the *Jakshy Kyz*—the "Good Girl" in Kyrgyz, which is a well-prescribed way of staying within the required norm. While this chapter does not claim the uniqueness of such prescriptions of goodness to only the Kyrgyz culture, it is necessary to analyze them as factors that precondition the creation and escape into queer chronotopes by queer people in Kyrgyzstan.

The first time women come across this concept is when they are little girls, in response to an act committed, which is seen by the adults as unseemly for a girl. In the recent comprehensive research commissioned by GIZ (Moller-Slawinski and Calmbach 2015) on youth in Kyrgyzstan, where more than 150 youth aged 14 to 24 from all regions and the capital city of the country were interviewed, the subject of *Jakshy Kyz* came out most often in response to questions on the role of women. Almost all of the respondents mentioned that a Kyrgyz girl must be "good," and good was conceptualized on three levels: emotional, domestic, and intellectual:

> On the emotional side, a woman should be kind, respectful, tender, polite, affectionate, friendly, humane, simple, friendly, understanding;

> On the domestic level, a woman is expected to be orderly, conscientious, neat, a good housekeeper, taking good care of husband and children;

> On the intellectual side, especially (but not exclusively) for young people in urban centers a woman should be clever, educated and intelligent. (Moller-Slawinski and Calmbach 2015, 25)

Interviewees of this chapter in a focus group discussion further developed the concept of *Jakshy Kyz*, identifying this normative image as non-monolithic, separating it into several composite parts:

• The Islamic good girl: reading Quran, obedient, compliant, second to husband;
• The traditional good girl: Kyrgyz, rural, not especially Islamic, domestic, respectful toward elders and husband;
• The cosmopolitan good girl: sexy, glamorous, preferably connected to show business, while also able to be a good wife and mother;
• The secular good girl: higher education, diploma, good-paying job, but not too high positioned, good wife and mother.

Often nationalist discourses represent themselves in debates about women and their role in society, starting from what they should wear, how they should act, and all the way to whom they should marry, thus bearing responsibility for the nation's destiny (Yuval-Davis 1997). In studying this connection, Yuval-Davis classifies all modern nation-states based on their "myth of origin" and how it treats the subject of women. The *Volknation* category in this classification is especially interesting in the framework of the research results, as it considers its women to be responsible for the biological reproduction of the nation and as such for the preservation of the purity of the nation.

> I would say that having a child, just as it was before, is a very important criterion of "goodness" as a woman. You do not have to have many children, at least one. What is interesting is that this idea is promoted in the first place by medical specialists, that my clients visit [respondent is a practicing psychologist] or which I visit myself. They translate the idea that any and all health problems that a woman of a reproductive age might be encountering are due to unrealized reproductive functions of her body. (Respondent R)

> In my experience a woman is considered "good" when she is married, and the earlier, the better. To be good this woman should be willing to obey orders from her husband, the husband's parents and other relatives, and be this calm, servile, caring, nurturing woman, who also is bringing up children. She has to be very respectful towards her husband's parents, which is manifested in her doing all the housework alone and always on time and better than expected. And if you do not like something or express your opinion, you are not good, you become a "bad" woman. (Respondent NS)

> I think the most normative image is that of the celebrity—many girls want to be beautiful and sexy, wearing high heels. Many men also want these kinds of girls. But currently the strongest image is also the hijab girl, because of the growing Islamization of our country and I think girls themselves understand that men are more attracted to these types of girls—subservient, servile, who allow the men to control and dominate over them. And I think some girls wear the hijab so they can get married quicker. As for the sexy girl image, even though men want to marry the "pure" ones in hijab, they also want someone sexy. Maybe they will not marry them, but they will go to their concerts, watch their movies and so on. (Respondent A)

Foucault's concept of disciplinary power and of docile bodies argues that individuals are under constant surveillance and regulation in ways that are often subtle and thereby seemingly invisible, leading to the normalization and acceptance of such systems (Gordon 1980). Foucault focuses on the body specifically as the sight of regulation, or more specifically "as object and target of power" (136) historically. The notion of "docility"—the point at which "the analyzable body and the manipulable body" are joined—is employed to illustrate how individuals within their bodies are subjected to institutional regulation (136). He continues by stating that "a body is docile that may be subjected, used, transformed and improved" (136).

The docile body that is *jakshy kyz* is regulated by the ubiquitous concept of *el emne deit* ("what will people say," translated from Kyrgyz). It is the question that every girl and woman is asked by her parents and family whenever there is danger of falling beyond the prescribed norms and as such, bringing shame onto the family and stigma to the girl in question. Daring to be different or to be one's self, a queer woman, is complicated:

> In my experience it is very difficult—I had to sacrifice my time and communication with family. I had to leave my house constantly, so other relatives would not see me. I saw how my mother was silently glad when I would tell her that I had better leave before the guests come, because of course she did not want them asking all the same questions—when are you getting married? When are you going to have children? So that is why I have stopped attending any of the extended family meetings and celebrations, communicating with them. At some point I have to leave my family because of the constant barrage of questions—why do you have to have short hair? Why do you like such aggressive sports like soccer and rugby? Why do you only have girl friends? Why do boys never call you on the phone—only girls? So for me it was very difficult. (Respondent N)

Some choose themselves over family, while others are suffocated by this inhumane choice:

> I am depressed by the impossibility of loving my girlfriend openly. No, nothing horrible will happen, should I ever come out, especially to my parents. But I just do not even want to think about how my mother might look at me. Father would not even learn about it, she would never tell him, and neither would I. And I wish I could share with my mother how much I love her and how much fun we have together, and how we achieve so many things, how passionate we are about feminism and human rights and contributing to our country. But I cannot, it is as if this body is not my own, my desires are not important. What is most significant is to not let my mother down, at whatever cost, so that she never has to feel ashamed for me in front of others. And so I stay silent, even though my heart aches. (Respondent S)

The concept of *el emne deit* is itself based on two notions deeply embedded in the Kyrgyz culture—those of *uyat* (shame*)* and *namys* (honor)—where the worst nightmare of any person or family would be to lose face (Satayeva 2017). Although theories about the guilt-shame-fear spectrum of cultures seem to have limited empirical evidence for such distinctions (Cozens 2018), these concepts are used as tools of disciplinary power. Their influence becomes all the more significant as these concepts do not have clear demarcations as to what exactly constitutes a shameful action, or one that tarnishes someone's honor—most likely this is where *el emne deit* comes in, in how these shameful or dishonoring actions may become public and be subjected to public scrutiny:

> As long as I don't mention to anyone that I'm queer, as long as I keep on joking my way out of all these marriage questions, I should be fine, my family should be fine. But it is tiring, so tiring! I am tired of always being the one that is "bad," even if I have several higher education diplomas, I have lived abroad, I help my parents, I am doing something good for my country—and still I am the "bad" one, whereas my cousin, who has been married three times now, is the "good" one. (Respondent NS)

It is interesting that several of the paper's respondents mentioned their financial stability as a key factor in protecting themselves from the *el emne deit* disciplining, at least within their immediate families, as it seemed like an excuse that their families could use when defending against the extended family's questioning of their daughter's or sister's singleness, or strange short hair, or masculine appearance:

> My brothers used to be proud that none of their sisters is divorced, that they are all married, well, except for me—but me, they could say, is the one that lives in London now, so this adds for them some level of coolness, as well as lets them off, because I am helping my family. Even before London I was always helping my family financially, as if I was buying my way out of this pit, then my parents would stop badgering me. (Respondent Zh)

But for those who could not boast such accomplishments and who did not have the activist backbone like the respondents of the paper, a voluntary or forced coming out (reportedly practiced by disgruntled exes within the non-activist queer women's communities in Kyrgyzstan) resulted in the women being submitted either to psychiatric wards (less common) or to a Muslim imam, who would perform some kind of religious rituals to "purify" the girl:

> This has not happened to me, thankfully, as my family is not so much into religion, but ever since I am with my girlfriend, who is not an activist at all and actually dislikes for us to always stand out in a crowd, I have learned of experiences of other queer girls who are not from the [capital city Bishkek] and who are not activists themselves. What happens is that their families take them to an imam, who can keep them in a closed-off room without food and water for

prolonged periods of time, forcing them to read and recite Qur'an. For many
the only option to be let out was to pretend they were cured. (Respondent A)

Compared to the situation of women in the Soviet Union, who were force-
fully de-veiled and encouraged to join the workforce, study, and join the
Party—the emancipated "Women of the Soviet East" (Schurko 2016)—the
ideal of the "good girl" is the opposite. In most cases, she is everything that
was supposed to have been lost throughout the decades of Sovietization of
Central Asia: docile, compliant, home-sitting, religious, pious, married, significant only inasmuch as she is part of a man. Remembering the inversion of
Von Clausewitz by Foucault, where power is a continuation of war by other
means, we see how religious and traditional norms of the Kyrgyz culture that
were once considered mere "vestiges" by a high-ranking Soviet official in the
1980s have wrestled their power back from the Soviet culture in Kyrgyzstan,
using a kind of speech warfare—the tools of disciplinary power here, which
subject everyone into a panopticon of *el emne deit.*

INSIGHTS INTO SOME CHRONOTOPES OF
BEING A QUEER WOMAN IN KYRGYZSTAN

As queer women struggle to find their place in the increasingly homophobic
and conservative public spaces of Kyrgyzstan, their self-narratives identify
several chronotopes that allow them to shift in and out of the good/bad girl
dichotomy, often at will. For the majority of the respondents, the spaces
where they felt like they were "good girls," accepted and recognized for who
they are, were their activist organizations:

> I felt most at ease when I joined my organization and started writing alternative
> reports, speaking at roundtables, meeting with our local decision-makers. Once
> they saw that I was serious, that I was not just some small girl, they would rec-
> ognize me and they would shake my hand. I finally felt like I was not the "bad
> girl" I was back home for my family, who kept on waiting for me to settle down
> and get married and leave this public life. (Respondent A)

Many of the respondents shared similar experiences. For others, these spaces
were sports or sports-related workspaces:

> In my experience it was pretty easy to be who I am at work and in sports—there,
> everybody respects you for being that. They respect my blue belt in karate,
> that I have travelled for sports competitions, that I am strong enough to fight
> a guy. All the male colleagues I had would talk of me as a "sister," they were

very accepting. It was this respect for everything that was shameful back home. When I was working in a security agency, my boss was a former police officer, and would speak of me as one of his most valuable workers, that he could rely on me. He would say: "If anything this small girl can overcome a two-meter tall guy." So in this sense in sports and security agencies, and other places like these, the same qualities that are unacceptable for a woman otherwise, are respected and valued. (Respondent N)

Some mentioned that spaces that used to be safe have become unsafe due to increased conservatism and the recent crackdown on LGBT rights in Kyrgyzstan:

> Previously I would have said the club, but not anymore. It is no longer a safe space, although it is the same space we used to attend before. Nowadays we only have one club, when before we used to have several. And even this club is a nomad, just like us [laughing], it keeps on moving from one place to another because the landlords of the space ask them to go once it becomes clear what kind of clientele comes to this club. Before? Before it was great—it was the only space we could relax and stop worrying about not being the way our families want us to be. (Respondent K)

In many of the self-narratives of the queer women interviewed or relayed during focus groups, the issue of agency cropped up constantly, as these chronotopes—where a queer woman's identity was "bad" or "good"—were open for escape or joining. They were not aware of the possibility of escaping from the "bad girl" identity while staying true to their queerness, but as they joined activism or befriended activists or simply hung on to their lives as they were, these options became apparent, also showing them that these options could be shared:

> We think differently, I guess, because we know that it is possible to live differently, maybe this was not only because of Labrys—for me it was when I was in soccer, for Marina it was when she was in martial arts. And in some parts of our life we realized that we do not have to be like our mothers, like our neighbors, or necessarily do what our families tell us to do. And I guess the reason I think we are an alternative to the "good girl" is because we were able to understand that it is possible to live differently. And for me this is the reason we exist—to let other people understand that there is a different life. That if someone is beating you, you do not have to live with that person. That is why I think we exist—to talk about women's dignity, that we do not have to be patient about insults and beatings, and that it is possible to walk away from this. (Respondent D)

The English-speaking activists among the respondents also indicated that traveling outside the country or meeting with foreigners allowed them to escape the labeling of "bad girl" and to bask a little in the identity of a "good girl":

> I remember my first Pride, it was in Berlin actually, in 2008, on Christopher Street, I think it's called. I was there for an IGLYO[4] event, and it was basically my first ever encounter with international LGBT organizing. I felt joy at finally being somewhere where I was accepted, where people could be whatever way they wanted, and I was appreciated for doing the work I was doing back home. Nobody was asking those stupid questions about marriage or when would I have a child, no one was interested in these material things that I hated for so long. I met with representatives of various European institutions and I could not imagine having the same kind of meetings and discussions back in Kyrgyzstan. (Respondent S)

What unites these narratives is the sense of constant shifting—identities being identified as either "good" or "bad" depending on the years (the setting of clubs), locations (inside and outside the country), spaces (family/work or sports), or people (parents/activists or foreigners)—all the same identities assessed as different depending on the socio-spatio-temporal context of the interaction.

CONCLUSION

This chapter attempted to identify some of the chronotopes of female queerness in Kyrgyzstan, specifically in Bishkek, while locating this study in the country's historical context of the women's movement, of religion's influence on gender and sexuality, as well as the different tools that are used to discipline the queer bodies in the country. While strongly influenced by religion (Islam and Orthodox Christianity), the Kyrgyz population relies heavily on the notion of *el emne deit* ("what will people say") in its judgments of ab/normality, based on the concepts of *namys* (honor) and *uyat* (shame). These concepts are most closely related to Foucauldian disciplinary power, which seeks to control the individual, manipulating the body into being useful and docile.

The concept of Bakhtinian "chronotopes" allowed this chapter to focus on the time-space configurations of the narrative identities of queer women in Bishkek in order to gain insight into them. Sharing their experiences of partitioning their lives and divulging certain narratives in certain spaces and certain times to certain people or groups of people, the respondents identified specific time-space settings that reinforced either of the "bad/good girl" dichotomies. What united these narratives was the sense of constant shifting—identities being identified as either "good" or "bad" depending on the years (one club over a period of time), locations (inside and outside the country within the same time period), circles (family vs. work or sports) or people (parents vs. activists or foreigners)—all the same identities assessed as different depending on the socio-spatio-temporal context of the interaction.

What gave hope to many respondents was the discovery that these chronotopes—where a queer woman's identity was bad or good—were open for escape or joining. They were sometimes not aware of the possibility of escaping from the "bad girl" identity for prolonged periods of time, but as they joined activism or befriended activists, these options became apparent, also showing them that they could be shared further with other queer women caught in these chronotopes. In this sense, LGBTQ activism facilitates the understanding of the fluidity of narrative identities and that they are free to shuffle to and from as desired, giving these women an idea of the alternative ways of being that are not submissive to the dominant discourses of the good or bad. This may be one way that the queer community in Kyrgyzstan can free itself from social bondage in the future—as the number of people joining the activist circle grows, so must their awareness of unrigidity of these shackles, which fall as soon as one shifts.

NOTES

1. Data from the State Committee on Religion in Kyrgyzstan: http://religion.gov.kg/ru/.

2. Human Rights Watch, "They Said We Deserved This: Police Violence Against Gay and Bisexual Men in Kyrgyzstan." 2014: www.hrw.org/report/2014/01/28/they-said-we-deserved/police-violence-against-gay-and-bisexual-men-kyrgyzstan.

3. Radio Free Europe/Radio Liberty, "Kyrgyz Fatwa Against Homosexuality Debated." 2014: https://rus.azattyq.org/a/fetva-protiv-geev-kyrgyzstan/25261350.html.

4. IGLYO—International Gay and Lesbian Youth Organization.

REFERENCES

Akiner, Shirin. 1997. "Between Tradition and Modernity: The Dilemma Facing Contemporary Central Asian Women." In *Post-Soviet Women: From the Baltic to Central Asia*, edited by Mary Buckley, pp. 261–304. New York: Cambridge University Press.

Bakhtin, M. M. 1988. *The Dialogic Imagination: Four Essays.* Austin: The University of Texas Press.

Blommaert, J., and F. De Fina. 2017. "Chronotopic Identities : On the Spacetime Organization of Who We Are." In *Diversity and Superdiversity: Sociocultural Linguistic Perspectives*, edited by A. De Fina, I. Didem, and J. Wegner, pp. 1–15. Washington, DC: Georgetown University Press.

Bonheur, S. M. 2016. "LGBT in Kyrgyzstan: From Anti-Gay Propaganda Bill to Hate Crime?" *OSCE Academy Brief* 35. Bishkek.

Botoeva, G. 2012. "Kyrgyz Migrant Workers: Does National Pride Mean Violence Against Women?" *Open Democracy Website.* https://www.opendemocracy.net/en/odr/kyrgyz-migrant-workers-does-national-pride-mean-violence-against-women.

Cozens, S. 2018. "Shame Cultures, Fear Cultures, and Guilt Cultures: Reviewing the Evidence." *International Bulletin of Mission Research* 42(4):326–336.

Foucault, Michel. 1995. *Discipline and Punish: The Birth of the Prison.* New York: Vintage Books.

———. 2003. *Society Must Be Defended: Lectures at the College de France 1975–1976.* New York: Picador.

Fragner, Berg G. 2001. "'Soviet Nationalism': An Ideological Legacy to the Independent Republics of Central Asia." In *Identity Politics in Central Asia and Muslim States*, edited by Willem van Schendel and Erik Zuercher. London: Tauris.

Go, J. 2012. "For a Postcolonial Sociology." *Theory and Society* 42(1):25–55. doi: 10.1007/s11186-012-9184-6.

Gordon, Colin. 1980. *Power/Knowledge: Selected Interviews and Other Writings 1972–1977, Michel Foucault.* New York: Pantheon Books.

Hoare, Joanna Pares. 2016. "Doing Gender Activism in a Donor-Organized Framework: Constraints and Opportunities in Kyrgyzstan." *Nationalities Papers* 44(2):281–298. www.tandfonline.com/doi/abs/10.1080/00905992.2015.1007344.

Huskey, Eugene. 2003. "National Identity from Scratch: Defining Kyrgyzstan's Role in World Affairs." *Journal of Communist Studies and Transition Politics* 19(3):111–138.

Jacques. J. 2018. "Fear and Loathing in Kyrgyzstan: How the LGBTQI Community Is Fighting Back Against Rising Discrimination." *Open Democracy Website.* www.opendemocracy.net/en/odr/fear-and-loathing-in-kyrgyzstan/.

Johnston, B. 1997. "Do EFL Teachers Have Careers?" *TESOL Quarterly* 31(4):681–712.

Jones, P. 2017. *Islam, Society, and Politics in Central Asia.* Pittsburgh: University of Pittsburgh Press.

Kandiyoti, Deniz. 2007. "The Politics of Gender and the Soviet Paradox: Neither Colonized, Nor Modern?" *Central Asian Survey* 26(4):601–623.

Lawson, J. 2011. "Chronotope, Story, and Historical Geography: Mikhail Bakhtin and the Space-Time of Narratives." *Antipode* 43(2):384–412.

Pushkin, M. 2017. "Critical Analysis of Bakhtin's Chronotope." *Humanitas* 5(10):425–447.

Razfar, A. 2012. "Narrating Beliefs: A Language Ideologies Approach to Teacher Beliefs." *Anthropology & Education Quarterly* 43(1):61–81.

Schiffrin, D. 1996. "Narrative as Self-Portrait: Sociolinguistic Constructions of Identity." *Language in Society* 25:167–203.

Schurko, T. 2016. "The Woman of the Orient: Soviet Gender Order in Central Asia Between Colonialism and Emancipation." In *Concepts of the Soviet in Central Asia*, edited by Georgy Mamedov and Oksana Shatalova, pp. 178–209. Bishkek.

Suyarkulova, M. 2016. "Fashioning the Nation: Gender and Politics of Dress in Contemporary Kyrgyzstan." *Nationalities Papers: The Journal of Nationalism and Ethnicity* 44(2):247–265.

Vaara, E., and A. Reff Pedersen. 2013. "Strategy and Chronotopes: A Bakhtinian Perspective on the Construction of Strategy Narratives." *M@n@gement* 16(5):593–604.

Yuval-Davis, Nira. 1997. *Gender and Nation.* Thousand Oaks, CA: Sage.

Section II

QUEER IN PUBLIC

Chapter 4

LGBT+ Rights, European Values, and Radical Critique

Leftist Challenges to LGBT+ Mainstreaming in Ukraine

Emily Channell-Justice

When comedian-turned-politician Volodymyr Zelensky was elected president of Ukraine in April 2019, his positions on major social and political issues were more or less unknown. It thus came as a surprise when he made a statement in support of the LGBT+ community in Ukraine. During a fourteen-hour press conference in the capital city of Kyiv, Zelensky faced a heckler who accused the president of being a "toadie" of George Soros and helping the billionaire "spread" the "perversity of homosexuality" (Maurice 2019). Zelensky responded,

> Regarding LGBT: I don't want to say anything negative because we all live in an open society where each one can choose the language they speak, their ethnicity, and [sexual] orientation. Let those people be, for God's sake!

While it certainly would have been nice for Zelensky to say something positive—rather than simply not saying something negative—it was the first time a Ukrainian president ever commented on the LGBT+ community in this way. Over the summer, Zelensky had been invited to the Kyiv Pride Parade by its organizers. He did not attend, but he issued a statement calling for the safety and security of everyone during the Parade. The Kyiv City Council promised support and tolerance precisely to show that Kyiv is a "European" capital (Kyiv City Council 2019).

Ukraine's relationship with "Europe"—real and imagined—has been a contentious one since its independence in 1991. Ukraine's leaders have vacillated between aspiring to be members of the EU and economic and political rapprochement with Russia, but in general, the population has been oriented toward Europe. A 2019 survey by the Il'ko Kucheriv Democratic Initiatives Foundation found that 53 percent of Ukrainians think that their country should ultimately become a member of the EU (Il'ko Kucheriv 2019). And a 2018 survey by the same foundation showed that 68 percent of respondents felt that Ukraine should pursue pro-European reforms, even if it does not ultimately become a member (Il'ko Kucheriv 2018).[1] A major turning point for Ukraine were the 2013–2014 Euromaidan protests, which began in November 2013 in response to then-president Viktor Yanukovych's decision not to sign an EU Association Agreement and instead to turn to Russian president Vladimir Putin's Eurasian Customs Union. Yanukovych had campaigned on a platform that promised an Association Agreement, and his decision came as a surprise (Kudelia 2014). People gathered around *Maidan Nezalezhnosti* (Independence Square) in Kyiv to protest, beginning what turned into the months-long Euromaidan protests.

While ultimately the protests turned into a movement to remove Yanukovych from office, focusing more on democracy and dignity than Europeanization, they indicated a significant shift in that they solidified that most Ukrainians saw Ukraine's future as part of Europe. But what it means to "be European" is hotly contested in Ukraine to this day. As I have argued previously, gender and sexuality are topics that are particularly sensitive in relation to discourses around Europe, inasmuch as they are perceived to be threatening to traditional values in ways that other "European values" such as a free press or rule of law are not (Channell-Justice 2017).[2]

This chapter explores the intersection of LGBT+ rights in Ukraine with Europeanization and leftist politics. It is framed by the question, to what extent are gay rights an essential component of Ukraine being "part of" Europe? Are safer Pride Parades and increasing LGBT+ activism in Ukraine a legacy of the 2013–2014 Euromaidan mobilizations? How does the connection between LGBT+ rights and Europeanization limit the acceptance of activist claims that are organized around rights (i.e., to work, to marriage, etc.)? I consider the criticisms of this rights-based framework through the lens of leftist activists, who were some of Ukraine's earliest allies of the LGBT+ community and who concomitantly present essential criticisms of European and Western frames of political activism. These activists see a disconnect between more visible types of recognition of LGBT+ people, such as Pride Parades and corporate efforts to include LGBT+ consumers, with the lived reality for LGBT+ people in Ukraine.

I have been working with leftist activists since 2012, when I began doing research with student and higher education activists who were also anarchists, anti-capitalists, and feminists. When this research began, LGBT+ issues were peripheral to their major concerns, which were organized around repressions of student activism at universities, the marketization of higher education in Ukraine, and the encroachment of religion in secular educational institutions. But by the time I returned to Ukraine in 2013 for ten months of fieldwork with these activists, many had an attitude that LGBT+ rights and recognition were an obvious part of their fight. While not necessarily integrated with NGO-based LGBT+ rights groups in Ukraine, many leftists felt that it was natural to fight for LGBT+ communities.

Thus, I draw here from formal interviews as well as informal conversations with leftists about their relationship with LGBT+ activism. Some of them are themselves part of the LGBT+ community, while others see themselves and leftists in general as natural allies. As diverse obstacles have prevented my attendance at a Pride Parade in Ukraine, I have discussed the events with various attendees over several years, getting a fuller picture of how these events unfolded thanks to numerous informal interviews and discussions. I combine these conversations with media analysis of Pride Parades in Ukraine and around the postsocialist world in order to contextualize the importance of Pride in leftists' critiques. I discuss two articles about LGBT+ activism in the leftist journal *Commons* (*Spil'ne*), published in 2015, to help elaborate on leftist perspectives on LGBT+ rights and homophobia at that time. Finally, throughout this paper, I have used the acronym "LGBT+." Most publications in Ukrainian or by Ukrainians tend to use LGBT, and Roman Leksikov's (2017) sound criticism of the application of the term "queer" leads me not to use the "Q" in this case. I revert to LGBT when citing an author or document that uses this acronym.

UKRAINE IN A HOMOPHOBIC NEIGHBORHOOD

Ukraine's neighbors have records of extreme attitudes toward the LGBT+ community. In an assessment of over 200 news headlines regarding Pride Parades, the majority reflects violence and canceled events, especially until 2013. Serbia, Poland, Hungary, and Lithuania hosted Pride Parades in 2010, but violent attacks on participants in Serbia led to Pride being banned there until 2014 (Associated Press 2010). Russian activists attempted to organize Pride in 2010, but in 2012, Russian courts banned Pride Parades in Moscow for 100 years (BBC News 2012; and see Stella 2013; Semykina [2019] states that Pride marches have taken place in St. Petersburg since 2010 regardless of legal permissions). Articles about Russia, Poland, Romania, and Ukraine especially focus on social and political attitudes rejecting Pride and visible LGBT+ activism. Far-right threats in Poland increased (Young-Powell 2019), and cities across Russia that considered approving permits for Pride Parades reneged on those promises for various reasons, such as claiming that the ban was to protect children (Osborne 2019). Violence remains an issue for the LGBT+ community, and Pride Parades still see counter-protests (Renkin 2009; Woodcock 2009).

Indeed, in the past decade, it appears that tolerance for homosexuality has decreased around Eastern and Central Europe (Radio Free Europe 2019). At the same time that these countries are becoming part of the EU or entering into economic agreements with the EU, the same tolerance that increases in Western Europe continues to decrease in places such as the Czech Republic, Slovakia, Bulgaria, Russia, and Ukraine. Poland's tolerance level, according to this measure, has remained nearly the same, but stories on the ground may indicate a different attitude; for instance, the mayor of Gdansk, who had explicitly pro-LGBT+ sentiments, was murdered in 2019 (Santora and Berendt 2019). Around the post-Soviet region, LGBT+ people remain marginalized, and often silenced, with their safety in constant jeopardy. In T'blisi, Georgia, far-right and Orthodox protesters caused violence to break out during the premier of a Swedish-Georgian film about a gay relationship in November 2019 (RFE/RL Georgian Service 2019). A man was killed in Tashkent, Uzbekistan, in September 2019, following his coming-out on Facebook (RFE/RL Uzbek Service 2019). A gay Donbas war veteran was assaulted in Ukraine because of his sexual orientation (RFE/RL 2019).

In this context, how are LGBT+ activists organizing in Central and Eastern Europe? What are the issues they prioritize, and why? Is the institutionalization of LGBT+ rights, such as same-sex marriage and non-discrimination, a European value? Will adopting laws to protect these rights change dominant homophobic attitudes? Do Pride Parades represent progress, and how? This chapter teases out these "mainstream" LGBT+ issues by considering radical leftist critiques of how gay rights are represented in Ukraine. In so doing, I consider that LGBT+ activism has many angles, including claims to rights, as well as critiques of those claims that are grounded in a wider critique of global capitalism. In other words, I see that it is essential to consider the complexity that radical critiques lend to LGBT+ activism, while at the same time not diminishing the work that visible, protected Pride Parades contribute to bringing LGBT+ communities into the forefront of conversations about Ukraine's political future.

POST-SOCIALIST LGBT+
COMMUNITIES AND ACTIVISM

As many have written before, discussions of gender and feminism have been largely unwelcome in the postsocialist world.[3] The same is largely true for discussions of sexuality, which, while a separate sphere of inquiry in U.S.-based scholarship, is often collapsed in post-Soviet region because gender and sexuality are often seen as threats with similar points of origination in the West. Early scholarship on non-heterosexual sexualities focused on the potential of newly independent countries to develop a gay rights movement that mirrored those in Western European and North American societies (Baer 2002; Essig 1999). The progression of LGBT+ activism in the region is often measured by the same standards, such as economic mobility or the legalization of gay marriage, as U.S.- and Western Europe-based gay rights movements (Leksikov 2017). Despite a generally negative attitude toward gay rights movements in the region, Hungarian researchers Judit Takács and Ivett Szalma (2014) have argued that the institutionalization of gay rights through legalizing same-sex marriage or a registered partnership system can lead to a decrease of anti-LGBT+ attitudes, and they advocate for such policy changes in Central and Eastern Europe, even if the majority of the population does not have tolerant attitudes to the LGBT+ population.

Like other places in the post-Soviet world, Ukraine has a poor track record on protections of LGBT+ rights (Martsenyuk 2012). As was the case with terms "gender" and "feminism" before, LGBT+ activism is regularly framed by regimes and by anti-LGBT+ groups as a Western import, either not a priority for activists or simply as not relevant for Ukrainians. In a research survey by the University of St. Gallen (2017a), a question indexing social distance found most Ukrainians to feel more distant from LGBT+ people than any other group of people. Using a Bogardus scale on which 1 meant that the respondent would accept the person as a family member and 7 meaning that they would exclude that person from entry in Ukraine, LGBT+ people scored a 6.2.[4]

But more recent research has shown that Ukrainians who encounter gay and lesbian-identified people in their lives, especially those who have gay and lesbian friends, have a significantly more positive attitude toward the gay and lesbian community than those who have no contact with gay and lesbian people, especially among young people. Kharchenko also found that students had a more positive attitude toward lesbians than gay men; students also expressed that homosexual people should be accepted in society and have equal rights as non-homosexual people (except for the right to get married), but that there were more pressing issues for most Ukrainians than discussing gay rights (2017, 116). While this data, as well as interviews with mothers of gay and lesbian children suggests that interaction with LGBT+ people will help make non-LGBT+ people feel less distant from LGBT+ people, these research examples feature very small and limited sample sizes, making it difficult to assess whether various communities in Ukraine may be more or less friendly to LGBT+ individuals (Martsenyuk and Kolesnik 2016).

Across postsocialist countries, LGBT+ rights have become contentious and often exemplify the relative "backwardness" of formerly socialist societies (Kulpa 2014). But these anti-LGBT+ and anti-gender campaigns are the result of the interplay of various interests. In the months leading up to the Euromaidan protests in Ukraine, the anti-European accession platform Ukrainian Choice (*Ukrainskyi Vybir*) placed posters around Kyiv that called the proposed Association Agreement "same-sex marriage" (*odnostatevyi shliub*). The organization was funded by Viktor Medvedchuk, an oligarch close to Vladimir Putin and then-president of Ukraine Viktor Yanukovych, and its mission was to threaten that Ukraine would have to adopt anti-discrimination legislation and protections for gay citizens if Yanukovych signed the Association Agreement (Shevtsova 2017).[5] As Hadley Renkin has argued, anti-European logics treat LGBT people as symptoms of a kind of modernity that is "taken to be antagonistic to the Nation . . . this symbolic status renders them powerful sites of nationalist hatred" (Renkin 2009, 24). Relatedly, Samuel Greene and Graeme Robertson (2019) have described how the Putin regime in Russia mobilized LGBT+ claims to rights as a "wedge issue," one that had previously been absent from mainstream politics but was used by the regime to stir up support for those in power and to encourage rhetoric about traditional and religious values being threatened.

Such policies have led LGBT+ communities in countries like Ukraine and Russia to continue to relegate sexuality to the private sphere in order to protect themselves, even as this also reinforces the marginalization of claims to rights (Kondakov 2014). Maryna Shevtsova provides an analysis of "invisible participation" (which I later refer to as "strategic invisibility") of LGBT+ groups during Euromaidan, arguing that their invisibility prevented violence, but it also prevented LGBT+ activists from being able to make claims on their rights after the protests ended. As she writes, "The LGBT activists at the Euromaidan prioritized the common political goals of the Euromaidan protesters over their own goal—recognition of the human rights of LGBT people" (2017, 167). This statement reflects the earlier conclusions from Kharchenko that most Ukrainians who do accept the idea of gay rights as human rights—including LGBT+-identified people themselves—prioritize other issues over their own claims on rights. Yet others have found that visibility and presence in the public sphere may provoke backlash that helps strengthen the framing LGBT+ activist groups use to claim rights (O'Dwyer 2018). Shevtsova concludes that Ukrainian activists' increased participation in international LGBT+ activism has ultimately increased their visibility and has raised the profile of LGBT+ activism in Ukraine (2017, 174).

These arguments are based on a hegemonic, Western assessment of the "effectiveness" of gay rights agendas and activism in Eastern Europe and the former Soviet Union. The rest of this chapter will focus on the intersection of leftist activism and LGBT+ activism, from which criticisms of these mainstream analyses of gay rights are leveled. But this paper suggests that rights discourses must exist to provoke the critiques that are of interest here. In other words, there must be a certain adherence to the idea that to be "modern" and "European" means to have Pride Parades and gay marriage. Without adherence to these ideas, there is no space for radical critiques of modernity, normativity, and sexuality. I use various examples of Pride Parades in Ukraine to elucidate the connections between rights discourses and radical critique.

PRIDE PARADES AND HOMOPHOBIC VIOLENCE IN UKRAINE

For the past four years, Kyiv has been the site of successful, largely safe Pride Parades. In 2019, about 8,000 people participated with the support of global organizations such as Amnesty International (RFE/RL Ukrainian Service 2019). In 2016, a march took place in central Kyiv with a large police presence, and by 2017, activists celebrated an entire week of Pride events, culminating in a parade on June 18. The 2017 parade was attended by at least 2,500 people, including British ambassador to Ukraine Judith Gough. Maksym Eristavi, one of the organizers, called the event more of a "celebration" than ever before, noting that this successful Pride Parade brought Ukraine even further out of Russia's orbit and closer to Europe (Penman 2017). In these recent years, organizers have begun to see the Pride Parade as a celebration, rather than the risky protest it was in the early 2010s. Many gay rights activists even claim that these safe and successful Pride Parades show that Ukraine is moving closer toward Europe. Despite the presence of right-wing counterprotesters, police protection has focused on the protests, and the events have unfolded without a major incident.

Yet Nash Svit, a monitoring network, documented 358 cases of actions motivated by homophobia or transphobia, discrimination, and other violations of LGBT+ rights in Ukraine that occurred in 2017 (34 cases) and 2018 (324 cases). Their report points out that the 2018 number is somewhat artificially inflated because of improved monitoring mechanisms, but there is also a real increase in violence against LGBT+ people by right-wing groups (this latter may be related to O'Dwyer's evidence that backlash against marginalized groups, such as the LGBT+ community, can ultimately help their visibility and thus their claims on rights and protections). Nash Svit's 2018 report "Overcoming Obstacles" provides detailed documentation of these homophobic and transphobic actions and also documents the increased visibility of LGBT+ activism across Ukraine (Kravchuk and Zinchenkov 2019).

Along with violence at Kyiv Pride Parades, the western city of L'viv has seen its share of homophobic violence. The city is often considered to be Ukraine's most European city since it spent much of the eighteenth and nineteenth centuries under Austrian rule and only came into the Ukrainian Soviet Socialist Republic in 1944. But this history has not necessarily led to city residents holding progressive, so-called European social views. In March 2016, activists attempted to hold an Equality Festival (*Festival' Rivnosti*) in the city. Law enforcement received a call alerting them to a bomb threat at the Dnister Hotel, where some events were to be held, and when the hotel was evacuated, around 200 masked aggressors threw stones and firecrackers at festival participants and the police officers escorting them out of the building (Prokopchuk 2016). While law enforcement stated that the aggressors did not seem to be representing one organization, the rest of the Equality Festival's events in L'viv were canceled or held as closed meetings to protect participants' safety.

Nash Svit's report also found that, in 2018, the city of Kryvyi Rih held an Equality March, in addition to Kyiv and Odesa, and other events were held in Kharkiv, Zaporizhzhia, Kherson, and Mykolayiv. The contrasting geography shows that organized, sanctioned Pride-related events have been appearing in recent years in eastern and southern cities such as those listed above, rather than in the west of the country. Whereas western regions may historically have stronger connections to the rest of Europe, residents of these regions also tend to hold more traditional values, especially regarding gender and family. Right-wing and traditionalist groups continue to counter-protest the Pride Parades, largely by promoting a "pro-family" and anti-gender agenda.[6] For instance, in 2017, the right-wing organization Right Sector called the Pride Parade "Ukraino-phobic" and invited people to join their counter-event through their Facebook page: "In order to prevent all kinds of destroyers of the Ukrainian traditional family and cultural heritage from holding their 'gay shabash,' we call on all conscious citizens to protect their honor, dignity, and fatherland (*Bat'kivshchyna*)." Given that national surveys from 2013, 2015, and 2017 all showed that family membership was Ukrainians' second-most dominant identity (male/female being first), using rhetoric of protecting the family is a resonant way of mobilizing people against the LGBT+ community (University of St. Gallen 2017b).

Despite the continued organization against the Equality March events, they have come a long way in a few years: in 2015, President Petro Poroshenko advocated for a safe, unimpeded event, but the mayor of Kyiv, Vitaly Klitschko, had suggested canceling it that year (Miller 2015). Then, a small group of activists held a Pride Parade, but they and their police protection were attacked by far-right activists (Amnesty International 2015). While twenty-five people were detained following the attack, nearly all of them have since been released without charges. Four were convicted of hooliganism, but they were not charged with a hate crime (Schaaf 2019). I will discuss the implications of the 2015 Equality March for leftists later on in this chapter. First, I delve into leftist activism in Ukraine and the ways leftists have leveled critiques against the mainstreaming of LGBT+ activism.

ALTERNATIVE ACTIVISMS: LEFTIST CRITICISM OF LGBT+ MAINSTREAMING

Radical queer and feminist activists have been skeptical of the centrality of Pride Parades in Ukraine, even as they usually participate. Many express criticisms that parades have the potential to gloss over demands for actual changes to protect LGBT+ people in Ukraine, or that parades are not reflective of more widespread attitudes toward LGBT+ people. The Pride Parade encourages people to present Ukraine as more accepting of LGBT+ people than it actually is. These critiques are resonant with Jasbir Puar's notion of "pinkwashing," or the "cynical promotion of LGBT bodies as representative of . . . democracy" (Puar 2013, 338). Kyiv's Pride Parades reflect a site in which criticisms of Ukraine's precarious future in a global, neoliberal capitalist economy play out in a moment that espouses progressive values and democratic representation but demands no substantive change.

This chapter takes seriously the intersection between LGBT+ activism in Ukraine and the broadly defined left. Framing leftist activism is the concept of self-organization (*samo-orhanizatsiia*), a key structure of the Euromaidan protests. Self-organization is the notion that if something needs to be done, and a person can do it, then they should simply do it. Leftists see self-organization as a basic political concept, and it has consistently framed their activism since I began my research in 2012. Self-organization allows activists to be inspired to work toward goals they make for themselves, rather than definitions or expectations established by outsiders. This framework helps us understand why leftists remain so critical of institutionalized Pride Parades and legalization of gay marriage, if they did not choose these priorities themselves. Many leftists are not convinced that a Europeanized version of a Pride Parade actually helps end discrimination and marginalization.

The following anecdote, told to me in an interview in April 2014 with a male leftist activist named Volodya, helps frame how leftists found the intersection between LGBT+ issues and the left.

> Basically, I am of leftist views. But the spectrum of "left" is really big, and I only became politicized so strongly in the last year and a half, and especially

during the time of the events on Maidan. [. . .] There is a big influence that I took part, and continue to take part in the last eight or nine years in tolerance projects and informal education about tolerance and anti-discrimination. Maybe especially it was the action for International Human Rights Day that made an impression on me, at the end of 2012. There was an action against the Law 8711, that's the so-called "homosexual propaganda" [law], and human rights activists as well as [student] activists came. And there was a Nazi attack. And it became clear to me that leftists support human rights and anti-discrimination, while the ultra-right does not.[7]

On the one hand, it makes sense that leftists would naturally position themselves opposite of the radical right. Relatedly, as critics of most political regimes but especially critical of then-president Viktor Yanukovych's time in power, it makes sense that leftists would be critical of Yanukovych's adoption of a Russian law such as the one against the spread of "homosexual propaganda." But on the other hand, given the marginal place of LGBT+ activism in Ukrainian society, what would motivate leftist activists, themselves also marginalized and threatened in Ukrainian politics, to so clearly link their values with LGBT+ rights?

Volodya expressed that LGBT+ rights and activism are crucial to political activity in Ukraine, especially as it is related to anti-discrimination, tolerance, and human rights. By framing LGBT+ rights as human rights, and as the radical right and the state work in tandem to repress those human rights, leftist allies of the LGBT+ movement present themselves as a political alternative that is more progressive, and possibly more "modern," than the current governing system. Importantly, Volodya associated the radical right with unprovoked violence, a tactic that leftists or other progressive groups would not use. He presented the use of violence as the opposite of respect for human rights in discussing the right-wing attack on the demonstration against the homosexual propaganda law: "Just violence, it was not clear to me why they jumped us, used tear gas. There wasn't any kind of provocation, just an attack." Volodya's view—that violence against a peaceful demonstration was as unacceptable as a law against "homosexual propaganda"—presents an arguably modernist idea of what progressive values are. The protection of human rights and the idea of tolerance of difference come from a globally hegemonic liberal democratic perspective. Without arguing against these values, I show here that ensuing attempts to implement some idea of gay rights as a sign of Ukraine's position in Europe or as a democracy have led to major criticisms of these efforts from leftist groups, who early on took risks to support LGBT+ claims long before mass mobilizations.

KYIV PRIDE'S PRECARITY

In June 2015, a year after the end of the Euromaidan mobilizations, LGBT+, feminist, and leftist activists organized an Equality March in Kyiv. About 250 people joined the march, protected by nearly 500 city police officers. Radical right-wing activists harassed and attacked the march, injuring several protesters and police officers, one severely. For Ukrainian leftist, feminist, and LGBT+ activists, who later set up a website to crowdfund the medical costs for the injured police officer, this march was a success. Despite the violence, and the cancellation of other Pride-related events following the march, the fact that a Pride Parade happened at all, and that police protected the marchers instead of joining their attackers, showed a significant shift in perceptions of protest and activism following the mobilizations on Maidan.

Russian LGBT+ activist and journalist Masha Gessen, however, compared the parade with one that year held in Warsaw, Poland, Ukraine's "more European" neighbor, which, Gessen described, "draw[s] thousands of people to an extravaganza of floats and flags that looks as much like a party as any other western Pride celebration" (2015). But leftist commentary on the situation of LGBT+ activism before the parade argued that discrimination on the basis of sexual orientation and gender identity were not a priority for the current administration, and thus opened those activists up to violence and harassment from the far right. Echoing Volodya's statements earlier, representatives of the far right felt empowered to use violence when they disagreed with the values being promoted, even if those values were supposedly part of Ukraine's "European" future.

In the leftist journal *Commons*, Denys Lavryk (2015) analyzed homophobia in the post-Euromaidan period. He described the contradictions in Ukraine's claims to move toward Europe and the ways it has—and has not—prioritized protecting the rights of sexual minorities. Lavryk argued that Euromaidan and the ensuing war with Russia has militarized many Ukrainians and created the space for the far right to commit violence with abandon. Further, his evidence from 2011 and 2012 showed that tolerance for LGBT+ people in Ukraine has decreased since 2002.[8] This combination of factors led to the mobilization of false notions about the LGBT+ community, as the threatening rhetoric of "Gayropa" (Gay+Europe) was meant to discredit the Euromaidan protests and EU integrationist politics. Thus, Lavryk argued, LGBT+ activists who wanted to participate in Euromaidan were more likely to choose the policy of "strategic invisibility" described by Shevtsova (2017; which she calls "invisible participation" in English; see also Martsenyuk 2014). Lavryk argued,

Experts believe that the most optimal strategy for combating homophobia is cooperation at the state and grassroots levels, when the efforts of state institutions in this sphere are supported by the educational activities of LGBT rights organizations and movements. However, against the background of the aggravation of the situation in the country, the growing role of right-wing militant organizations, and the neglect of the new authorities to protect minority rights assumed in the context of Euro-integration, the prospect of such a strategy remains questionable.[9]

Despite right-wing and pro-Russian attempts to connect Europeanization with the threat of LGBT+ rights, Lavryk pointed out that state institutions have *not* effectively integrated LGBT+ rights into their priorities for European integration. Rather, state actors have allied themselves with right-wing organizations and expanded the militarization of society, turning a blind eye to anti-LGBT+ activism at the hands of the far right. Thus, Lavryk remained critical of the idea of the EU as a "life vest" that will support Ukraine in overcoming homophobia. He was critical of the orientation of LGBT+ activists who attempt to mimic "Western" ideals and values in their communities—and, as he pointed out, not all European countries have real protections for LGBT+ rights. Lavryk argued that the LGBT+ community lacked a critical lens onto Euromaidan, which "did not allow the LGBT+ community to consolidate foremost with other groups that experience discrimination (ethnic, religious, linguistic) but forced it to enter the general mainstream pro-European discourse." These attitudes, plus the "strategic invisibility" policy, have preserved the homophobia present in Ukrainian society, rather than fought against it.

In this context, the 2015 Equality March took place. Activists were aware of threats from the far right and that they would likely not be protected by law enforcement. But leftists who participated in the 2015 march felt that the march was still a significant experience. Zakhar Popovych was one leftist activist at the Equality March, bloodied by the right-wing thugs, who wrote in *Commons* about why it was so important to go to the Equality March. Putting the attack on the march in the context of a general promotion of violent acts by right-wing groups and echoing Lavryk's assessment above, Popovych (2015) linked LGBT+ rights to human emancipation from the constraints of capitalism:

The exclusion and creation of stigmatized minorities has been a common method of the existence of a capitalistic world system since its inception. [. . .] Today, the artificial stigmatization, criminalization, and social exclusion of social groups: migrants, national and religious minorities, LGBT people—is perhaps the most important way of legitimizing the barriers between the exploited of the capitalist system, both between different countries and within each country. Only real, effective solidarity between all the excluded and the exploited (whoever that may be) is the only guarantee of a successful struggle for real emancipation and overcoming the capitalist system of human exploitation by man.

Thus, Popovych makes LGBT+ rights an essential component of leftist ideals of equality and solidarity. LGBT+ people are part of the exploited groups in capitalism, so their liberation is part of all our liberation from capitalist exploitation. Popovych was also hypercritical of the mainstreaming—and pinkwashing, though he did not use the word—of the Equality March. He wrote,

> It will be possible to allow ourselves not to support "gay parades" only if they finally turn into "*vyshyvanky* parades" with the president-oligarch at the front.[10] Only then will "pride" really have nothing to do with the fight for human rights, as the traditional Mother's Day has nothing to do with feminism and the fight for women's rights. Then, maybe it will be worth launching our own "Equality March," like our comrades from the Feminist Offensive did a few years ago on the 8th of March.[11]

Popovych is drawing from themes of self-organization to describe ways to promote the intersection of LGBT+ rights with leftists' general goals. If self-organization is fundamental to the ways leftists organize themselves, then the appropriation of LGBT+ activism—which should have a critical, anti-capitalist bend to it—can be reversed with a return to self-organization.

Since 2015, Kyiv's Pride Parades have gotten closer to Gessen's idealistic vision. A few years later, I discussed the Pride Parades with a feminist and LGBT+ activist. In 2017, the Kyiv parade saw a right-wing presence, but there was not mass violence against participants. The city organized special metro cars to take protesters from the event once it was over to help protect them from any roving would-be attackers. Some 5,000 police were mobilized for that event, and police did indeed stand with the protesters (Janjevic 2017). But these visibly successful events are not indicative of a more widespread acceptance of LGBT+ rights in Ukraine. Right-wing activists promote the idea that LGBT+ people threaten traditional gender norms and family structures. This is precisely what makes leftist and radical activists skeptical: the appearance of a successful Pride Parade with rainbows and drag queens makes Ukraine appear to be more accepting of LGBT+ citizens than it actually is. According to Natalia, a leftist, feminist, and queer activist, who attended the Pride Parade in 2017, "We can do that here when there are thousands of other people and a police cordon, but not every day."

While Leksikov and Rachok (2020) have used a critical lens to understand the application of Puar's homonationalism on Ukraine, here, I would like to draw Puar back into this discussion. Puar argues that homonationalism is a "facet of modernity and a historical shift marked by the entrance of (some) homosexual bodies as worthy of protection by nation-states, a constitutive and fundamental reorientation of the relationship between the state, capitalism, and sexuality" (2013, 337). In the example of Ukraine, we do not see that some LGBT+ bodies are worth protecting; rather, we see that all LGBT+ bodies are *only sometimes* worth protecting—only when Ukraine is making a claim on a European identity. Here, pinkwashing is a promotion of LGBT+ bodies as representative of a European-style, non-discriminatory democracy, which is anything but secure in Ukraine, especially for LGBT+ people.

As Puar points out, these processes are inevitably linked to capitalism. As capitalist and democratic development in Ukraine continue to go hand in hand, and as leftists continue to levy their critiques largely in relation to the country's economic precarity, a discussion of the intersection of LGBT+ identity and capitalist development is merited here. While Puar describes the normalization of "the production of a gay and lesbian tourism industry built on the discursive distinction between gay-friendly and not-gay-friendly destinations" (2013, 338) for instance, here, I consider how companies in Ukraine do or do not mobilize around a perceived LGBT+ audience, and I use leftist critiques to discuss the reception of these campaigns.

PINKWASHING CAPITALIST PROGRESS

Some businesses, especially international companies with stores in Ukraine, have shown their support for Ukraine's LGBT+ community. A Ukrainian ridesharing company, Uklon, ran a Valentine's Day ad campaign with the tagline "I love you" (with "love" as the logo for the company) and featuring both male and female same-sex couples. As a Facebook post commending Uklon pointed out, the company's services were regularly two times cheaper than an international company like Uber in the city of L'viv—the post's author's only complaint was that many cars still do not have seatbelts. In another instance, the cosmetics company Lush has a strong anti-discrimination policy for its employees, even in Ukraine where such policies are not the norm. Their store in Kyiv faced harassment because of its inclusive policy (Bond and Vlasova 2017) but, as activist Natalia pointed out, if she and other LGBT+-identified people cannot afford to shop at such stores, is visibility really helping the everyday problems LGBT+ people face because of discrimination?

At the same time, the Ukrainian Corporate Equality Index, which measures practices and politics of equality in businesses in Ukraine, has begun to measure the levels of information and protection for LGBT people. In 2016, their report measured only how inclusive companies were regarding gender and disability, but in 2017, they measured inclusivity for LGBT people, as well. While the majority of companies that had the highest scores regarding LGBT inclusivity and non-discrimination were either NGOs or international companies, the work to measure LGBT protections independently from other kinds of discrimination is perhaps an important step toward potentially securing economic stability and protections for the LGBT community in Ukraine. Or, more cynically, perhaps such measures serve no real function other than to show, on paper, that Ukraine is meeting European standards to encourage foreign investments.

Leftists continue to be critical of the business focus of these types of promotions of LGBT+ rights that promote comfortable ideas rather than the ongoing problem of economic inequality. Natalia and other leftists are skeptical of institutionalized LGBT+ events and would instead prefer to keep their focus on intersectional activism: to Natalia and her partner, working for LGBT+ rights also means working against other kinds of discrimination, including against people of color or of other ethnicities. As Natalia put it, "If we want to talk about equal rights, then we have to actually do them." This further means recognizing the ways that LGBT+ people of color, or lesbian mothers, or LGBT+ people with disabilities, face even greater discrimination than people like Natalia and her partner. Because institutions, corporations, and the Ukrainian government are not focused on intersectional human rights, leftist LGBT+ activists must continue to level these critiques and work toward inclusive change.

CONCLUSION

In this chapter, I have argued that the intersection of LGBT+ discourses with leftist activism levels significant criticisms about the mainstreaming of LGBT+ rights. Whereas Pride Parades make Ukraine look safe and tolerant of LGBT+ people, leftists' focus on the use of violence and lack of everyday safety corroborate monitoring organizations' conclusions that homophobic violence has increased in Ukraine since Euromaidan. While a Europeanized, modernized version of a Pride Parade, such as those taking place in Kyiv since 2017, is an institutionalized recognition of LGBT+ rights, leftist activists are not convinced that such events actually help end discrimination and marginalization. Because leftist interest in LGBT+ causes is intimately connected to their commitment to the liberation of all oppressed people, leftists are intensely critical of these surface measures that only represent equality but do little to support LGBT+ people in their everyday lives.

Perhaps turning the discussion away from Europe and focusing more on community building and self-organization would help make equal rights a reality for LGBT+ people in Ukraine. In a context where openly identifying as LGBT+ remains unsafe, it is small communities, such as leftist activists, who create the space for LGBT+ people to be themselves and feel supported among others. While these localized practices may not explicitly fall under widely accepted definitions of activism, they continue to be meaningful for those LGBT+-identified people who may otherwise struggle to find accepting spaces. Further, these everyday practices of tolerance frame the vision that leftist activists have of themselves, just as Volodya described in 2014.

NOTES

1. This number has fluctuated since 2013, peaking at 59 percent for EU integration in January 2016. The percent of the population that supports EU integration is now about the same as it was in 2013, 2017, and 2018. The percent of the population that would prefer entering the Eurasian Customs Union with Russia and Kazakhstan has been steadily decreasing since 2016 and is now around 10 percent (Ukrains'ka Pravda 2018).

2. This comparison does not mean to indicate that Ukraine has established a free press or rule of law.

3. There is an extensive body of literature on this topic; see the review in Channell-Justice 2017. Some significant early contributions to this literature are Drakulic 1991; Funk and Mueller 1993; Gal and Kligman 2000.

4. The middle values of the scale were as follows: 2=close friend, 3=neighbor, 4=colleague, 5=inhabitant of Ukraine, 6=tourist. The questions in the survey dealt mostly with ethnic groups (Arabs, Africans, Roma, Turks, etc.), and it is notable that most respondents were likely to feel like neighbors or colleagues (values 3 or 4) with internally displaced people from Crimea and the Donbas, as well as with Russians and Crimean Tatars.

5. These protections were established in Ukraine in November 2015 (see Shevtsova 2017, 171).

6. Regarding anti-gender campaigns in Poland, see Graff (2014).

7. Personal communication.

8. As Lavryk rightly states, however, there have been very few polls on this topic, and the questions often vary, meaning that this data must be considered critically and is not necessarily representative.

9. Translation by the author.

10. *Vyshyvanky* are traditional Ukrainian embroidered shirts, so here, Popovych is indicating that the parades would have to become "Ukrainian" or even "national" to be not worthy of support by leftists.

11. Although Feminist Offensive is no longer a functional organization, feminists and LGBT activists organize a demonstration on March 8 to promote feminism and women's rights.

REFERENCES

Amnesty International. 2015. "Ukraine: Homophobic Violence Mars Gay Pride Rally in Kyiv." *Amnesty International*, June 6, 2015. www.amnesty.org/en/latest/news /2015/06/homophobic-violence-mars-gay-pride-rally-in-kyiv/.

Associated Press. 2010. "Serbia Police Clash with Far-Right Rioters at Gay Pride March." *The Guardian*, October 10, 2010. www.theguardian.com/world/2010/oct/ 10/serbia-police-rioters-gay-pride.

Baer, Brian James. 2002. "Russian Gays/Western Gaze: Mapping (Homo)Sexual Desire in Post-Soviet Russia." *GLQ* 8(4):499–521.

BBC News. 2012. "Gay Parades Banned in Moscow for 100 Years." *BBC News*, August 17, 2012. www.bbc.com/news/world-europe-19293465.

Bond, Kate, and Anastasia Vlasova. 2017. "Gay and Displaced on the Front Lines of Ukraine's Conflict." *UNHCR*, September 15, 2017. www.unhcr.org/en-us/news/ stories/2017/9/597ef1fc4/gay-displaced-frontlines-ukraines-conflict.html.

Channell-Justice, Emily. 2017. "'We're Not Just Sandwiches': Europe, Nation, and Feminist (Im)Possibilities on Ukraine's Maidan." *Signs: Journal of Women in Culture and Society* 42(3):717–741.

Drakulic, Slavenka. 1991. *How We Survived Communism and Even Laughed*. New York: W. Norton and Company.

Essig, Laurie. 1999. *Queer in Russia: A Story of Sex, Self, and the Other*. Durham, NC: Duke University Press.

Funk, Nanette, and Magda Mueller. 1993. *Gender Politics and Post-Communism: Reflections from Eastern Europe and the Former Soviet Union*. New York: Routledge.

Gal, Susan, and Gail Kligman. 2000. *The Politics of Gender After Socialism*. Princeton, NJ: Princeton University Press.

Gessen, Masha. 2015. "The Assault on Kiev Pride." *The New Yorker*, June 6, 2015. www.newyorker.com/news/news-desk/the-assault-on-kiev-pride.

Graff, Agnieszka. 2014. "Report from the Gender Trenches: War Against 'Genderism' in Poland." *European Journal of Women's Studies* 21(4):431–435.

Greene, Samuel, and Graeme Robertson. 2019. *Putin v. the People: The Perilous Politics of a Divided Russia*. New Haven, CT: Yale University Press.

Il'ko Kucheriv Democratic Initiatives Foundation. 2018. "European Integration in the Dimension of Public Opinion [Yevropeis'ka intehratsiia u vymiri hromads'koi dumky]." September 28, 2018. https://dif.org.ua/article/evropeyska-integratsiya-u -vimiri-gromadskoi-dumki.

———. 2019. "Ukraine's European Integration: Dynamics of Public Opinion [Yevropeis'ka intehratsiia Ukrainy: dynamika hromads'koi dumky]." December 5, 2019. https://dif.org.ua/article/evropeyska-integratsiya-ukraini-dinamika-gromads koi-dumki.

Janjevic, Darko. 2017. "Ukraine LGBT Community Marches Through Kyiv for Gay Pride Parade." *Deutsche Welle*, June 18, 2017. www.dw.com/en/ukraine-lgbt-com munity-marches-through-kyiv-for-gay-pride-parade/a-39297276.

Kharchenko, O. 2017. "Attitudes and Stereotypes of Students Toward People with a Homosexual Orientation [Stavlennia ta stereotypy studentstva shchodo liudei z homoseksual'noiu orientatsiieyu]." *Current Problems of Sociology, Psychology, and Pedagogy* 2(33):105–118.

Kondakov, Alexander. 2014. "The Silenced Citizens of Russia: Exclusion of Non-Heterosexual Subjects from Rights-Based Citizenship." *Social and Legal Studies* 23(2):151–174.

Kravchuk, Andrii, and Oleksandr Zinchenkov. 2019. *Overcoming Obstacles. LGBT Situation in Ukraine in 2018.* Kyiv: Nash Svit Center.

Kudelia, Serhiy. 2014. "The Maidan and Beyond: The House that Yanukovych Built." *Journal of Democracy* 25(3):19–34.

Kulpa, Robert. 2014. "Western 'Leveraged Pedagogy' of Central and Eastern Europe: Discourses of Homophobia, Tolerance, and Nationhood." *Gender, Place, and Culture* 21(4):431–448.

Kyiv City Council. 2019. "Mykola Povoroznyk: 'A Safe Equality March Is a Possibility to Show Kyiv is a European Capital' [Mykola Povoroznyk: 'Bezpechnyy Marsh Rivnosti—mozhlyvist' pokazaty, shcho Kyiv—yevropeys'ka stolytsia']." June 21, 2019. https://kyivcity.gov.ua/news/mikola_povoroznik_bezpechniy_marsh_rivnos ti__mozhlivist_pokazati_scho_kiv__yevropeyska_stolitsya/.

Lavryk, Denys. 2015. "Homophobia in Ukraine: Tendencies of the Post-Maidan Period [Homofobiia v Ukraini: tendentsii postmaidannoho period]." *Commons [Spil'ne]*, May 18, 2015. https://commons.com.ua/uk/gomofobiya-v-ukrayini/.

Leksikov, Roman. 2017. "Post-Soviet Queer as the Colonial Theory and Practice." *Current Problems of Sociology, Psychology, and Pedagogy* 2(33):5–14.

Leksikov, Roman, and Dafna Rachok. 2020. "Beyond Western Theories: On the Use and Abuse of 'Homonationalism' in Eastern Europe." In *LGBTQ+ Activism in Central and Eastern Europe: Resistance, Representation, and Identity*, eds. Radzhana Buyanteva and Maryna Shevtsova. Cham: Palgrave Macmillan. Pp. 25–50.

Martsenyuk, Tamara. 2012. "The State of the LGBT Community and Homophobia in Ukraine." *Problems of Post-Communism* 59(2):51–62.

———. 2014. "Human Rights for the LGBT-Community and Euromaidan [Prava liudyny dlia LHBT-spilnoty i Yevromaidan]." *Commons [Spil'ne]*, October 15, 2014. https://commons.com.ua/uk/prava-lyudini-dlya-lgbt-spilnoti-i-yevromajdan -2013-2014/.

Martsenyuk, Tamara, and V. Kolesnik. 2016. "Factors of the Parents of Homosexual Children Involvement into the LGBT Movement in Ukraine [Chynnyky zaluchennia bat'kiv homoseksual'nykh ditey do LHBT-rukhu v Ukraini]." *Sociological Research Notes of Kyiv-Mohyla Academy* 187:67–75.

Maurice, Emma Powys. 2019. "Ukraine President Volodymyr Zelensky Shuts Down Homophobic Heckler During Press Conference." *Pink News*, October 14, 2019. www.pinknews.co.uk/2019/10/14/volodymyr-zelensky-ukraine-president-press-co nference-heckler/.

Miller, Christopher. 2015. "Ukraine's President Voices LGBT Support in a First for the Country." *Mashable*, June 5, 2015. https://mashable.com/2015/06/05/ukraines -poroshenko-supports-pride-parade-in-kiev/.

O'Dwyer, Conor. 2018. "The Benefits of Backlash: EU Accession and the Organization of LGBT Activism in Postcommunist Poland and the Czech Republic." *East European Politics and Societies and Culture* 32(4):892–923.

Osborne, Samuel. 2019. "Russian City Allows Gay Pride Parade then Bans It 'Because Children Might See It.'" *Independent*, July 15, 2019. www.indepe ndent.co.uk/news/world/europe/russia-gay-pride-parade-ban-strezhovoy-children -nikolay-alexeev-a9005381.html.

Penman, Maggie. 2017. "Organizer Says Pride Parade in Kiev More of a 'Celebration' This Year." *NPR*, June 18, 2017. www.npr.org/sections/thetwo-wa y/2017/06/18/533424039/organizer-says-pride-parade-in-kiev-more-of-a-celebr ation-this-year.

Popovych, Zakhar. 2015. "Why It Was Important to Go to the 'Equality March' [Chomu varto bulo yty na 'Marsh Rivnosti']." *Commons [Spil'ne]*, June 10, 2015. https://commons.com.ua/uk/chomu-varto-bulo-jti/.

Prokopchuk, Dmytro. 2016. "Clashes Took Place in Lviv During LGBT-Community Actions [U L'vovi stalysia sutychky v khodi provodennia aktsii LHBT-spilnoty]." *Deutsche Welle*, March 19, 2016.

Puar, Jasbir. 2013. "Rethinking Homonationalism." *International Journal of Middle East Studies* 45:337–339.

Radio Free Europe. 2019. "How Europeans View Homosexuality." *Radio Free Europe/Radio Liberty*, October 22, 2019. www.rferl.org/a/how-europeans-view-homosexuality/30230588.html.

Renkin, Hadley. 2009. "Homophobia and Queer Belonging in Hungary." *Focaal: European Journal of Anthropology* 53:20–37.

RFE/RL. 2019. "Gay Veteran of Donbas War Attacked in Kyiv." *Radio Free Europe/ Radio Liberty*, October 1, 2019. www.rferl.org/a/gay-veteran-of-donbas-war-att acked-in-kyiv/30192819.html.

RFE/RL Georgian Service. 2019. "Protesters Clash with Police at LGBT Film Premiere in Georgian Capital." *Radio Free Europe/Radio Liberty*, November 8, 2019. www.rferl.org/a/protest-against-lgbt-gay-film-sweden-georgia-tbilisi-then-w e-danced/30260713.html.

RFE/RL Ukrainian Service. 2019. "Thousands Join Pride Parade in Kyiv." *Radio Free Europe/Radio Liberty*, June 23, 2019. www.rferl.org/a/gay-pride-parade-ki cks-off-in-kyiv/30015061.html.

RFE/RL Uzbek Service. 2019. "Murder in Tashkent: Killing of Gay Man Spotlights Plight of Uzbek LGBT Community." *Radio Free Europe/Radio Liberty*, September 16, 2019. www.rferl.org/a/killing-of-gay-man-spotlights-plight-of-uzbek-lgbt-com munity/30167271.html.

Santora, Marc, and Joanna Berendt. 2019. "Mayor's Funeral Unites Gdansk: His Killing Exposed Poland's Deep Divides." *New York Times*, January 19, 2019. www.nytimes.com/2019/01/19/world/europe/poland-gdansk-mayor-funeral-pawel -adamowicz.html.

Schaaf, Matthew. 2019. "Is Ukraine Turning the Corner on LGBT Rights?" *Open Democracy*, July 2, 2019. www.opendemocracy.net/en/odr/ukraine-turning-corne r-lgbt-rights/.

Semykina, Kseniia. 2019. "The Media's Construction of LGBT Pride Parades in Russia." *The Journal of Social Policy Studies* 17(2):281–292.

Shevtsova, Maria. 2017. "Learning the Lessons from the Euromaidan: The Ups and Downs of LGBT Activism in the Ukrainian Public Space." *Kyiv-Mohyla Law and Politics Journal* 3:157–180.

Stella, Francesca. 2013. "Queer Space, Pride, and Shame in Moscow." *Slavic Review* 72(3):458–480.

Takács, Judit, and Ivett Szalma. 2014. "Gays in the Neighborhood? European Attitudes about Homosexuality a Quarter Century After the Fall of the Soviet Union." *Reviews and Critical Commentary: A Forum for Research and Commentary on Europe*, May 8. http://real.mtak.hu/12724/1/2014_Gays_in_the_Neighborhood_Cr itCom.pdf.

Ukrains'ka Pravda. 2018. "Ukrainians Support Entry to the EU and NATO [Ukraini pidtrymuyut' vstup do YeS i NATO]." November 13, 2018. www.pravda.com.ua/ news/2018/11/13/7198061/.

University of St. Gallen. 2017a. "Post-Maidan Ukraine (2015 and 2017)." Survey Infographics—Post-Maidan Ukraine (2015). Last modified 2017. www.uaregio.org /en/surveys/data-visualisations/survey-infographics/post-maidan-ukraine-2015/.

———. 2017b. "Identities and Regionalism." Survey Infographics—Identities. Last modified 2017. www.uaregio.org/en/surveys/data-visualisations/survey-infogr aphics/identities/.

Woodcock, Shannon. 2009. "Gay Pride as Violent Containment in Romania: A Brave New Europe." *Sextures* 1(1):7–23.

Young-Powell, Abby. 2019. "Warsaw Pride Kicks Off Amid Growing Far-Right Threats and Street Attacks Against LGBT+ Community." *Independent*, June 8, 2019. www.independent.co.uk/news/world/europe/warsaw-pride-lgbt-poland-gay -rights-far-right-attack-homophobia-a8950101.html.

Chapter 5

Queering the Soviet Pribaltika

Criminal Cases of Consensual Sodomy in Soviet Latvia (1960s–1980s)

Feruza Aripova

In light of growing homophobic sentiment and post-Soviet nostalgia for queer invisibility, including the legal and social exclusion of homosexuals from the public sphere, this work seeks to interject and disrupt current political mythology of a traditionalist narrative by examining the effects of the stigmatization of homosexuality through legal and medical discourses.[1] In its attempt to deconstruct the Soviet myth of queer invisibility and move beyond the Russo-Soviet historical discourse, this article explores subaltern queer existence and resistance in the Baltic region during the late Soviet period, particularly in Soviet Latvia. By using criminal files of men arrested and sentenced for consensual sodomy in Soviet Latvia, it seeks to construct the elements of a collective memory by mapping clandestine representations of queer lives, subjectivities, and existing networks. Moreover, the article looks at the public cruising spaces as sites of collective memory, subversion, and defiance amid the desexualized totalitarian state.

The second Soviet "sexual" revolution, from the 1960s through the 1980s, was not "launched in laws and decrees from above . . . but exploded in social change and lifestyle," contends historian Dan Healey in his latest monograph *Homophobia from Stalin to Sochi* (2017, xv). He further argues that "political stagnation blocked public debate and no decisive policymaking gave shape to this spontaneous 'sexual revolution' from below of the late Soviet era" (Healey 2017, xv). Despite the liberalization of "sexual" practices such as decriminalization of abortion in 1955 and the relaxation of divorce laws in the 1960s, the public silencing of sexuality continued from the suppression of any explicit reference to homosexuality that characterized the Stalinist era (Healey 2014, 237). Homosexuals continued to be charged with social, legal,

95

and medical deviance, a charge that was reflected in the new Soviet Criminal Code of the 1960s. Yet despite repression, men continued to seek sexual encounters with other men in defiance of the law.

Since the early 1990s, a growing body of scholarship on Soviet sexualities emerged in its attempts to diversify and decenter Western sexualities. A closer reading of the scholarly literature on the subject of sexuality in Russia and its former borderlands, including Igor Kon's *The Sexual Revolution in Russia* (1995), Dan Healey's *Homosexual Desire in Revolutionary Russia* (2004), and Daniel Schluter's *Gay Life in the Former USSR* (2001) demonstrates the fluidity and complexity of sexual development due to the combination of historical, geographical, social, and cultural specificities over time.

A profound shift in the development of subaltern queer histories in the post-Soviet context took place within the past decade. Attempts to historicize queer memory by shedding light on hidden same-sex history in the Baltic region include Rita Ruduša's collection of oral histories *Forced Underground* (2014) that reveals stories of homosexual men and women in Soviet Latvia as well as Ineta Lipša's monograph *LGBTI People in Latvia: A History of the Past 100 Years* (2018). Lipša's current work-in-progress, titled "Diaries of Irbe," is a microhistory that offers a rare glimpse into the queer subculture in Soviet Latvia. Kaspars Alexands Irbe, a resident of Jurmala, documented his queer experiences throughout the early to late Soviet periods (2018, 49–50). Other projects on queer histories in the Baltic republics during the Soviet period include Augustas Čičelis's ethnographic research on men with same-sex attractions during the late Soviet period in Lithuania (2011) as well as Jaanus Samma's "Not Suitable For Work. A Chairman's Tale" artistic project. The artist's exhibition is based on the criminal case of Juhan Ojaste, a chairman of a collective farm in Soviet Estonia who was arrested and sentenced to one-and-a-half years of hard labor for his homosexual encounters in the 1960s (Samma et al. 2015).

The sexual revolution led to significant changes in the lives of homosexual men and women whose invisible active existence continued to subvert the Soviet system from within by means of gender performativity and creation of secret networks and gatherings, particularly in major Soviet metropoles. At the same time, the Soviet government increased surveillance and further persecution of homosexuals, including in the Baltic republics. With the development of the new Criminal Code of the Republics of the Soviet Union in 1961, the punishment for consensual intercourse between men varied from imprisonment for two years in the Estonian Soviet Socialist Republic (SSR)(Article 118, Paragraph 1 of the Criminal Code) (Rebane 1968, 308–309). Male sodomy in the Lithuanian SSR was punished for up to three years (Article 122, Paragraph 1) ("Lietuvos Tarybų Socialistinės Respublikos Baudžiamasis Kodeksas" 1961). The penalty for male same-sex intercourse in the Latvian SSR resulted in imprisonment for up to five years (Article 124, Paragraph 1) (*Ugolovnyĭ Kodeks Latviĭskoĭ Sovetskoĭ Sotsĭalisticheskoĭ Respubliki* 1961, 47–48). Moreover, in Soviet Latvia, the surveillance of homosexual men from the 1960s to the late 1980s was instigated by the policy of combating sexually transmitted infections due to widespread anonymous sex and spread of venereal diseases (Lipša 2018, 67).

The majority of primary sources for this article consist of a few criminal cases of men arrested and sentenced for consensual sodomy under Article 124, p.1., of the Criminal Code of the Latvian SSR. Article 124 had two separate clauses dealing with consensual same-sex acts as well as sexual violence.[2] It served as a common denominator for rape, child abuse, and consensual sex in the sense that it did not consider whether the sexual act had been performed by mutual consent. The criminal cases discovered at the State Archive of Latvia ranged from consensual same-sex in public (LVA 2178-1-3823, 1), private (LVA 2178-1-2278, 90-91) and carceral spaces (LVA 1623-1-6987, 101) to rape of an inmate (LVA 1623-1-660, 36) and sexual assault and murder of a minor (LVA 865-4a-2195, 154).[3] Despite the specific nature of each committed crime, criminal cases that violated both clauses fell under the same legislation.[4] The figures for sodomy convictions for all three Baltic Republics ranging from 1961 to 1991 (see table 5.1) do not distinguish between consensual and forced same-sex acts. Nor does the data indicate any cases of hate crimes committed on the grounds of homophobia. Does the coalescence of consensual and violent explain the widespread negative public perception of homosexuality in Soviet and post-Soviet space, including Latvia? Undoubtedly, widespread same-sex interactions (either forced or consensual) informed the public view of associating homosexuality with criminality and pathology.

Working with the archival state documents that reflected the ways in which those individuals had been perceived by state officials raises the question of subjectivity. How should we treat the official sources that reflected the criminal and deviant gaze of Soviet officials regarding homosexuality? How did those engaged in homosexual activities view themselves? Ann Stoler in *Along the Archival Grain: Epistemic Anxieties and Colonial Common Sense* points to the "archival turn," a shift from "the archive-as-source to the archive-as-subject," and emerging questions about the changing role of the archive in "rereading the histories of colonialism to those of gay rights" (2010, 44–45). The role of the Soviet archive is instrumental when it comes to shaping, reimagining, and legitimizing knowledge about queer experiences. The archive sheds light upon invisible fragments of queer lives despite the state's homophobic legislation and surveillance. It brings forward the existing queer subjectivities, embodied in non-identitarian sexual ambivalence and complexity of non-normative desire, stories of sexual dissent existing on the margins of the Soviet experience.

HISTORICAL BACKGROUND

Consensual sodomy was decriminalized in Soviet Russia from 1922 to 1934, according to the 1922 criminal code (Engelstein 1995, 162–165). However, the policies on criminalization of male same-sex desire varied in the Baltic republics. Prior to the Soviet annexation in the 1940s, Estonia was the only country in the Baltic region where consensual same-sex acts were legal. Punishment was applied only in cases of violence or involving a minor (Veispak 1991, 108). Historian Ineta Lipša in *LGBTI People in Latvia: A History of the Past 100 Years* indicates that during the interwar period (1918–1940), Latvia retained the form of the Russian sodomy law (2018, 17). Male same-sex intercourse, referred to as "pederasty," was punishable by imprisonment for at least three months. The law, however, did not apply to women. The punishment for sodomy according to the revised Latvian Penal Law of 1933, Article 496, was imprisonment without a definitive period of time. That could also mean that the penalty for male sodomy could be shortened (Lipša 2018, 17).

One of the most prominent raids on homosexuals took place in 1926 in Riga, Latvia. Known as "The Black Carnation Club Scandal," it received local media coverage. Upon arresting several homosexuals at the apartment where they had frequent gatherings, the police began criminal investigation and further consulted forensic experts to conduct physical examinations of the arrested. As a result, homosexuals, comparable to drug addicts, were categorized as a threat to the public by medical experts. By elaborating on existing stereotypes, the media accused homosexuals of violating the gender order by being "passive" and corrupting the youth (Lipša 2018, 18–19, 23). Despite sodomy legislation during the interwar period, Riga had a number of public spaces where homosexuals could meet, ranging from the public toilets to Vērmanes garden to special restaurants and cafes that ran their own entertainment programs for men with same-sex attractions (Lipša 2018, 27).

The Soviet sodomy ban was extended to all three Baltic republics upon the Soviet annexation in the 1940s. State-sanctioned homosexual persecution in Latvia during World War II and its aftermath took on many forms. After the first Soviet occupation in 1940–1941, the government implemented Article 154a of the RSFSR Criminal Code in the Latvian SSR that punished homosexuality for a period from three to five years (Lipša 2019, 100). Deportations of the local population and massive arrests included homosexuals who were most likely charged based on political accusations (Lipša 2018, 49). During the Nazi occupation from 1941 to 1944, citizens were subjected to different penal laws. It was up to the German or Latvian courts to conduct civil trials and punish the offenders (Lipša 2018, 52). Despite the dual criminalization of homosexuality on the territory of occupied Latvia, homosexual subculture, including cruising for sex in public spaces, drag parties and even same-sex weddings, continued to exist. (Lipša 2018, 54–55). The second Soviet occupation in 1944 reinstituted the criminalization of same-sex acts (Lipša 2019, 100). The total number of men sentenced under Article 154a from 1945 to 1960 came to 34 (Lipša 2018, 60).

The new Article 124.1 of the revised Criminal Code of the Latvian SSR in 1961 punished consensual same-sex acts between men for up to five years. The court files related to the criminalization of male homosexuality included detailed descriptions of personal lives, testimonies of witnesses, and references from workplaces. It contained descriptions of the cruising spaces, number of sexual partners, frequency of the same-sex acts, and the amount of alcohol consumed, if any. The legislation did not prohibit same-sex relationships between women. While discussing the draft of the new criminal code, the acting head of the City Executive Committee Militia Department did propose applying the criminal offense for "satisfying sexual desire among persons of the same sex" to women, a practice that did not fall under the category of "sodomy," yet posed a public threat (LVA 938-6-66, 82). The proposal to criminalize same-sex relations between women never made it into the law (Lipša 2018, 62).

The majority of the archival sources reflect the experiences of men with same-sex attractions, since women's sexuality was not a part of the criminal legislation. Female same-sex relationships existed equally under the system that "institutionalized heteronormativity through criminalization and medicalization of same-sex desire" and "channeled women's sexuality into reproduction through the notion of motherhood as an essential duty to the state" (Stella 2015, 43). The Estonian art writer and curator Rebeka Polsdam's interviews with lesbian women who lived throughout the late Soviet era reveal that in the 1980s to early 1990s, women spread information about gatherings or parties by word of mouth.

> When they were going from Tallinn to Tartu they stopped in Poltsamaa (a small detour) to tell an old schoolmate that a month from now there's going to be a gathering in there-and-there. Somewhat unfortunately these gatherings ended up rather dramatically, since all the couples switched, and, as if in a chair game, some were left with nothing. (Samma et al. 2015, 92)

Women equally subverted gender order and private sphere to form their own circles and networks driven by same-sex desire. Concealed from the public and conveniently presented as a female companionship, "lesbian networks" existed in mainly private spaces.

SAME-SEX AND THE CITY: DEFYING THE LAW

This section of the article delves into the actual stories of people deemed criminals for engaging in consensual same-sex acts. Careful excavation of the fragments of lives and experiences of those arrested and imprisoned for same-sex acts in the Soviet Union, the so-called "archiving as process" (Stoler 2010, 20), provides a glimpse into an invisible queer existence that flourished despite repressive sexual politics and continuous government surveillance from the 1960s and onward. The law and potential imprisonment for consensual sodomy did not prevent men from manipulating public spaces and lavatories, creating coded language, and living "double" lives. Ordinary Soviet citizens, conventionally portrayed as having no agency, created their own discourses by being "vnye" (Rus. *inside/outside*) in Alexei Yurchak's formulation, a concept of living within the system, yet remaining relatively "invisible" (2006, 131–133). Queer men subverted the legal and medical establishments by creating alternative spaces and clandestine networks to pursue same-sex desire.

> I have never sought homosexual encounters in the place of my residence [Joniškis, Lithuania] . . . therefore, I would come to Riga to have sex with men. Frequently, I would find my partners at the square in front of the Latvian State Opera and Ballet Theater. I would usually meet them once a month, whenever I visit Riga. I have always done the following: I would sit on the bench and someone would usually come up. It all happens in the dark . . . I do not know the names of my sexual partners (an excerpt from Alexas Markevičius' court testimony).[5] (LVA 1623-1-6432, 6)

Markevičius' story was not unusual. He began coming to Riga in search for sexual partners. Close-knit community and social norms typical of a small town made Markevičius seek alternative adventures in the city that provided relative freedom of movement and anonymity. On June 29, 1985, Alexas Markevičius and Janis Mednis, a native of Riga, Latvia, were convicted of consensual sodomy in Riga and were subsequently sentenced to two years in a labor-corrective colony (LVA 1623-1-6432, 200). The third person involved, Nikolai Petrov, a native of Vorkuta, Russia, who happened to be in Riga while vacationing, was released due to lack of evidence (LVA 1623-1-6432, 5, 14, 70–71, 79–80).

Despite the ideological nature of state documents, archival files conveyed the active voices of hidden same-sex existence. Public lavatories in Riga served as meeting hubs for same-sex engagements. By the inscriptions in public bathrooms, Markevičius figured out that "there are quite a few people who are engaged in this type of activity" (LVA 1623-1-6432, 54). He received a few propositions to engage in same-sex acts and quickly realized that Riga offered multiple possibilities of that kind. His trips to Riga specifically revolved around seeking same-sex encounters with other men whom he only knew by their first names, for example, Volodya, Janis, Sasha, and so on (LVA 1623-1-6432, 54). It is impossible to determine how many men flocked to metropoles like Riga in order to participate in the emerging same-sex community, which was quite diverse. Maris, one of the respondents interviewed by Rita Ruduša in *Forced Underground,* claims that the "community of homosexuals" was comprised of multiple nationalities and numerous married men (2014, 31). Like the metropolitan men with openly "homosexual interests," archival cases reveal stories of men like Markevičius who came to Riga because they were aware of their desires. Small towns like Joniškis did not provide possibilities to search for sexual partners in public spaces. Moreover, it was nearly impossible to keep one's sexuality a secret.

Contrary to the official Soviet "sexless" ideological narrative, the testimonies of the defendants often revealed explicit details mixed with elements of interpersonal relationship drama when describing same-sex encounters. Alexas Markevičius, for example, testified that upon meeting Janis Mednis at the public square in front of the theater, they went to the apartment that belonged to Nikolai Petrov.

> After having a few drinks in the apartment, we took off our clothes and laid on the couch. . . . First, the man had sexual intercourse with Mednis, upon which Mednis turned towards me and I sexually engaged with him, and finally I turned around and Mednis had sex with me. . . . Petrov became slightly upset when we decided to leave . . . Mednis and I departed from each other when he told me he would "go for a walk," which meant to "hunt" for new sexual partners. At the same time, he got upset that I wanted to go for another "walk" myself. He scolded me for screwing around and I hit him in response. (LVA 1623-1-6432, 7, 9, 10)

The landscape of the city made it possible for Soviet queer men to subvert the existing social order and instead build an alternative one by constructing private networks for gathering and negotiating their sexuality by adopting various strategies of private and public visibility. The thriving clandestine networks and gatherings, the so-called *kruzhki* (Rus. circles of friends), flourished despite repressive sexual politics and continuous government surveillance. In his article "The Secret Life of Moscow," published in *Christopher Street,* G shares his experience of meeting "like-minded" people in one of those circles in Moscow in the 1980s (1980, 19). Personal connections served as the point of entry and access to those circles. Similarly, in Soviet Lithuania, small private circles served as "privileged spaces of communication between men during the 1980s (Čičelis 2011, 36). One of the Estonian respondents, interviewed by Jaanus Samma, testified to the existence of "various closed underground circles," including dissident ones, that operated on a model based on a circle of friends," including "salons for men" in Soviet Estonia in the 1980s (Samma 2013).

Fear of imprisonment and forced psychiatric treatment did not prevent queer men from searching for partners in public spaces like *pleshkas* (Rus. public same-sex cruising spaces), parks, bathhouses, beaches, and public bathrooms, thus confirming Henri Lefebvre's "right to the city" as a means of claiming urban spaces. In his essay, Lefebvre points out to the impulse to satisfy specific human needs, including the need to "accumulate energies and to spend them, even waste them in play," with sexual satisfaction being one of the needs. He further argues that those needs are "not satisfied by those commercial and cultural infrastructures which are somewhat parsimoniously taken into account by planners" (Lefebvre et al. 1996, 147). In Soviet Moscow, the meeting places for men revolved around the Kremlin and Red Square, including a little garden in front of the Bolshoi Theater and an underground toilet in the Alexander Gardens near the Kremlin Wall (Healey 2017, 99). In Soviet Lithuania, men transformed public sites into so-called "contact zones." They ranged from the train stations and public bathrooms in major Lithuanian cities to public sites such as Lenino (Lukiškių) Square in the center of Vilnius as well as the park in front of the movie theater "Kronika" in Vilnius (Čičelis 2011, 33). Palanga's male beach in the Soviet Republic of Lithuania was transformed into the Soviet Homointernational and attracted men with same-sex attractions from all over the USSR (Čičelis 2011, 46). In Soviet Estonia, one of the main cruising sites was Victory (Freedom) Square in Tallinn along with Hirve Park and Harjumägi Hill (Samma 2013). Similarly, multiple landmarks in Riga, stretching from the Freedom Monument to the State Opera and Ballet Theater to the banks of the City Canal, served as alternative spaces for same-sex opportunities and signified that type of redefinition of social spaces. A Lefebvrian perspective allows us to challenge and "redefine" the power of the state and argue for agency and defiance in the hands of the Soviet citizens, and in this case queer men, who were not mere victims of the law. On the contrary, they maintained agency by utilizing urban landscapes for search and pursuit of same-sex desire throughout the late Soviet period.

In "Homosexuality and the City: An Historical Overview," Robert Aldrich argues that "urban centers have been conducive to homosexual expression whether integrated into or transgressive against social norms" (Aldrich 2004, 1719). Historically, those who experienced sexual desire toward the same gender have been both marginal and central to the city. In spite of being "consigned to the fringes," they continued "subverting normative standards of behavior, carving out social niches," and so on (Aldrich 2004, 1719). Stories of men seeking same-sex rendezvous in urban spaces have been described by Matt Houlbrook in his book *Queer London*. Young Cyril arrived in London in 1932 to immerse himself "within networks of public and commercial sociability constructed by men like him," and hence, associating sexual selfhood, the pursuit of same-sex desire, and the city (2006, 3). "Being queer" for Cyril was "equated with the cultural experience of urban life" (Houlbrook 2006, 3). George Chauncey in *Gay New York* provides an example of a young man who moved from Michigan to New York City in the 1920s and points out how the city's landscapes, including parks, streets, and various monuments, served as cruising centers for same-sex encounters (2003, 160). Robert Beachy's *Gay Berlin* elaborates how Berlin's openness in the 1920s freed one of the protagonists to explore his sexuality (2015, X). Similarly, in his article "Moscow," Dan Healey describes Pavel, a seventeen-year-old peasant who relocated to Moscow from the Smolensk region in 1912 and subsequently sought and developed sexual relations with men at the Prechistenskii (Gogol) Boulevard (2003, 46–47).

George Chauncey contends that the history of gay resistance goes beyond formal political organizing "to include the strategies of everyday resistance that men devised in order to claim space for themselves in the midst of hostile society" (2003, 5). By applying James Scott's concept "weapons of the weak," a kind of resistant social practice, he demonstrates an array of various tactics used by gay men for communicating and claiming space in New York City (Chauncey et al. 2003, 5). When it comes to regular Soviet citizens, they employed similar daily tactics to construct spheres of cultural and social autonomy, including the production of queer spaces. Generating those milieus and practices was not necessarily perceived as a form of political resistance to the socialist state (Yurchak 2006, 34). Those temporalities existed *vnye*, "simultaneously inside and outside the system" (Yurchak 2006, 128).

Unlike in other world metropoles such as New York, London, or Paris where men, in fact, migrated from Europe or rural America to find "work, a homosexual circle of acquaintances and a definite social life" (Chauncey et al. 2003, 135), the Soviet government maintained strict surveillance of its citizens by imposing the internal passport and *propiska* system, requiring proof of residence in the passport. One could not easily relocate to a different city or republic, unless they were assigned by the workplace or local or regional authorities. That, however, was not an obstacle for Nikolai Petrov, single, a native of Vorkuta, who owned an apartment in Riga (Rus. *propisan*) as the result of an exchange for his one-bedroom in Sverdlovsk. Most of the time, he lived in Vorkuta while working for the Palace of Pioneers as the head of the club for young pilot-cosmonauts. He usually came to Riga during school holidays, vacations, or on business trips (LVA 1623-1-6432, 71). The apartment was most likely used for designated purposes. According to Markevičius' testimony, he wanted to sexually engage with Mednis at the public square. Mednis, in turn, suggested that they go to an apartment nearby that belonged to Petrov, a man he met earlier at the bridge (LVA 1623-1-6432, 7). All three men subsequently engaged in same-sex acts in Petrov's apartment. Later, Petrov denied any involvement in the act of sodomy. "I was mainly curious to meet and observe homosexual behavior," he stated in his testimony (LVA 1623-1-6432, 14–15). He was eventually released for lack of *corpus delicti*, reinforced by an excellent reference from employer in Vorkuta that stated that Petrov was "politically literate and ideologically convinced person, who instructed young pioneers" (LVA 1623-1-6432, 80, 101).

Despite Khrushchev's housing initiative, getting one's own apartment was extremely difficult, even for respectable married couples (G 1980, 16). The policy of virtually nonexistent private real estate ownership did not affect Varlens Kalniņš (b. 1936), a single man and native of Latgale, Latvia who owned an apartment in the city of Ogre, twenty-two miles east of Riga (LVA 2178-1-2278, 90). According to the court verdict and testimonies of Gustavs Kroms and Alexander Stoyanov, the apartment was often used for the purpose of sexual engagements between men. In December 1970, Kalniņš and Stoyanov (b. 1952), a native of the Perm region who worked at the Bolderaja plant in Riga, engaged in consensual same-sex acts at Kalniņš' apartment. In January 1971, Kalniņš and Kroms (b. 1937) committed consensual acts of sodomy where Kirš performed as both an active and a passive partner. According to the testimony of Kalniņš' neighbor, who often informed authorities of ongoing suspicious activities, multiple men visited the apartment, including Ivan Tulik, who lived there for some time (LVA 2178-1-2278, 90–91). Varlens Kalniņš also admitted that he had multiple sexual partners (Stanislav, Ajvar, German, Ivan) in Ogre and in Riga. Kalniņš, Kroms, and Stoyanov eventually admitted to their engagement in consensual same-sex activity while intoxicated, without giving it much thought. All three defendants were convicted in violation of Article 124, p.1., of the Criminal Code of the Latvian Soviet Socialist Republic and sentenced to one year in prison, including mandatory labor (LVA 2178-1-2278, 92). Despite the fact that state surveillance extended deep into the private sphere, the following cases demonstrate multiple attempts to manipulate and utilize private spaces to defy the existing state monopoly of the housing system and challenge the law.

If any big city could be a site of sexual freedom and same-sex expression, the Soviet city represented socialist utopian ideals. The idea of the socialist city embodied ideological significance: it was symbolic of modernity, progress, and the family as the cornerstone of society. "The Soviet regime embraced the family unit as not only compatible with socialism, but one of society's basic building blocks" (Kotkin 1996, 242). Recreational spaces that revolved around organized leisure for working people, including parks and public squares, were designed to reflect socialist ideals and morals and foster a sense of collectivism. Queer men, however, appropriated public sites into spaces of same-sex pursuits and possibilities by transforming the city into the center of unconventional behavior contrary to existing social values. The tiny square in front of the Latvian State Opera and Ballet Theater, comparable to the lower part of the Champs Elysées in Paris as "the most concentrated site of homosexual encounters," served as a point of entry for male newcomers (Jackson 2009, 29). The surrounding trees and bushes provided the necessary cover for men to have sexual contact. "When it got dark, I sat on the bench in front of the fountain near the State Opera while men passed by looking at me," continues Markevičius, "I went into the bushes with some stranger where we sexually engaged with each other while taking turns" (LVA 1623-1-6432, 6).

In his article "The Theory of Pleshka," artist Yevgenyi Fiks argues that "the memory of homosexuals of Soviet times is not registered in the space of the history and geography . . . their (under-)subjectivity forever dissolved in the city itself" (2018, 304). He further elaborates how public cruising spaces could be conceptualized as places of absences of Soviet gay history, subjectivity and self-identification (Fiks 2018, 304). Soviet urban spaces as collective sites of memory, for example, the public square in front of the State Opera in Riga, serve as connections to the invisible queer past and its social groups. By evoking emotions, memories, and imagination; they "restore" the historical queer subject to the present. In addition to the State Opera's public square that was used for same-sex rendezvous, the public park on Bastion Hill in Riga was another site of possibly becoming a silent monument to collective memory.

The way in which homosexual behavior constituted a transgression against public order in the eyes of Soviet authorities became apparent in the criminal case of Edgars Vitols and Petr Grigor'yev, arrested for having sex in the public park on Bastion Hill on Christmas Eve in 1979 (LVA 2178-1-3823, 1). Public urban spaces, reflective of the socialist ideological order, were especially prone to systematic police surveillance. Since men looked for sexual partners in the streets and parks, they became subjected to the power of state law. Detaining individuals in the midst of sexual intercourse often served as evidence for criminal charges. Edgars Vitols and Petr Grigor'yev were caught in the midst of their sexual activity and arrested on the spot. The representative of the night patrol (Rus. *nochnaiia militsiia*), who happened to be one of the eyewitnesses, testified that he was observing two men having sexual intercourse where Grigor'yev was an "active" partner (LVA 2178-1-3823, 3). In the process of detention, Grigor'yev made an attempt to hit Vitols (LVA 2178-1-3823, 29). Similar to Markevičius, Edgars Vitols, a native of the Ventspils region in the Latvian SSR, initially came to Riga in summer 1979 to have a random sexual encounter with a stranger in front of the Latvian State Opera and Ballet Theater. On the evening of December 24, 1979, Vitols went to a movie theater, consumed two bottles of alcohol and went for a walk around the Bastion Hill area where he met Petr Grigor'yev (LVA 2178-1-3823, 14). While not being able to recall exactly who initiated the sexual contact, Vitols confirmed that the sexual encounter was mutually consensual.

One suspects that Grigor'yev possessed some knowledge about the purpose of the Bastion Hill area, hence his rendezvous in search for men on the cold December night. However, he portrayed himself as a victim and claimed he had never engaged in homosexual acts prior to this incident. Grigor'yev recalled being intoxicated when he ran into a stranger in the park and asked him for a cigarette,

> I sat next to him on the bench. Then I realized that someone's hands were touching me, followed by unbuttoning my pants. All I knew that I really wanted to sleep. Then the unimaginable happened which I would never forgive myself for. Not fully realizing my course of actions, I surrendered myself to him. Then the police officers came and took us to the station. (LVA 2178-1-3823, 9)

The duration of punishment varied for so-called active vs. passive, "practicing" versus "accidental" homosexuals like Grigor'yev. In his testimony, he claimed he had never been sexually involved with men before (LVA 2178-1-3823, 9, 41). With his admission of guilt, in addition to his obligation as a husband and a father of a two-year-old child, reinforced by a positive reference from his employer, the criminal charges were dropped (LVA 2178-1-3823, 40, 59). Edgars Vitols, characterized as "passive" homosexual was sentenced for violating Article 124, p.1 (LVA 2178-1-3823, 40, 61).

A criminal case often required a physical assessment of the defendant by the medical experts. Forensic doctors, like medical experts in the 1920s in interwar Latvia, provided their expert opinion upon conducting a physical exam of the accused. With the establishment of sexopathology in the USSR in the 1960, an attempt to bring sexuality under medical control by seeking psychological factors in sexual behavior, queer men and women became the objects of psychiatric and medical intervention (Kon and Riordan 1993, 95). Some of the methods of medical treatment revolved around hypnosis, the use of antipsychotic drugs like aminazine or electroshock therapy to "transform" homosexual men and women into heterosexuals (Sviadoshch 1991, 158–159). The court files based on Article 124 of the Soviet Latvian Criminal Code speak to the widespread belief that one could trace a pattern of "anatomy of deviance" based on medical and psychiatric reports along with anatomical assessment of a person's body. By examining the size of the penis or looking for visible signs on the person's rectum to define whether the partner was active or passive, the links between anatomy and deviance became inseparable in the opinions of the medical experts

In addition to the extended sentence, "practicing" homosexuals were often "effeminized" by medical experts. A prominent Soviet Latvian sexologist Jānis Zālītis in his book *Mīlestības Vārdā* (1981), one of the most influential texts that promoted "correct sexual practices," claimed that sexual perversions, including homosexuality, developed as the result of both parents using substances (alcohol, tobacco or drugs) during pregnancy (Lipša 2018, 78–79). He further argued that homosexual men "consider themselves to be the members of the opposite sex by wearing their type of clothes and taking women's jobs. Those people like to cook, bake and look after children. They tend to grow long hair and look very feminine" (Zalytis 1985, 82). The feminization of homosexual men, comparable to the existing stereotypes of the 1920s in Latvia, was demonstrated through the case of Edgars Vitols. The forensic psychiatric committee from the Riga Republican Psychiatric Hospital, comprised of the chairman and the deputy head physician of the hospital, the head of the forensic department, and a number of resident doctors, conducted physical exams and provided a report in connection with the crime. Vitols was categorized as a passive and effeminized homosexual (LVA 2178-1-3823, 50–52). An excerpt from Vitols's medical report states the following:

> He once tried having sex with a woman but instead experienced an aversion. Since his childhood, Vitols liked to cook, sew and knit. He liked to cross-dress in women's clothing and shoes. . . . Since the age of eight or nine, he began experiencing same-sex attraction. He envisioned himself in the position of a woman. Vitols subsequently engaged in same-sex acts and always had a role of a "passive" partner. (LVA 2178-1-3823, 50)

At the end of the report, Edgars Vitols was diagnosed with sexual perversion in the form of homosexuality (LVA 2178-1-3823, 52). Mandatory anal examinations conducted on men, especially passive homosexuals, to "prove" their homosexuality were integral to the investigation process. The experts pointed out the degree of laxity of the anal sphincter when inserting the finger. They also took a swab from Vitols's anus to determine whether it contained any sperm. In the eyes of the forensic experts, those signs closely correlated with the passive form of homosexuality. They argue that Vitols committed systematic acts of sodomy as a passive partner (LVA 2178-1-3823, 18–19). Similarly, Markevičius, who used to come to Riga from neighboring Lithuania had undergone a similar set of procedures upon which the experts "proved" that he sexually engaged with other men as a passive partner (LVA 1623-1-6432, 23).

Police surveillance, including random night raids, broke down the umbrella of anonymity within the urban setting, especially when it came to the performance of a double life, an ability to negotiate one's sexuality in public. The city was a perfect cover for Anatolii Alfeyev, born in 1945, a native of Oryol. A member of VLKSM (Rus. All-Union Leninist Young Communist League), Alfeyev completed a University degree and worked as a mechanical engineer. The fact that he had a one-year-old son allows us to imagine that Alfeyev was seemingly happy with his family life (LVA 2178-1-2291, 15). However, that did not prevent him from pursuing and acting upon same-sex desires at the Kirov park in Riga at eleven o'clock at night on May 22, 1972, when he met Janis Skratinš. Skratinš was a native of the Cēsis region in Latvia and, just like Alfeyev, he belonged to Communist Youth League. While intoxicated, both men engaged in sexual activity based on mutual consent and Alfeyev performed the role of an active partner. Disrupted in the midst of their sexual intercourse by the night patrol, Alfeyev and Skratinš were subsequently detained while Skratinš resisted the arrest by trying to attack the representative of *nochnaia militsiia* (LVA 2178-1-2291, 15).

Upon their arrest, both defendants felt deeply remorseful about the night incident by blaming it on the alcohol. Moreover, Alfeyev's wife testified in his favor by describing her spouse as a good family man. "I never noticed any deviations in our sexual interactions," she added (LVA 2178-1-2291, 16). Another witness, the brother of Janis Skratinš described his brother as someone who is good and humble. "He rarely drinks and takes care of our elderly mother who lives in the village" (LVA 2178-1-2291, 16). Additional positive references from employers reaffirmed the court's decision not to isolate Alfeyev and Skratinš from the society and instead, sentenced them to one year of corrective labor with additional retention of 20 percent of their monthly salary (LVA 2178-1-2291, 17). This case demonstrates that the city, despite its ideological aspirations, provided space for men to construct double lives and identities in order to participate in a flourishing homosexual scene.

In case of Alfeyev, Grigor'yev and many others who were married, double life or identity performance was often employed as a means of protection from societal mores, draconian legislation, and the medical gaze. Living double lives constituted one of the cracks in the Soviet system during late socialism. Maris, one of the respondents in *Forced Underground*, had to learn how to maneuver between his family and hundreds of same-sex partners, many of whom remained anonymous (Ruduša 2014, 32). Many of his same-sex partners were married (Ruduša 2014, 31). Maris's entire life revolved around identity performance and continuous negotiation of public and private. The so-called "heterosexual façade" helped him to maintain his "hobby" (Ruduša 2014, 32). His same-sex desire was active only during "business hours," from nine to five, when he cruised around streets, city landmarks, and public bathrooms in search for sexual partners (Ruduša 2014, 31). Upon returning home every night, Maris had to rethink his entire day, "Everything you say has to be edited, you have to think which places to mention, which to avoid and how to describe day at work. Hide it deep, and put a lid on it" (Ruduša 2014, 32). The heterosexual family for Maris was "the core of society, and the gold standard" where "homosexuals have a lastingly unhappy life" (Ruduša 2014, 33). To this day, the respondent is convinced that his family was not aware of his "hobby" despite the fact that he contracted gonorrhea at some point and had to be locked in an institution with other men with STDs (Ruduša 2014, 32). Marriage of convenience was one way to conceal a divided existence in a society that promoted heteronormative social order.

CONCLUSION

Archives in the post-Soviet space allow us to assemble the fragmented elements of a collective memory by deconstructing and telling the personal stories of *queeroes*, nonheterosexual "criminal and deviant" invisible people subjected to the legal and medical gaze. In "The Theory of Pleshka," Yevgeniy Fiks argues that "the post-Soviet queer subject must declare their rights to Soviet history and return to their historical pleshkas" (Fiks 2018, 305). Mapping and locating queer voices adds legitimacy to the Soviet queer experience. It also allows for an opportunity to chart a queer underground by tapping into social networks in public spaces amid the socialist state. Soviet queers "performed" docility rather than internalized its concept. Multiple stories speak of invisible queer resistance in urban settings, including manipulating public spaces in the socialist city reflective of ideological purposes, creating coded language, living double lives and "owning" lavatories. Despite continuous police surveillance and tracking "sexual transgressions" in urban spaces, men continued to invisibly "penetrate" the law. The public spaces of same-sex encounter become visual silent monuments of queer collective memory, and hence, must be commemorated and reclaimed.

The Soviet homophobic legacy continues to affect the current development of LGBTQ rights in the Baltic region. The former Baltic Republics of Lithuania, Latvia, and Estonia, full-fledged members of the EU, remain a site of contestation and battleground for LGBTQ rights despite continuous attempts of activists, artists, and a number of regional historians to challenge Russian homophobic hegemony by attempting to revive local queer histories and hosting annual Baltic Prides as markers of LGBTQ visibility. Queer voices continue to be suppressed in the context of the neo-homophobic nationalist or neo-traditionalist narratives promoting "traditional family values." In Latvia, the Parliament once again rejected proposed partnership legislation that would extend its protection to the same-sex couples.

The first Riga Pride took place in July 2005 and faced an enormous opposition from the public protesters who threw eggs and tomatoes at the participants (Goba 2010). In the aftermath of Riga Pride, contemporary Latvian politicians have been employing various homophobic tropes, reminiscent of the Soviet era, by linking homosexuality to "Western decadence" and "immoral" valued supposedly foreign to Latvia (Mozaika 2007, 43). Other homophobic tropes, embodied in modern religious nationalism, emphasize the value of the traditional heterosexual family, which excludes LGBTQ by default (Mozaika 2007, 22). Homosexuality is also perceived as a trend that hinders potential birth rate and might contribute to the decrease of population (Mozaika 2007, 30). For instance, Inese Šlesere, a member of LLP (Latvijas Pirma Partija) during the plenary session of the Parliament in 2005 firmly advocated for a "traditional family being the greatest value of the country." She further contended that "only by strengthening and defending it, we can overcome the demographic crisis and avoid a looming demographic catastrophe for Latvia" (Mozaika 2007, 23).

Why do queer voices matter? During one of the Prides, a random man approached Linda Freimane, one of the founders of the LGBTQ organization "Mozaika" and admitted that he was punished for his homosexual activities during the Soviet period (Freimane 2017). In the context of Soviet silencing of same-sex desire and rising homophobic nationalism, recovering queer histories is instrumental for the region's popular and collective memory. Those arrested and imprisoned for consensual sodomy have not been recognized as active citizens subverting the Soviet regime. The historical acts of same-sex defiance revolving around negotiating public and private spaces, identity performance and sex, challenge the idea of Soviet queer invisibility as well as the imagined homogeneity of modern Latvian history.

APPENDIX

Table 5.1   Sodomy Convictions in the Baltic Republics, 1961–1991

Year	Lithuanian SSR	Latvian SSR	Estonian SSR
1961	19	6	3
1962	3	11	4
1963	5	3	5
1964	5	14	10
1965	4	9	5
1966	4	20	8
1967	3	12	17
1968	9	6	1
1969	12	10	2
1970	11	7	13
1971	5	6	2
1972	3	10	13
1973	9	4	8
1974	11	13	6
1975	5	3	6
1976	9	5	6
1977	7	19	5
1978	24	17	12
1979	13	13	10
1980	6	12	15
1981	7	5	2
1982	9	10	4
1983	14	8	5
1984	10	12	4
1985	3	16	9
1986	8	10	3
1987	4	3	6
1988	4	0	1
1989	6	4	0
1990	Data unavailable	3	4
1991	Data unavailable	1	Data unavailable
Total	232	272	189

Source: GARF (State Archive of the Russian Federation). "Svodnye (godovye) statisticheskie otcheti o raspredelenii osuzhdennykh po stat'iam Ugolovnogo Kodeksa po SSSR i soiuznim respublikam" (f. 10a)
1961 (GARF, 9492-6-58); 1962 (GARF, 9492-6-69, 178, 186, 206); 1963 (GARF, 9492-6-81); 1964 (GARF, 9492-6-91); 1965 (GARF, 9492-6-102); 1966 (GARF, 9492-6-112); 1967 (GARF, 9492-6-128); 1968 (GARF, 9492-6-141); 1969 (GARF, 9492-6-151); 1970 (GARF, 9492-6-161); 1971 (GARF, 9492-6-177); 1972 (GARF, 9492-6-193, 57,65, 85); 1973 (GARF, 9492-6-205, 54, 62, 82); 1974 (GARF, 9492-6-221, 59,67,87); 1975 (GARF, 9492-6-239, 56, 64, 84); 1976 (GARF, 9492-6-254, 63, 71, 91); 1977 (GARF, 9492-6-271, 66, 74, 94); 1978 (GARF, 9492-6-285, 64, 72, 92); 1979 (GARF, 9492-6-302, 66, 74, 94); 1980 (GARF, 9492-6-317, 67, 75, 95); 1981 (GARF, 9492-6-328, 58, 66, 86); 1982 (GARF, 9492-6-368, 55, 63, 93); 1983 (GARF, 9492-6-393, 61, 69, 88); 1984 (GARF, 9492-6-427, 52, 59, 80); 1985 (GARF, 9492-6-466, 51, 59, 79); 1986 (GARF, 9492-6-500, 55, 63, 83); 1987 (GARF, 9492-6-533, 53, 63, 81); 1988 (GARF, 9492-6-555, 54, 62, 82); 1989 (GARF, 9492-6-579, 49, 57, 83); 1990 (GARF, 9492-6-605, 53, 77); 1991 (GARF, 9492-6-650, 40).

NOTES

1. I am immensely grateful to Irina Roldugina (Oxford University) and Uladzimir Valodzin (European University Institute, Florence) for sharing the data on sodomy convictions in the Soviet Union, obtained from the State Archive of the Russian Federation (GARF).

2. 124.1—The act of sodomy (Lv. *pedarastija*) is punishable by imprisonment for up to five years. 124.2—The act of sodomy, committed by using violence or threats of violence, taking advantage of the victim or the victim's dependent position, as well as a minor, shall be punished by imprisonment from three to eight years (*Ugolovnyĭ Kodeks Latviĭskoĭ Sovetskoĭ Sotsĭalisticheskoĭ Respubliki* 1961, 47–48).

3. State Archive of Latvia (Lv. Latvijas Valsts Arhivs (LVA).

4. Historically, sodomy laws punished any same-sex encounters between men whether or not men had consented.

5. Unless otherwise stated, all translations are the author's. All the names have been changed to maintain the respondents' confidentiality.

REFERENCES

Aldrich, Robert. 2004. "Homosexuality and the City: An Historical Overview." *Urban Studies* 41(9):1719–37. https://doi.org/10.1080/0042098042000243129.

Beachy, Robert. 2015. *Gay Berlin: Birthplace of a Modern Identity.* New York: Vintage Books.

Chauncey, George, Jessica Shatan, Archie Ferguson, and Vicki Gold Levi. 2003. *Gay New York: Gender, Urban Culture, and the Making of the Gay Male World, 1890–1940.* New York: BasicBooks.

Čičelis, Augustas. 2011. *Reading Between the Lines: Spatial Communities of Men with Same-Sex Attractions in Late 20th Century Lithuania.* Central European University.

Engelstein, Laura. 1995. "Soviet Policy Toward Male Homosexuality: Its Origins and Historical Roots." In *Gay Men and the Sexual History of the Political Left,* edited by Gert Hekma, Harry Oosterhuis, and James D. Steakley. Binghamton, NY: Haworth Press.

Fiks, Yevgeniy. 2018. "Theory of Pleshka." In *Art and Theory of Post-1989 Central and Eastern Europe: A Critical Anthology,* edited by Ana Janevski, Roxana Marcoci, and Ksenia Nouril. New York: The Museum of Modern Art.

Freimane, Linda. 2017. "Importance of Historical Research and Documentation on LGBTI in Latvia." Presented at the "LGBTI History - Research and Documentation: How to Advance LGBTI Rights through Historical Perspective" Conference, Riga, Latvia, November 3.

G. 1980. "The Secret Life of Moscow." *Christopher Street* 4(7):15–22.

Goba, Kaspars. 2010. *Homo@lv.* Documentary. Elm Media, Elmmedia.

Healey, Dan. 2003. "Moscow." In *Queer Sites: Gay Urban Histories Since 1600,* edited by David Higgs. London: Routledge.

————. 2014. "The Sexual Revolution in the USSR: Dynamics Beneath the Ice." In *Sexual Revolutions*, edited by G. Hekma and A. Giami. London: Palgrave Macmillan.

————. 2017. *Russian Homophobia from Stalin to Sochi*. New York: Bloomsbury Academic.

Houlbrook, Matt. 2006. *Queer London: Perils and Pleasures in the Sexual Metropolis, 1918–1957*. Chicago: University of Chicago Press.

Jackson, Julian. 2009. *Living in Arcadia: Homosexuality, Politics, and Morality in France from the Liberation to AIDS*. Chicago: The University of Chicago Press.

Kon, Igor' Semenovic, and James Riordan. 1993. *Sex and Russian Society*. Bloomington: Indiana University Press.

Kotkin, Stephen. 1996. "The Search For the Socialist City." *Russian History* 23(1/4): 231–261.

Lefebvre, Henri, Eleonore Kofman, and Elizabeth Lebas. 1996. *Writings on Cities*. Oxford: Blackwell.

Lietuvos Respublikos Seimas. 1961. "Lietuvos Tarybų Socialistinės Respublikos Baudžiamasis Kodeksas." https://e-seimas.lrs.lt/portal/legalAct/lt/TAD/TAIS.204 65?jfwid=-fxdp782c.

Lipša, Ineta. 2018. *LGBTI People in Latvia: A History of the Past 100 Years*. Riga: Dardedze Hologrāfija.

————. 2019. "Categorized Soviet Citizens in the Context of the Policy of Fighting Venereal Disease in the Soviet Latvia from Khrushchev to Gorbachev (1955– 1985)." *Acta Medico-Historica Rigensia* 12:92–122. https://doi.org/10.25143/ amhr.2019.XII.04.

Mozaika. 2007. "Homophobic Speech in Latvia: Monitoring the Politicians." www.i lga-europe.org/sites/default/files/Attachments/latvia_-_homophobic_speech_in_lat via_english.pdf.

Rebane, Ilmar, ed. 1968. *Ugolovnyĭ Kodeks Ėstonskoĭ SSR. Kommentir. Izd.* [Po Sostoianiiu Na 1 Ianv. 1968 g]. Tallinn: Ėėsti raamat.

Ruduša, Rita. 2014. *Forced Underground : Homosexuals in Soviet Latvia*. Riga: Mansards.

Samma, Jaanus. 2013. *Untold Stories*. www.jaanussamma.eu/stories/.

Samma, Jaanus, Eugenio Viola, and Martin Rünk. 2015. *Not Suitable for Work: A Chairman's Tale*. Berlin: Sternberg Press.

Stella, Francesca. 2015. *Lesbian Lives in Soviet and Post-Soviet Russia: Post/ Socialism and Gendered Sexualities*. Basingstoke, UK: Palgrave Macmillan.

Stoler, Ann Laura. 2010. *Along the Archival Grain: Epistemic Anxieties and Colonial Common Sense*. Princeton, NJ: Princeton University Press.

Sviadoshch, A. M. 1991. *Zhenskaĭa seksopatologĭia*. Izd-e 5-perer. i dop. Kishinev: Izd-vo "Shtiintsa.

Ugolovnyĭ Kodeks Latviĭskoĭ Sovetskoĭ Sotsialisticheskoĭ Respubliki. 1961. Riga: Latviĭskoe gos. izd-vo.

Veispak, Teet. 1991. "Homosexuality in Estonia in the 20th Century: Ideological and Juridical Aspects." In *Sexual Minorities and Society: The Changing Attitudes Toward Homosexuality in the 20th Century Europe: Papers Presented to the International Conference in Tallinn, May 28–30, 1990*. Tallinn, Estonia: Institute of History.

Yurchak, Alexei. 2006. *Everything Was Forever, Until It Was No More: The Last Soviet Generation*. Princeton, NJ: Princeton University Press.

Zalytis, Janis. 1985. *Meilės Vardu*. Kaunas: Šviesa.

Chapter 6

Queer People and the Criminal Justice System in Ukraine

Negotiating Relationships, Historical Trauma, and Contemporary Western Discourses

Roman Leksikov

The issue of LGBTI+-criminal justice relationships has become one of the most debated questions in Western academic and activist environments (Perry 2008; Peterson and Panfil 2013).[1] From the 1970s onwards, in most Western countries, LGBTI+ people organized to overcome the problems of invisibility, silence, and marginalization as well as criminalization by state institutions. During this time, queer communities that were previously subjects of criminalizing policies by institutions of state violence (such as the police) now have become the subject of state protection, while anti-queer hate speech has become criminalized and anti-queer hate crimes have started to be punishable under the law. In this way, the very notion of homophobic and transphobic hate crimes was constructed (Tiby 2007). This shift caused a broad debate between two opposing camps of academics and activists.

On the one hand, liberal LGBTI+ movements often rely on state support and expect state institutions to protect them from homophobic and transphobic acts. This approach is generally based on the theory of retributive justice[2] and several other criminological theories, like rational choice theory,[3] and this position implies that expanding policing and incarceration practices are effective and ethical ways to deal with crime. On the other hand, radical and left queer movements often strongly oppose this way of thinking and promote the opinion that expanding policing and the criminal justice system will never protect vulnerable social groups from assault, crime, and discrimination. To prove their position, radical queer activists often appeal to the terms "carceral feminism" and "carceral queer movement" (Spade 2015) to argue for the impossibility of making structural changes by dealing with the effects instead of the causes.[4] They criticize the attempt to individualize structural problems and argue that the first approach only reinforces and strengthens existing social inequalities, and they try to emphasize the problem of queer investment into justice institutions and retributive justice (Ball 2014, 548–549; Meyer 2014).

Although both these paradigms are theoretically grounded and rely on ethical reasoning, there is little sociological research that examines how both these approaches work in practice. Queer criminology is a newly born branch of social research and is not yet institutionalized. As Mathew Ball argues, the construction of opposing camps as described above is not helpful when conducting comprehensive studies on the relationships between LGBTI+ people and the criminal justice system (2016, 56). Moreover, these two approaches simplify social reality because, for instance, there are examples of how different criminal justice institutions may treat LGBTI+ people differently in the same society at the same time (Dwyer 2014, 156). My data from Ukraine shows the complexity of attitudes of LGBTI+ people—victims of hate crimes—to the criminal justice system, the evolution of queer narratives and imagination of criminal justice, and how different outcomes of interaction between LGBTI+ people and criminal justice institutions might appear in different settings.

This chapter examines the following questions among Ukrainian LGBTI+ communities. What are the attitudes of Ukrainian LGBTI+ people who fell victim to hate crimes toward the criminal justice system? How do they perceive the role of the criminal justice system and its institutions in the process of sexual citizenship acquisition,[5] or, vice versa, the construction and maintenance of structural homophobia and transphobia? How do the victims renegotiate their vision of relationships between LGBTI+ people and the criminal justice system after victimization and collaboration with the police? What are the motivations of Ukrainian LGBTI+ people to engage with the police and the judicial system? I put a specific emphasis on the issue of the queer vision of the penitentiary system in contemporary Ukraine, exploring the presence and absence of cultural trauma post-Soviet LGBTI+ people might experience as a consequence of homophobic and transphobic politics of late Soviet and early post-Soviet carceral systems and the police. In this regard, I am concerned with establishing patterns of cultural trauma construction and their difference in relation to similar queer political process in North American countries (the United States and Canada).

METHODOLOGY

The empirical part of the research was conducted with three methods: interviewing, ethnographic observation, and document analysis. I conducted twenty-two in-depth interviews with (a) victims of homophobic and transphobic hate crimes, who then interacted with the police and the judicial system regarding their cases, and (b) human rights activists and NGO workers who deal with these issues. While my initial goal was much more ambitious—going to the field, anticipating conducting thirty to fifty interviews—when I started the recruitment process, it appeared that the studied group was much more difficult to access than I had previously expected. First of all, very few LGBTI+ people in Ukraine elect to interact with the criminal justice system after being assaulted. Most of the victims remained silent and did not press any charges. Secondly, even those who pressed charges were afraid to disclose this information, understanding that they could be re-victimized if their personal information were revealed. Moreover, because Ukraine is a weak state, these people realized that it is almost impossible to protect their rights with the help of the law and legal tools if a researcher disclosed their personal data or somehow behaved unethically toward them. And even though I used several channels of recruitment simultaneously (mailing lists and postings from trusted human rights organizations, snowball method, etc.), it did not help to recruit more than twenty interviewees. Last but not least, for some people who experienced violence, to remain silent and never talk about the past events is a way to heal their trauma and avoid triggering. While more possible participants might exist, it would require more time and resources than were accessible during this data collection.

This research used two kinds of questionnaires. The first was used to conduct interviews with victims of violence who then interacted with the police. The second one was used among NGO workers. The first questionnaire consisted of two parts. The first part contained questions about the violent experience and further interaction with the police, while the additional attachment contained questions about the interaction with the judicial system and the experience in a courtroom for those participants who went through this stage. Because the number of these people is tiny (five persons), there is no reason to distinguish this part of the research into a separate study. Thanks to the existence of the "Only State Registry of Court Decisions" (Ukr: *Iedynyi reiestr sudovykh rishen'*), I was able to discover all the relevant court verdicts before conducting interviews with my participants to have more meaningful conversations and better fact-checking. The analysis of documents was focused on all court decisions and documents in relevant court hearings which could be found in the Only State Registry of Court Decisions of

Ukraine and in the annual reports of human rights NGOs ("Nash Svit" and "Social Action Center," as well as OSCE-Ukraine).

Besides this, I also took ethnographic field notes, which were incorporated in the final text of the chapter, for three reasons. First, sometimes meaningful interactions or communication appeared beyond the official interviewing process. Secondly, some of the valuable data for this research was found in the social, cultural, and political context, such as in a court hearing on a relevant case that I attended. Moreover, I sometimes noticed contradictions and inconsistencies in the information provided to me by my interviewees, or specific features of their behavior, which made me reinterpret, examine, and critically reflect on their responses. All information was coded in an open way (instead of a focused one), meaning that no themes and categories were predetermined.

HISTORICAL TRAUMA TOWARD THE CRIMINAL JUSTICE SYSTEM AND QUEER POLITICS OF MEMORY IN NORTH AMERICA

Even though this chapter, first and foremost, aims to shed some light on the relationships between Ukrainian LGBTI+ communities and the criminal justice system, it is important to analyze patterns of these relationships in American and Canadian societies for several reasons. First, as the global cultural and political superpower and hegemon, the United States not only invests in the Americanization of politics and discourses around the globe but also becomes the "original example" for Eastern European countries (like Ukraine) that after the disappearance of Eastern Bloc turned to the epoque of "aspiring Westernization." This might be easily illustrated by how Russian LGBTI+ activists adopted the American queer movement's heritage, political narratives, and vision of the political future since the first American-Russian queer festival in 1991 (Kon 1997, 256); how Ukrainian LGBTI+ activists reproduce and abuse the American rhetoric of homonationalism under completely different settings (Leksikov and Rachok 2020); or how Ukrainian think tanks and opinion-makers support the application of U.S.-produced practices of zero-tolerance policing, over-policing and overincarceration. Shortly after anti-police sentiment became mainstream in American and Canadian queer politics, the same argument popped up in Ukrainian queer discourse, being completely detached from the local context. Secondly, it is very useful to review the North American context of the issue because it helps us to understand the current processes in Ukraine in terms of their temporal sequence. Of course, here I am by no means arguing about the certain linear temporality of queer movement development, but I rather offer an analysis of the timeline of the construction of cultural trauma from the criminal justice system's violence in North American queer communities, which will be helpful to understand recent development of the Ukrainian LGBTI+ vision of the criminal justice system.

Anti-police and anti-penitentiary sentiment among queer political groups in North America has clearly been on the rise during recent years. For example, significant media attention was given to incidents around Toronto Pride (Casey 2019) and Edmonton Pride (Wakefield 2018)—just two examples worth mentioning. In both cases, a substantial number of queer activists argued for banning uniformed police officers from marching in Pride Parades. Slogans like "The police have nothing to be proud of" and "There are no queer-friendly cops" as well as "No pride in police violence" became popular and widespread across the United States and Canada. Various academic and activist discourses oppose the engagement of criminal justice system officials in the LGBTI+ movement, but two main modes of reasoning are most relevant to this paper: current social issues in policing and the expression of historical trauma.

Regarding current social issues in policing, anti-police queer activists support their position with the following arguments. First, LGBTI+ people are still being overpoliced and over-arrested for the same types of misdemeanors when compared to their cisgender and heterosexual counterparts (Stern 2013). Second, the police do not effectively investigate hate crimes against queer people. For example, it took law enforcement authorities seven years to find the serial killer Bruce McArthur, who killed eight men in the Toronto Gay Village. Finally, the police are systemically engaged in racial profiling activities and repressions against homeless and poor people, and thus, as an institution, policing reproduces structural inequalities (Spade 2015; Haritaworn 2015). In addition to these reasons, there is another way to explain an emerging anti-police sentiment in the queer milieu: in the contemporary queer political imaginary, the police seems not only to be a structurally homophobic, transphobic, and racist institution in the transhistorical perspective, but it is also a source of intergenerational cultural trauma. The history of the blatant persecution of queer people in the twentieth century by police forces makes even younger generations of queer people experience and express this resentment.

The first set of arguments might constitute the basis for further studies, and here I would like continue to draw on the notion of intergenerational trauma as well as the political imaginary of the police as a structurally and transhistorically queer-oppressing institution, and how this notion and imaginary shape the relationships between queer people and the criminal justice system nowadays in Ukraine in comparison to North America. First of all, regarding cultural or intergenerational trauma, it is crucial to highlight and remember that it is always socially mediated, because the generations that live with trauma are neither survivors nor witnesses of the traumatic events. Thus, the discourse of collective trauma takes the social consciousness of the group that experienced the trauma out of the social reality, focusing on a constructed imaginary of the past (Alexander 2014). But what is even more interesting is how this discourse of intergenerational trauma around policing tends to erase and neglect the evidence of structural violence against LGBTI+ people worldwide and in North America in particular. Alexander argues:

> In creating a compelling trauma narrative, it is critical to establish the identity of the perpetrator, the "antagonist." Who actually injured the victim? Who caused the trauma? This issue is always a matter of symbolic and social construction. Did "Germany" create the Holocaust, or was it the Nazi regime? Was the crime restricted to special SS forces, or was the Werhmacht, the entire Nazi army, also deeply involved? Did the crime extend to ordinary soldiers, to ordinary citizens, to Catholic as well as Protestant Germans? Was it only the older generation of Germans who were responsible, or were later generations responsible as well? (2014, 15)

This opens another perspective on the analysis of emerging queer trauma toward the police; thus, the following questions should be seriously considered for further analysis. Why is it that the main subject of resentment among queer people is that police merely reproduce social inequalities as well as homophobic and transphobic policies, when the police also produce them? One might argue, drawing on Michael Lipsky's theory of street-level bureaucracy, that police officers always have the capacity of agency to use their own judgment in the process of decision-making. However, this argument seems to be more than problematic. For example, Mary Pat Baumgartner (1991, 129–163) and Martha Feldman (1991, 163–185) show that police officers' (and all legal officials') discretion is, indeed, strictly patterned by a range of factors and is thus very predictable. Moreover, this decision-making is subject to social control and depends on the opinion of one's professional group. As Feldman specifies, social and professional control of the discretionary behavior of legal officials is related to formal training and informal socialization and the aspiration to perform encouraged and appropriate behavior. These factors do affect the decision-making of police officers regarding the treatment of LGBTI+ people because the public expression of attitudes toward sexual and gender minorities is highly regulated by the cultural norms of a given society and by the institutional norms or professional culture of law enforcement agencies. Whether this informal regulation undermines the notion of street-level agency of law enforcement officers or not, it makes us look for the factors which shape and pattern the process of "decision-making" by police officers instead of relying on an explanation that favors agency as subjects of power and authority. Ultimately, this discussion brings up the core "structure vs. agency" debate. This standpoint demonstrates explicitly how decisions, which may be seen as a result of someone's agency, are indeed predetermined and patterned, which should make us challenge the dichotomy of structure vs. agency.

Returning to the discussion, it makes sense to go further and analyze how this discourse designates the police as individually responsible for structural violence against queer people, neglecting the other components of this structural violence. This discourse, as we can conclude from Alexander (2014), places responsibility on the police for the entire system of homophobic and transphobic structural violence. And this designation opens up myriad problematic questions. If queer pride politics aim to ban institutions that are actively engaged in structural violence against LGBTI+ people (in the past or present) from being a part of the pride movement, why is it exclusively about the police, and not about the healthcare system or religious organizations, which are still welcome in pride parades throughout the continent?

The role of the healthcare industry in reinforcing structural violence against LGBTI+ people cannot be overestimated. Especially in the United States, due to the absence of universal healthcare coverage and treatment prices that have become increasingly unaffordable in the last few decades, many of for-profit healthcare providers tend to be lobbyists against the single tax-payer system, which allows them to monopolize the market and, rejecting any state price regulations, increase their profits. This phenomenon led scholars to call the contemporary U.S. healthcare system the "medical industrial complex" (Rosenthal 2017) as an analogy with the "prison industrial complex."

This discursive turn reflects another pattern of social and political reality in contemporary American society. The prison and police system, in conjunction with the for-profit healthcare system, became the two main branches of the institutional infrastructure of structural violence. The prison system uses overincarceration to contribute to the highest incarceration rates in the world, and the for-profit healthcare system limits access to healthcare, thus cutting the life chances of underprivileged social groups. The input of the medical industrial complex in structural violence against queer people, once again, cannot be overestimated, especially considering the response of the complex to the AIDS epidemic, which dramatically reduced the life chances of gay and bisexual men, trans people and sex workers (Hunt 1988). Other examples of the contributions of the medical-industrial complex to structural violence against queer people include medical violence against trans and intersex people as well as the involvement of medical institutions in conversion therapy practices. Even though the problem of limited access to healthcare in Ukraine has completely different reasons, and there is no way we can talk about the Ukrainian healthcare system as the "medical industrial complex," some of my participants (as we can see from the excerpts below) indicate that their lives were more traumatized by the healthcare system rather than police.

A similar argument can be made about religious organizations, from the slightly different perspective of cultural violence. In accordance with Galtung (1969), Gilligan (1997), Christie et al. (2001), cultural violence constitutes a system of norms, discursive practices, and acts that normalize and reinforce structural violence by producing, reproducing, and enhancing anti-queer narratives, religious organizations became the main agent of cultural violence against LGBTI+ people, and hence, widely invested in structural violence against queer people. Nevertheless, the representatives of healthcare professions and religious organizations, unlike police officers, were never banned from pride events in North America in recent years, and, unlike police, they have not been designated as responsible for inflicting systemic harm to the LGBTI+ community. And once again, here we can see how fast this discourse was borrowed and developed by Ukrainian queer activist groups: the annual festival KyivPride received a lot of criticism every year for the "engagement of" and "collaboration with" the police (ФРАУ 2017); however, the participation of religious organizations was neither brought up nor condemned. Of course, this by no means denies the engagement of the police and penitentiary in reproducing the social order and structural violence, including sexual, gender, and racial inequalities. Rather, it suggests that contemporary queer cultural trauma in North America is based on a very limited, biased, and particular imaginary of past and present, and this anti-police discourse aims to personalize and assign responsibility to a certain institution for the structural violence experienced by queer people rather than reflect on structural violence itself. The next part of this chapter examines how the queer vision of the criminal justice system in the context of structural violence has been developed in Ukraine in light of the reproduction and imposition of the North American vision and politics analyzed above.

UKRAINIAN LGBTI+ PEOPLE AND THE CRIMINAL JUSTICE SYSTEM: CRUEL OPTIMISM

After developing the landscape of the relationships between queer communities and the criminal justice system in the contemporary United States and Canada, we can now turn to the empirical data from Ukraine to consider whether queer visions of the criminal justice system in Ukraine correspond with "borrowed" and imposed discourses and politics from North America, and whether we can talk about the construction of cultural trauma toward the criminal justice system within Ukrainian LGBTI+ communities. Here, I draw largely on the responses of my participants' interviews; however, I begin with a representative anecdote from my fieldnotes to make my argument.

When I met Jan, one of my interviewees in Kharkiv and a relatively famous artist and LGBT activist, I noticed that he was proud to have been born and reside in this city, so I decided to give him a compliment on his lovely hometown: "You know, Jan, the city center is so clean and well-kept, I am really excited, it's not a dirty and messy place like we have in Kyiv." He replied, "Yes, I still cannot understand why the Kyiv city government cannot clean up the city center. Come on, this is the capital! It must be cleaned up! It's unbearable: once you arrive at the central railway station and see all these dirty and stinky bums. . . . Why not order the police to throw all these fucking bums out and clean the territory around in the same way? That's so easy, and it has to be done!" While he is a vulnerable queer person and an activist, Jan supports the policing of homelessness and policing of the poor, supports the notorious approach of urban space policing in accordance with broken windows theory, and operates according to statements which obviously carry racist and classist implications.

In Ukraine, the relationship to the police has not been comprehensively discussed among LGBTI+ organizations and communities. Moreover, the LGBTI+ movement remains ideologically unstructured, operating with a more utilitarian approach. Thus, an analysis of these attitudes and their dynamics is warranted. Furthermore, the settings in which Ukrainian LGBTI+ people have to elaborate their attitudes toward the criminal justice system obviously differ from similar settings in North American or Western European societies. Hence, this dichotomy (the criminal justice system as the protector and hope of queer people vs. the criminal justice system as the oppressor) would not be able to describe the complexity of these attitudes and their dynamics in a Second World country like Ukraine.

During this study, each participant was asked several questions regarding their attitudes toward the criminal justice system. First, I asked, what was their motivation to interact with the police and press charges? And what did they expect if they did so? This question is relevant because of the general sentiment toward police in Ukrainian society, which are also prominent among its marginalized groups. People overall are rather skeptical or even hostile toward the police, and their attitudes might have improved only slightly after the police reforms of 2015. And even though this reform was aimed at restructuring the police and accelerated staff rotation, as well as creation and implementation of the new policies that were supposed to advance human rights protection in policing (such as "Police Ombudsman" and "Police of Dialogue), in 2019, according to two representative quantitative studies, only 30 to 32 percent of Ukrainian adults "trusted" the police as an institution (Кобзін et al. 2019; Мониторинг Общественных Настроений Украинцев 2019). Secondly, I asked my participants whether they believe that the current form of criminal (retributive) justice in Ukraine can be effective in reducing gendered and sexual violence and can rehabilitate or educate convicts. Last but not least, I took note when my participants were talking about their attitudes toward the police and criminal justice system beyond the official interview process.

Most of the participants admitted that they did not trust the police; nor did they believe that police officers would help them in a critical situation or would investigate an assault. One of the interviewees, Alex, explained his action in the following way:

> I didn't expect that the police would help at all, I was just convinced that I should do at least something, at least press charges. So I thought, why not try? Perhaps something would come out of it. Perhaps a miracle would happen. So I did. I don't trust the police at all. My family has very complicated relationships with all law enforcement authorities.

Another participant, Igor, who was a victim of three violent attacks, admitted:

> I am an LGBT activist. If I keep silent, it means that I've fucked up as an LGBT activist. After the first attack, I had certain expectations from the police. After the second attack, I had them too. But after the third attack, when I saw the same situation. . . . You know there was a press conference in Kyiv, and the same lady from the police was telling us that "it is so important to investigate hate crimes," so I've directly asked her, "Why don't you investigate them then?" And she, of course, replied that it's "so difficult, so difficult." So after that press conference, I've finally realized that it just makes sense to say "fuck it" for all this stuff and move away from this country. Cause there are no changes. These crimes were not investigated in the past, nor are they in the present. And even when the police already know who committed an attack, there are witnesses, and there are video recordings and stuff—they always let it go.

Here, we see that victims initiated interaction with the police without trusting or believing in this institution, or that they held onto trusting police and relying on their help, already having (multiple) experiences of failure of the police to investigate offenses against them and to prosecute offenders. Such irrational actions and hopes can hardly be explained in any other way than as manifestations of "cruel optimism." Lauren Berlant (2011) reflects on this phenomenon of maintaining attachment to problematic objects, which in fact only create additional obstacles for the person's endeavors and aspirations, though they are still considered objects of hope and optimism. We can see how Ukrainian LGBTI+ people maintain their hopes and positive attachment to the police and criminal justice system, regardless of their real attitudes toward this institution and their previous experience of interaction with it.

RETRIBUTION, RESTORATION, REHABILITATION OR PREVENTION: WHAT TYPE OF JUSTICE DO UKRAINIAN QUEER PEOPLE ASPIRE TO?

Another issue I have examined concerns attitudes toward the criminal justice system and retributive justice among victimized LGBTI+ people. During the last century, the criminal justice and prison systems in the USSR and the post-Soviet space became a source of homophobic and transphobic violence, as well as the primary space of its concentration. Queer women rarely suffer from gay and trans bashing in women's penitentiaries; however, gay, bisexual, and non-heteronormative men are frequent victims of systematic and widespread attacks, violence, rapes, humiliation, and segregation (Mogutin and Franeta 1993). Hence, some scholars conclude that prison culture itself is one of the most significant factors in the development of homophobic and transphobic sentiment in the post-Soviet space (Kon 1997). This issue made me rethink the perspective of using the criminal justice system as a tool to reduce or eliminate homophobic and transphobic violence in contemporary Ukraine. Moreover, I suspect that the criminal justice system and the penitentiary may be the central site for the cultural trauma that Ukrainian queer people experience, as it is the case in contemporary North American societies. In fact, late Soviet/early post-Soviet societies and North American countries in the twentieth century share the same features of mistreatment and persecution of LGBTI+ people by the criminal justice system: ceremonial rape and sexual abuse of suspected queers behind bars, police raids, and surveillance. This history and memory became a source of the vision of the criminal justice system as inherently homophobic and transphobic and as the origin of rape in contemporary critical queer discourse in the United States and Canada, which was described in the beginning of the chapter. Consequently, going to the field, I expected to observe the same process of trauma construction among my respondents, and therefore the same vision and imagination of the criminal justice system and its place in queer politics and everyday lives of LGBTI+ people. It was surprising that most of my interviewees expressed reasonably positive attitudes and expected that the criminal justice system would help to prevent anti-queer violence. For example, one of the interviewees, Olena, commented on her opinion on a sentence her attackers received:

> Well, of course, two years of a conditional sentence is also good, but I think they should go behind bars. Of course, that's obvious that they will not become cleverer in prison, but the real sentence may be motivation for those who are going to commit the attacks in the future as well as for the organizers of these mass attacks. If no one is sentenced, then these guys and girls will think that

they can do it again. But if they are sentenced. . . . It's not that I want her to be imprisoned, but I just hope it will be a lesson to other potential attackers.

Several participants, including Oleksandr and Andrii, argued that it is very important to advance hate crime legislation and policing, because the law frames public consciousness and shapes ethical and legal norms. In accordance with their point, the fear of prosecution is an effective restraining factor which helps to drop the level of bias-motivated violence, and advanced hate crimes legislation will assert legal emancipation of marginalized social groups, including LGBTI+ people, and abolish victim-blaming culture in such cases.

The majority of queer people in my study do rely on the educational function of the criminal justice system, yet at the same time, they believe that tougher sentences and incarceration of the attackers will be an ineffective measure to prevent new episodes of gay and trans bashing. Moreover, it is obvious from the pieces above that almost all my participants adhere to ideas of legal idealism (Attwooll 1998), which seem to be contradictory to their own experiences of interaction with law enforcement bodies and the criminal justice system. However, some participants were skeptical about the instrumentalization of the criminal justice system and were reflecting on the alternative justice measures. As another interviewee, Oleh, said:

> Honestly, I don't know. . . . Fortunately, I have nothing to do with the criminal justice system . . . to make it tougher, it may work both ways: either prisoners will become calmer, or they'll become even crueler. There is no third option. And since there is pressure from cellmates, I think they will become even more brutal and it will get worse.

A similar statement of skepticism was also expressed by another participant, Mariia, who commented upon the specific situation in Ukrainian prisons as not being conducive to re-education and rehabilitation:

> If we had a prison with normal psychologists, social workers, and staff that really cares and invests efforts into rehabilitating convicts, as is done in some other countries, where it [the prison sentence] might be a really useful and helpful experience for criminals . . . But instead, they [convicts in Ukraine] will just wash toilets there [in prison]. So if in some countries imprisoned people may achieve new levels of development, I am pretty sure that in our prisons one can only fall down and never be lifted up. Or at least it happens pretty seldom. And when you see TV shows about prisons abroad, you understand that it really makes sense: people cook for themselves, they are engaged in social life, read books, work out, live in normal conditions, so they feel like humans, and not

just as . . . I'm sorry, a piece of shit. So I think it doesn't make sense to sentence anybody in our country.

Later, Mariia also added that she indeed believes that only probation may be an effective educational and rehabilitation measure, as well as a preventative tool. She, as well as several other participants, assumed that convicts on probation would probably refrain from reoffending even when being tempted to do so because they have to avoid a real sentence. However, she was the only participant who thought that probation would contribute to discouraging violent offenders from committing assaults, whereas several other interviewees, who at first admired the idea of restorative or preventative justice for their offenders, expressed strict disbelief in the rehabilitation possibilities of probation, going back to the endorsement of incarceration and retributive justice. I suggest that these two participants do not think that the criminal justice system is an effective tool for reducing anti-queer violence; however, one of them still expresses a belief that the penitentiary system may successfully rehabilitate offenders, if it is well organized and well-funded, a situation that, in her opinion, is already successfully implemented in the countries of the generalized and idealized "West," what might be another example of "aspiring Westernization" among Ukrainian LGBTI+ people.

Though it may seem like the majority of participants are too hopeful regarding the possibility of successful instrumentalization of the criminal justice system, it must be noted that none of them expressed a belief in the potential of the Ukrainian criminal justice system to rehabilitate offenders. However, a lot of them believe that sentences and incarceration may be an effective tool of social change in terms of prevention of new offenses. These same beliefs pushed a total majority of my participants to interact with the criminal justice system after experiencing violence, which also may be understood as a form of cruel optimism (Berlant 2011).

Moreover, this cruel optimism toward the criminal justice system has been reinforced in the contemporary Ukrainian queer imaginary quite recently, after the police reform that took place in 2015. The queer vision and imagination of "the new police" has perfectly reflected the general social reaction that was shaped on the basis of binaries. They perceived the old militia and the new police through the dichotomous dispositions of "archaic vs. modern," "past vs. future," "Soviet vs. European," and hence "obscurantist vs. tolerant and progressive," "repressive vs. protective." Many LGBT people, as well as LGBT and human rights organizations hoped that this reform would significantly improve the relationships of LGBTI+ people with law enforcement institutions and would completely reshape practices of policing of homophobic and transphobic violence. Such points of view, though much rarer, are still expressed today.

CONCLUSIONS: DENIAL OF TRAUMA
FOR RESTORING THE RELATIONSHIPS
WITH THE NATION-STATE

As surprising as it might sound, the total majority of my interviewees, even those of them who were already young adults in the late Soviet and early post-Soviet times, knew almost nothing about homophobic and transphobic practices in the milieu of police and penitentiary that were the most widespread in that time. Here, I am referring to so-called "subbotniks," "lists," and "lowering down" in prisons. In the Soviet period, "subbotniks" were the practice of "voluntary" engagement of citizens in public space maintenance on Saturdays, and later, the same word was used to describe police raids on LGBTI+ venues or sex-work venues with the purpose of extortion of bribes and free sexual services. "Lists" refers to the practice of late Soviet and post-Soviet police to unlawfully collect the personal data of queer people with the purpose of further management of queer lives. Finally, "lowering down" was the widespread ritual of rape in late-Soviet and post-Soviet prisons, when the men who were or were perceived by the inmates as gay, trans, effeminate, or even heterosexuals, who performed oral sex on women, were "lowered down" to serve as sources of sexual services for the "real men" behind bars (Могутин и Франета 1993; Symkovych 2018).

The fact that the majority of my interviews admitted to not knowing about these practices and phenomena is even more suspicious if one considers the fact that these practices and rituals left prison culture a long time ago and successfully infiltrated the cultural mainstream. Thus, there is a chance that this is an example of a conscious denial and attempt to push out traumatic events from memory instead of simple ignorance. As one of my interviewees, Alex, said: "To be honest, I don't know what was going on behind bars . . . and I don't want to know. I have no connections to that world, and I don't care." And since I have received similar replies from my interviewees many times, such an attitude seems to be a pattern. Moreover, such a strategy of refusal and denial of the traumatic past looks even more patterned if analyzed through the lens of a cultural trauma theory. As Alexander (2002, 19–20) and Lipstadt (1996, 195–214) point out, the phase of denial and avoidance of the past is the first stage in the process of cultural trauma construction. Drawing on the classical example of Holocaust and post-Holocaust era, the authors point out that the resilience and forgettance stage is shaped by the multiple factors: after these events have finished, the people who experienced traumatic events attempt to charge themselves with a "can-do" mentality," trying to cut off the past from the present, while the younger generation of a traumatized social group encourages them to "go over" the past, depreciating their experiences. Thus, such a stage can continue for several dozen years.

However, in the case of LGBTI+ people in contemporary Ukraine, such denial and forgettance also has an additional background. My interviewees are ready to "forgive" the criminal justice system its past and present practices of persecution of queer people in order to get protection from the police and penitentiary because for them it signifies recognition by the state and the criminal justice system of their vulnerability as a social group. Secondly, it would signify that the LGBTI+ community, as a social group, has become the subject of legal relationships in the field of criminal law. The third general narrative which appears in this discussion may seem more problematic, especially for scholars of queer studies and critical criminology. It is apparent that such an endeavor is a result of the attempt to reconcile queer identities with national identities and a feeling of belonging to the nation-state. This aspiration requires victimized queer people to feel an ability and will of the nation-state they feel they belong to, to protect and secure them, and in this way, they try to gain access to their sexual citizenship. This aspiration may be especially strengthened by the experience of everyday homophobia, heterosexism, and transphobia from a variety of institutions, collectives, and social groups. In these settings, the strong self-identification of LGBTI+ people with the nation they feel they belong(ed) to may be undermined and affected.

In her talk "Who Marches the Nation-State?: Performing Transnational Citizenship and Pride in Brighton Beach," Alexandra Novitskaya argued that due to the exclusion of Russian LGBTI+ citizens from the nation-state discourse, they feel like aliens in their own country (Novitskaya 2018), and Ukrainian LGBTI+ people often feel the same: as I would call it, "the national identity disorder." In this situation, the appeal to an institution of the state, which, on the one hand, embodies the nation, and, on the other hand, is expected to be understanding, loyal, accepting, rational and educated as a counterweight to the "aggressive," intolerant, "archaic," "dull" and "obscurantist" society, and is expected to protect and secure its LGBTI+ citizens, and thus, to recognize their belonging to the nation-state by its superior authority (the criminal justice system), seems to be the apparent step to restore the national identity. Moreover, these differences in the vision of the criminal justice system among queer people in contemporary North America and Ukraine show us how the imagination of "the West" and of "the queer West" in Ukraine contradicts current queer politics and discourses in, for example, North American countries. Ukrainian queer people mostly continue to carry an imagination of "the queer West" as a legally idealistic dream about " law and order" and protection of the criminal justice system with an emphasis on retributive justice, while the perception of the legal and justice systems among North American queer people has drifted into an anti-police resentment and denial of the current criminal justice practices.

NOTES

1. Pseudonyms are used throughout this chapter.

2. Retributive justice as an ethical concept implies that an offender must be punished to suffer to an extent relatively equivalent to those sufferings experienced by the victim of their crime. Thus, the notion of retributive justice focuses on punishing an offender as the main accomplishment of justice.

3. In criminology, rational choice theory implies an approach to understand and analyze crimes and misdemeanors as rational social actions that are made by autonomous social actors after processing and analyzing advantages, disadvantages, and consequences of their actions and acting within the capacity of making deliberate choices.

4. The terms "carceral feminism" and "carceral queer movement" usually refer to feminist and queer political approaches that build on the belief that harsher penal measures and increased incarceration of those who commit offenses against women or LGBTI+ people are effective and ethical tools to deal with anti-women and anti-queer crimes. These terms also signify the relevant advocacy aspirations, which are directed at the creation and enforcement of relevant legislation and state policies.

5. The term "sexual citizenship" refers to the recognition of rights of non-heterosexual and non-cisgender persons by the state and normalization, as well as representation, of gender and sexual diversity by the social institutions and in public life.

REFERENCES

Alexander, Jeffrey C. 2002. "On the Social Construction of Moral Universals." *European Journal of Social Theory* 5(1):5–85.

Alexander, Jeffrey C. 2014. "Culture, Trauma, Morality and Solidarity, Vol. 1 No. 2: Simon Shoah: Intervention." In *Methods. Documentation*, 156–166.

Attwooll, Elspeth. 1998. "Legal Idealism." In *Routledge Encyclopedia of Philosophy*, edited by Edward Craig, 510–514. London: Taylor & Francis.

Ball, Matthew J. 2014. "What's Queer About Queer Criminology?" In *Handbook of LGBT Communities, Crime, and Justice*, edited by Dana Peterson and Vanessa R. Panfil, 531–555. New York: Springer-Verlag.

———. 2016. "The 'Prison of Love' and Its Queer Discontents: On the Value of Paranoid and Reparative Readings in Queer Criminological Scholarship." In *Queering Criminology*, edited by Angela E. Dwyer, Matthew J. Ball, and Thomas Crofts, 54–79. Basingstoke, UK: Palgrave Macmillan.

Baumgartner, Mary Pat. 1992. "The Myth of Discretion." In *The Uses of Discretion*, edited by Keith Hawkins, 129–162. Oxford: Clarendon Press.

Berlant, Lauren Gail. 2011. *Cruel Optimism*. Durham, NC: Duke University Press.

Casey, Liam. "Pride Toronto Members Won't Allow Uniformed Police to March in the Parade." *Global News*, January 24, 2019. https://globalnews.ca/news/4877398/pride-toronto-police-uniformed/.

Christie, Daniel J., Richard V. Wagner, and Deborah Du Nann Winter. 2008. *Peace, Conflict, and Violence: Peace Psychology for the 21st Century*. Delhi: Indo-American Books.

Creswell, John W. 2007. *Qualitative Inquiry and Research Design: Choosing Among Five Traditions*. Thousand Oaks, CA: Sage.

Crouch, Mira, and Heather Mckenzie. 2006. "The Logic of Small Samples in Interview-Based Qualitative Research." *Social Science Information* 45(4):483–499.

Dwyer, Angela. 2014. "Pleasures, Perversities, and Partnerships: The Historical Emergence of LGBT-Police Relationships." In *Handbook of LGBT Communities, Crime and Justice*, edited by Dana Peterson and Vanessa R. Panfil, 149–165. New York: Springer-Verlag.

Edwards, Rosalind, and Janet Holland. 2013. *What Is Qualitative Interviewing?* The 'What Is?' Research Methods Series. London: Bloomsbury Publishing.

Feldman, Martha. 1992. "Social Limits to Discretion: An Organizational Perspective." In *The Uses of Discretion*, edited by Keith Hawkins, 163–185. Oxford: Clarendon Press.

Galtung, Johan. 1969. "Violence, Peace, and Peace Research." *Journal of Peace Research* 6(3):167–191.

Gilligan, James. 1997. *Violence: Reflections on a National Epidemic*. New York: Vintage Books.

Gorton, Donald Esq. 2011. *Anti-Transgender Hate Crimes: The Challenge for Law Enforcement*. Report. Boston: The Anti-Violence Project of Massachusetts.

Hunt, Charles W. 1988. "AIDS and Capitalist Medicine." *Monthly Review* 39(8):11.

Leksikov, Roman, and Dafna Rachok. 2020. "Beyond Western Theories: On the Use and Abuse of 'Homonationalism' in Eastern Europe." In *LGBTQ+ Activism in Central and Eastern Europe*, 25–49. Cham: Palgrave Macmillan.

Lipsky, Michael. 2010. *Street-Level Bureaucracy: Dilemmas of the Individual in Public Services*. New York: Russell Sage Foundation.

Lipstadt, D. E. 1996. "America and the Memory of the Holocaust, 1950–1965." *Modern Judaism* 16(3):195–214.

Novitskaya, Alexandra. 2018. "Who Marches the Nation-State?: Performing Transnational Citizenship and Pride in Brighton Beach." Paper presented at the 117th Annual Meeting of the American Anthropological Association, San Jose, CA, November.

Perry, Barbara. 2008. "Hate Crimes (Bias Crimes), Criminal Justice Responses." In *Encyclopedia of Interpersonal Violence*, edited by Claire M. Renzetti and Jeffrey L. Edleson, 308–309. Thousand Oaks, CA: SAGE Publications, Inc.

Perry, Barbara, and Shahid Alvi. 2012. "We Are All Vulnerable." *International Review of Victimology* 18(1):57–71.

Peterson, Dana, and Vanessa R. Panfil. 2013. "Introduction: Reducing the Invisibility of Sexual and Gender Identities in Criminology and Criminal Justice." In *Handbook of LGBT Communities, Crime, and Justice*, edited by Dana Peterson and Vanessa R. Panfil, 3–13. New York: Springer-Verlag.

Rosenthal, Elisabeth. 2018. *An American Sickness: How Healthcare Became Big Business and How You Can Take It Back*. New York: Penguin Books.

Spade, Dean. 2011. *Normal Life: Administrative Violence, Critical Trans Politics, and the Limits of Law*. Brooklyn, NY: South End Press.

Stern, Mark Joseph. 2013. "You Can Still Be Arrested for Being Gay in Red-State America." *Slate Magazine*, August 5. https://slate.com/human-interest/2013/08/gay-people-are-still-being-arrested-for-having-consensual-sex-in-some-red-states-like-louisiana.html.

Stotzer, Rebecca L. 2010. "Seeking Solace in West Hollywood: Sexual Orientation-Based Hate Crimes in Los Angeles County." *Journal of Homosexuality* 57(8):987–1003.

Stotzer, Rebecca L. 2014. "Bias Crimes Based on Sexual Orientation and Gender Identity: Global Prevalence, Impacts, and Causes." In *Handbook of LGBT Communities, Crime and Justice*, edited by Dana Peterson and Vanessa R. Panfil, 45–65. New York: Springer-Verlag.

Symkovych, Anton. 2018. "Do Men in Prison Have Nothing to Lose But Their Manhood? Masculinities of Prisoners and Officers in a Ukrainian Correctional Colony." *Men and Masculinities* 21(5):665–686.

Tiby, Eva. 2007. "Constructions of Homophobic Hate Crimes: Definitions, Decisions, Data." *Journal of Scandinavian Studies in Criminology and Crime Prevention* 8(2):114–137.

Wakefield, Jonny. 2018. "Pride, EPS Keep Lines of Communication Open After Controversies over Police in Parades." *Edmonton Journal*, June 10. https://edmontonjournal.com/news/local-news/pride-eps-keep-lines-of-communication-open-after-controversies-over-police-in-parades.

Weber, Max. 1995. "The Nature of Social Action." In *Weber: Selections in Translation*, edited by Garry Runciman, 7–32. Cambridge: Cambridge University Press.

World Values Survey. Report. 2014. Accessed February 26, 2019. www.worldvaluessurvey.org/WVSDocumentationWV6.jsp.

Кобзін, Д., С. Щербань, К. Коренева, and А. Черноусов. 2019. *Оцінка Діяльності Національної Поліції України За Допомогою Опитування Громадської Думки*. Харків, Україна: ХІСД.

Кон, Игорь Семенович. 1997. *Клубничка на березке: сексуальная культура в России*. Москва, РФ: ОГИ.

Могутин, Ярослав, and Соня Франета. 1993. "Гомосексуализм в советских тюрьмах и лагерях." *Новое время*.

"Мониторинг Общественных Настроений Украинцев (20–24 Ноября 2019 Года)." Украина - Исследования - Социологическая группа "Рейтинг". Accessed April 15, 2020. http://ratinggroup.ua/ru/research/ukraine/monitoring_obschestvennyh_nastroeniy_ukraincev_20-24_noyabrya_2019_goda.html.

"ФРАУ." ФРАУ - сьогодні ніякої іронії, сарказму чи алегорії.... Accessed April 15, 2020. www.facebook.com/fraugroup/photos/a.793646954043536/1552526294822261/?type=3&theater.

Section III

DECOLONIZING QUEER PERFORMANCE

Chapter 7

Stifled Monstrosities

Gender-Transgressive Motifs in Kazakh Folklore

Zhanar Sekerbayeva

Dedicated to my grandparents—you are in my heart

The history of gender-transgressive practices in Kazakhstan may be traced all the way from the shamanistic traditions of the Kazakh people (Basilov 1976, 156; Alexeev 1984, 216) through tsarist Russia to the Soviet Union.[1] Gender-transgressive practices were part of a normalized reality not only in Kazakhstan but also in Central Asia as a whole, long before the globalized spread of knowledge or influence of feminism. Besides shamanism, cross-dressing and transgender motifs are fixed in Kazakh folklore in tales which use heroines and queer themes that may not otherwise be publicly discussed. This chapter explores stories such as "Zheztyrnak" and "Malukhan the Beauty" (Sidel'nikov 1971, 155–164) and other characters in Kazakh folklore, like the seven-headed Zhalmauyz Kempir in the story of "Qarauirek" (Kaskabasov et al. 2011, 117–122) to argue that the history of Kazakh folklore included records of queer characters who went beyond gender norms, who transgressed, who had alternative desires and chose alternative behavior. These stories provide a glimpse into the background of these transgressive characters who create the potentiality for a queer rethinking of folklore.

Transgressive motifs were not articulated by Russian Empire ethnographers and scholars, who traveled across Central Asian colonies, whose first goal was understanding the colonization process with its expansion of language, culture, civilizing of *inorodtsy* (a legal term with a negative connotation for the description of non-Russian populations). Historian Marina Mogil'ner argues in her work (2013) that studying racial superiority and inferiority was a part of the flourishing anthropology in Russia, as it was for science in the colonizing Western countries. It is very consistent with other Russian ethnographers who saw fieldwork as a possibility to gather remnants of "primitive" life of tribes that may disappear (Mogil'ner 2013, 59). That is why traces of any gender "deviance" collected by ethnographers had been described as either a great sin (in case of the Uzbek *bachi*) or just an exotic difference of inferior native people. This chapter attempts to rectify this sti-fling of the gender-transgressive motifs in Kazakh folklore by re-telling and re-analyzing the stories of monsters that had much too intimate relations with humans, and by virtue of doing so, had allowed them to transgress as well. I start with a brief overview of the Kazakhstani modern context and move to the challenges of the Russian tsarist period where ethnographers used colonial optics in recording Kazakh folklore. Their Russo-centrism led to a simplification of the diverse mythological pantheon of creatures of Turkic tribes, but at the same time kept the traces of a queer layer, in an unexpected way, such as in the case of Dudar Kyz. This is a modest attempt to unfold the meanings of these fairy tale enchantments.

REREADING FAIRY TALES

Since my bilingual childhood to today, I cannot give any examples of folklore characters which I met that reflected me or my queer lived experiences and that I could have identified with. I never read any books that "got" me— nothing echoed in me, although I read about diverse heroic male adventures, animals' magical help, stories of good and evil in the human path that can be easily intermixed. I did not realize what I was searching for for so many years. A close friend helped me to find out the object of the long search. Once she told me a story of how she went to a city park and looked for women like herself in the woods because she could not succeed in finding them in litera-ture or cinema. She was eagerly looking for queer women. After some time she managed to meet one such a beautiful person. We understood that we should stop looking for any queerness in classical Russian or Kazakh litera-ture and maybe should start our search in Kazakh folklore, with its examples of powerful women, though they were depicted in very monstrous patterns or interpreted in only one narrow understanding of being.

How can folklore help in understanding queer or transgressive practices? And why is it important? Transsexuality (like homosexuality) in Kazakhstan is considered gender "deviance" in public discourse and even a sin, which influences the attitudes of the general population toward transgender and transsexual people, or people who might appear as transsexual (Alma-TQ 2016, 7–10). Newspapers, online media, or TV shows that raise the issue of trans people only raise it from a negative point of view, where all participants, including journalists, psychologists, and judges criticize trans participants on camera (Jurttyn Balasy 2018). Coverage of trans people's life stories in mass media is done with a scandalous gradation, when journalists ask their interviewees about intimate details of their lives and focus only on such depictions. Often it is accompanied by the personal transphobic attitude of reporters who cannot erase their own hatred, fear, and anxiety. And such hate speech in the media causes not only public opinion against any queer characteristics but also leads to physical violence. In 2013, the house of a trans man was burned down after his participation in a Kazakhstani TV show "Nasha Pravda" (KTK 2013; see also Sekerbayeva 2021).

Public narrative toward any gender diversity in Kazakhstan is strongly negative, and backlash and hatred are fueled by references to the history of the country, traditions, past times where everything "fit the order." But it is a rather ungrateful endeavor to appeal to ancestors, who may turn out to be much more accepting people, with a wider understanding of society. When studying folklore, we may see that our histories contain a plethora of transgressive practices, examples of breaking gender norms, and it becomes easier to understand that queerness has always been woven into Kazakh social fabric. For modern Kazakhstan, the traditional opposition of East versus West, where the West is the ideological invader, may be reversed, pointing to a possible situation in the past where "an oriental elaborated plot had actually been carried westward with great fidelity in the transmission" (Schlauch 1944, 208). Such a view was expressed by folklorists Emmanuel Cosquin (1886, 22) and Alexei Veselovski (1872) and developed by Kaarle Krohn (1926, 28) who established the principles of the "Finnish School" of folklore studies, which define the geography of the plot by classifying different variants of one fairy tale. Another significant researcher, Victor Zhirmunsky (1979, 48, 213, 334–335, 397), wrote several articles about the influence and infiltration of the Turkic epos into Western culture, where he compared the epic tales of "The Odyssey" with "Alpamysh Batyr," the Russian folk tale Swan Maiden with "Edige and Tokhtamysh," and the Scottish ballad "Edward" with the poem "Kozy Korpesh and Bayan Sulu." Thus, Zhirmunsky studied international folklore influences and, in particular, found the thematic and subject similarities of the works of Kazakh folklore with Russian, Scottish, Old Icelandic oral-poetic works of other peoples.

Looking at contemporary folklore studies, it is possible to find queer and feminist analyses of the narratives, allowing us to read fairy tales with new meanings beyond gender stereotypes (Bacchilega 1997, 6; Turner 2015, 44). Additionally, there are works where folk stories were rewritten by authors, such as Emma Donoghue's *Kissing the Witch: Old Tales in New Skins* (1997) and William Holden's *A Twist of Grim: Erotic Fairytales for Gay Men* (2010) and anthologies *Happily Ever After: Erotic Fairy Tales for Men* (Michael Ford 1996); *Sleeping Beauty, Indeed & Other Lesbian Fairytales* (JoSelle Vanderhooft 2009); *So Fey: Queer Fairy Fiction* (Steve Berman 2009).

Related to this, Kazakhstani collections of research, articles, and essays queering folklore are rare, solitary cases. There are only two examples at hand: the poetry paper "Ышшoodna" (2016) (*Yshsho Odna*, in English "One More"—a noncommercial newspaper, each issue of which has different editors and themes; Issue 5 was dedicated to gender politics) and the collection of poetry "Pod Odnoi Oblozhkoi" (2018), where a literary representation of gender differences was presented. Remarkably, "Ышшoodna" was published in a format of *samizdat*—self-published literature—and contributors Mariya Vilkoviskaya and Ruth Jenrbekova stressed the challenging situation in the afterword (2016, 47–48):

> Like any self-publishing, it means, firstly, an unfavorable cultural climate, where modernity, with all its variety of artistic languages, has been squeezed out into the field of private initiative, and secondly, a growing awareness that art and literature exist inside relations of power, which means the choice between assimilation and autonomy (i.e., between compromise and resistance) is faced by each participant in the process. In this sense, our current "semi-underground" situation is not much different from the Soviet one. But if in Brezhnev's times the pressure was explicitly ideological, then the current ruling ideology (which we generically refer to as patriarchal) no longer resorts to theoretical arguments, shamelessly reinforcing its eternal imperative to maintain the status quo by forced normalization practices. It is not surprising that in such a situation, gender and sexuality become markers, with the help of which the images of "strangers" or "lower people" are constructed, which are modern untimely. Not only do women fall into this category, but in general the whole variety of bodies and subjectivities, which differ from the archaic heteromasculine norm. Thus, to declare today your identity as inconsistent with the officially approved canon from a purely personal case is once again turning into a political one—regardless of whether it takes place in the territory of art or literature, in the media or just on the street.

CHALLENGES IN AN ETHNOGRAPHIC APPROACH

The history of Kazakh literature goes back to Turkic nomadic tribes, who inhabited the whole territory of Central Asia. The migratory character of living in the region influenced the type and form of early folklore, which was a particularly oral tradition until the nineteenth century (Winner 1980). Nomadic oral and, later, written traditions were not a pure subject without external influences; on the contrary, they absorbed Irano-Arabic literature's impacts.

The question that has remained most challenging is about the periodization of Turkic literary heritage. Even though it is not the main aim of the chapter, it is important to provide an overview to enhance contextual understanding. Seit Kaskabassov (2013, 82) suggested that the history of oral-poetic oeuvre started from the second half of the eighteenth century and can be divided into four stages: (1) the eighteenth century and first half of the nineteenth century; (2) the middle of the nineteenth century to the 1920s; (3) the Soviet period; (4) the independence period, from 1991. Another authoritative folklorist, ethnographer Serikbol Kondybai, divided the history of Kazakh mythogenesis into three stages (2005, 7): proto-Turkic, from the end of the Neolithic and Eneolithic to the first through third centuries BC; Turkic itself from the first through third centuries BC to the fourteenth to fifteenth centuries, and Kazakh itself from the fifteenth century and beyond. However, there are three great literary monuments which survived, and one of them allows us to start the periodization of early nomadic folklore at least from the eleventh century (Winner 1980, 27): Mahmud al-Kashgari's Diwan lughat at-Turk (1077); recordings of the Russian ethnographer Vasilii Radlov "Obraztsy Narodnoi Literatury Turkskikh Plemyon Zhivushchikh v Yuzhnoi Sibiri i Dzhungarskoi Stepi" (1866–1907); recordings of Kazakh ethnographer Shokan Valikhanov "Sochineniya. Zapiski Imperskogo Russkogo Geographicheskogo Obshchestva," XXIX (1904). These works lead to the idea that the roots of Kazakh folklore might go deeper than its documentation and interpretation by folklorists of the nineteenth century.

Tsarist imperial policy was interested in the peripheries, and materials about the style of local people's lives, traditions, and beliefs had to be gathered. Created in 1845, the *Russkoe Geographicheskoe Obshestvo* (RGO) implemented research into the everyday lives of the Russian and non-Russian *inorodtsy*, populations beyond the empire's borders (Vaskul 2013, 115–116). It aimed to bring to light the environment outside of the Russian Empire, where its folk observed primordial customs unlike than those who lived inside of the native land. According to the "Svod Zakonov o Sostoyaniyakh" (Code of Laws on Conditions) (article 762), *inorodtsy* were divided into the following categories: Siberians; Samoyeds of the Arkhangelsk province; nomads of the Stavropol province; Kalmyks in the Astrakhan and Stavropol provinces; Kyrgyz of the Inner Horde; nomads of the Akmola, Semipalatinsk, Semirechensk, Ural and Turgai regions; nomads of the Turkestan region; the population of the Trans-Caspian region; highlanders of the North Caucasus; and Jews all over the empire (Andreevskii, Arsen'ev and Petrushevskii 1894, 224–225).[2] In 1850, a special department of the RGO discussed a project regarding the comprehensive survey of one *narodnost* (nation), using it as an example for any *inorodtsy* research afterward. The chair of the RGO, Nikolai Nadezdin, described such a method:

> For experience and sampling it may be possible to do something practical and interesting about one tribe, specifically *mordva*, of which we have

several curious samples from the two main governorates. (Nizhegorodskiy and Simbirskiy1850, 1(1))

Undoubtedly, Kazakh folklore studies should be revised in search of a decolonial interpretation of the canon through an analysis of original texts (before translation or recording), in light of the rising importance of oral tradition, which was accepted as primitive rather than unique or remarkable regarding the Turkic folk canon. Decolonizing means to challenge mono-centrism, particularly Eurocentrism and Russocentrism, in Central Asian countries' cultural imaginary and stand in an unsubordinated position to the general colonial storytelling history that prevailed with European narratives, theories, terminology, and expertise. Oral literature was deemed less developed than written tradition (Milgnolo and Tlostanova 2007, 109–123). In Kazakh folklore, female images survived different historical and mythic times, political and linguistic regimes, the colonial past, and the modern flourishing of patriarchy, which kept traces of being queer, rebellious, and powerful in the form of horrendous monstrosities. In the next section I will discuss three common characters, Zhalmauz Kempir, Zheztyrnaq, and Albasty, which in their essences compound the monstrous, unexplained, and illicit gestures and actions.

FEMALE MONSTROSITIES IN KAZAKH FOLKLORE: ZHALMAUZ KEMPIR, ZHEZTYRNAQ, AND ALBASTY

Considering the character of work on folklore-ethnographic databases it is no surprise that exploratory colonial politics influenced scientists and military staff who were responsible for the recordings and interpretation of Turkic fairytale heritage. One of the examples of the "imperialization" of plots is the figure of Zhalmauyz Kempir,[3] a demonic creature in the image of an old lady that was instantly compared and named as only a version of Baba Yaga from Russian folklore (see Image 7.1). For example, here is a representative description of the character:

> Far away, in another country, lived Yalmauz-Kampir (Baba Yaga), a terrible gluttonous old woman. She has a head like a large Kyrgyz yurt and a mouth like a door. When she eats, she swallows whole sheep at a time. She prepares food for herself in a huge cauldron, which has 40 ears, so that 40 people can lift it. In this boiler, 40 sheep or other animals are cooked. She rushes quickly, like a whirlwind; therefore, when she appears, a strong wind also occurs. Baba Yaga changes its appearance, depending on the circumstances. In her power are 40 strong Devas, and it is impossible to resist it without magical power. Baba

Yaga's children are voracious monsters just as she is. They, even at a young age, can devour whole carcasses. Most of all, Baba Yaga loves human meat and, in order to get her favorite food, she walks around the cities, under the guise of a beggar, and takes small children to her by deception. (Ostroumov 1906, 1)

Interestingly enough, in "Kazakhskie Narodnye Skazki" (1983), Zhalmauz Kempir was named in the text as Baba Yaga (1983, 15).

Even footnotes afford an oversimplified equation: Zhalmauz Kempir is Baba Yaga. In another collection of the same year named "Zolotaya Bita" (1983) the creature is presented as Zhalmauz Kempir with the epithet "Old Woman-Gluttonous Mouth" (1983, 28). The book "Skazki Narodov Mira" (Fairy Tales of the World) was published in 1995, with volume 10 dedicated to the fairy tales of people of Siberia, Central Asia, and Kazakhstan which, however, did not express either the diverse bestiary and classification of terms, nor the differentiation between supernatural creatures with their specific functions, roles, and symbols. For instance, the book gathered forty ethnic folk tales and, in cases where there are mentions of female monsters, like Albasty, Mystan Kempir, Zhestyrnak, Zhalmauz Kempir—they are all simply called *starukha* ("old woman" in Russian). In the attached vocabulary of "Skazki Narodov Mira" it is also challenging to find more examples of demonic beings that are commonly known to Turkic people, aside from *Abbasy* (monster of Yakuts), *Devas* (common Turkic evil), *Jinn* (common Turkic spirit), *Kele* (Chukot devil), and *Chzhinchi* (Dungan evil spirit). In

Image 7.1 Zhalmauz Kempir. From Batyrlar Turaly Ertegiler. Almaty: Aruna Baspasy, 2015, 91. Artist T. Vishnyakova.

"Miphy Narodov Mira. Entsiklopediya" (Myths of the Peoples of the World 1980, 1005–1006) the section regarding Turkic folklore represents Kazakh folklore very briefly. This significant lack of information moved geography teacher Serikbol Kondybai to create the Kazakh mythological dictionary in 1993. He prepared his first book, *An Introduction to Kazakh Mythology* in 1996–1997, and it was published only in 1999. The contemporary works of Kondybai are considered some of the most important contributions regarding the mythopoetic oeuvre in Kazakhstan. In sum, Russian language interpretations of Central Asian folklore were far too narrow and not thorough enough for comprehensive understanding and differential analyses.

Returning to one of the omitted female monsters, Zhalmauyz Kempir was instantly compared with and called only a version of Baba Yaga from Russian folklore (Ostroumov 1906, 9). According to Professor Assima Ishanova, the Kazakhs had their own mythology and folklore, no less ancient than Russian:[4]

> Zhalmauz Kempir is not like Baba Yaga, neither externally by behavior, nor by semantic fullness. Zhalmauz is a devourer, she has seven heads, but she may be a savior. She does not fly on a broomstick. Zhalmauz goes back to the cult of the patron mother, and this is indicated by, according to researcher Serikbol Kondybai, her features of shamanism, using magic, being a mistress of tribal fire, mistress of the land of death.

Baba Yaga in Slavic folklore is a creature from chthonic empire who has a daughter and three sisters of the same name. As an illustration, she is presented as an old beast and ancient witch, a snake (Rogachevskaya 1998, 425–430). Baba Yaga can be very aggressive, especially if somebody comes as an unexpected guest (Warner 2010, 124) who steps over her domain. Yaga threatens to eat an intruder, though in some tales that intention is possible to avoid. Some folk narrators emphasize the grotesqueness of her nose, breasts, buttocks, or vagina ("zhopa zhilena, manda mylena," Onchukov 8). Interestingly, her nose, teeth, and pendulous breasts are made from iron. Quite remarkable also is the fact that she suckled at the breasts of lovely women. In "The Legless Knight and the Blind Knight" (Afanasyev 1861, 171–172):

> The merchant daughter remained with them; the *bogatyri* (heroes) revered her, loved her, recognized her as their full sister; they themselves are on the hunt every now and then, and the named sister is forever at home: she runs the whole household, she cooks dinner, and she launders the laundry. So Baba Yaga, a bone leg, walked into their hut and sucked at the white breasts of the red damsel, a merchant's daughter. Barely the heroes go hunting, and Baba Yaga is already right there!

This can be interpreted as hidden sexuality, a queer act of the Russian witch when she absorbs the power of young females. Nikolai Novikov notes her role as an enchantress, avenger, and insidious detractor (176). Her queerness is also depicted in her beast features, as a creature with hypertrophied parts of the body: "one lip on the earth, another lip in the skies"; "the nose has grown into the ceiling"; "in one corner the legs, in the other head"; "Baba Yaga sits, her chest shuts the stove"; "tits across the threshold, snot through the garden, raking soot with tongue" (Rogachevskaya 1998, 425–430). She has a tremendous mouth that indicates exorbitant gluttony. She has a bone leg, one eye, iron nose, and clay face. Mikhail Chulkov writes in the book *Abevega Russkikh Sueverii, Idolopoklonnicheskikh Zhertvoprinoshenii i Svadebnykh Obryadov, Koldovstva, Shamanstva i Prochego* (Alphabet of Russian Superstitions, Idolatrous Sacrifices and Wedding Common Rites, Witchcraft, Shamanism and Other):

> The Slavs revered the infernal goddess, portraying her as a monster, sitting in an iron mortar and having an iron finger, they offered a bloody sacrifice to her, thinking that she enjoys the shedding of blood. (1786, 324–325)

Professor Assima Ishanova stressed in an interview[5] that Kazakh chthonic beings show traces of shamanism. This is confirmed by Zhalmauz's inherent functions of a shaman, mistress of a family fire, mistress, and guardian of the "land of death" (Meletynskii 1990, 672). Additionally, the development of Zhalmauyz Kempir could be seen from the merging of two images (Kondybai 2005, 115): the mythological mother and the historical servant of a cult (female priestess). Later these images began to mix and become one.

Zhalmauyz Kempir is known for her cannibalistic addictions, appearing as a woman with seven heads and a kidnapper of children. In addition, she asks her victims to suck their blood from a finger which can be considered an intimate and sexual act, for example, in "Qarauirek" (Karazhanova 2016, 53; Kaskabasov et al. 2011, 117–122):

> With the fire extinguished, Sarqyt went in search of her brothers to take a flint from them, when out of the corner of her eye she saw a distant fire. When she went to get the fire, there was the seven-headed Zhalmauyz Kempir. It was her eye that shone in the dark.
>
> "My dear, welcome, why have you come here?"—asked the hag.
>
> "I have come to ask for fire,"—the girl replied.
>
> "If you let me suck on your thumb, I shall give you fire, but if you don't, then I shall not. And if you refuse, I shall swallow you!"—said the old hag. Sarqyt quaked with fear.

"I agree then,"—she said and gave up her thumb. As the old hag sucked on her
finger, the girl went pale.

And it is not just about the act of sucking blood itself, but also about
Zhalmauyz Kempir secretly visiting the chosen girl, and about the subordination of Sarqyt, who is afraid to tell her brothers about such a bond, an unusual
partnership (see Image 7.2). The misfortune to meet Zhalmauyz Kempir was
associated with the desire to ignite the extinguished fire, because Sarqyt
showed greed for food and lost vigilance over the hearth—thus she violated
societal expectations about her gender role.

Image 7.2 Zhalmauz Kempir From Qial-gazhaiyp Ertegiler. Almaty: Aruna Baspasy,
2015, 21. Artist Assol Sas.

The character of Zhalmauyz Kempir, according to Kazakh folklorist Seit Kaskabassov (2014), undergoes a number of significant changes: from powerful ancestress of the clan to a purely evil creature who degrades herself to the level of a person creating domestic atrocities. Kaskabassov described her as an "insidious schemer" (2014, 51). He also accents references to existing matriarchy in Turkic nomadic tribes, which influenced the dynamics of an antagonist and helper of heroes:

> The image of the Zhalmauyz Kempir also dates back to the real progenitor. Some of the traits and actions of Zhalmauyz Kempir and her good attitude to the hero, help, advice bring her closer to the prototype: the head of the female genus named babies, adopted children, gave advice to young people in marriage, defended the rights and interests of relatives; was the keeper of the unwritten laws of the race, customs, traditions; judged, sometimes stood at the head of the army. The universality of the functions of the matriarch served as a good basis for creating a cult. People attributed to her supernatural properties, even considered her a sorceress, capable of engaging in a fierce battle with evil invisible spirits. So the shamans appeared in the primitive maternal genera, protecting the relatives from misfortune. (2014, 45)

Images that influenced the evolution of Zhalmauyz Kempir are connected to archaic mythological females. First, Mother-Ingle (*Ot Ana*) or Grandmother Khal (*Khal Azhe*), who guard the fire in a yurt and punish people, usually young women, if the fire goes out. She sucks blood or swallows personages, returning them in better health and physical condition (a repeated plot throughout with *Samruk Bird* and *Alyp Kus*). The second type of fabulous woman is Mother-Water who gives a child (or takes it) or helps a hero to find a spouse. In order to foster a child, she gives her breast to suck (Kondybai 2011).

Zhalmauyz Kempir has zoomorphic features, such as references to birds (owl, swan, raven, dove, horse, snake); several heads (from seven to seventy); birds' legs and beak. Zoomorphism connects her to another colorful and monstrous character of Kazakh folklore, Zheztyrnaq. They are half human and half animal—an essential component in theorizing monsters (Heinz Mode 1973, 7).

Zheztyrnaq is the copper-clawed (*zhez*—copper, *tyrnaq*—nail) and the copper-beaked (a feature that is not always presented) being that transgresses gender norms and expresses interconnections with animalism.

Hatto (1994) mentions the hybridity of Zheztyrnaq in her half-woman and half-animal nature, which points to shamanistic patterns. Such ideas are echoed in the work on "Myphologiya Predkazakhov" (The Mythology of Pre-Kazakhs) of Serikbol Kondybai (not yet published and only available online).

Image 7.3   Zheztyrnak. From Erlik Ertegileri. Almaty: Aruna Baspasy, 2015, 68. Artist Marat Komekov.

On the side, a creature appears in the guise of a beautiful woman who can seduce a hunter and possesses great power, including a piercing voice that can kill birds and small animals (see Image 7.3). She herself can turn into animals and inanimate objects. The character's gender ambivalence develops in "Zheztyrnaqi, Peri i Mamai" (The Zheztyrnaqs, Peri and Mamai) where Zheztyrnaq exists in both status—male and female (Sidel'nikov 1971, 56–62). In Divaiev's description, Zheztyrnaq is genderless and close to animals rather than humans (1903, 2). Importantly, the Kazakh language itself is gender neutral and the pronoun *ol* refers to she, he, or it at the same time. Additionally, when using words *adam* or *kisi* (both mean human being), which occurs in folklore, it is very problematic to guess the gender because these words do not have a gender component, and as such they do not indicate definitively whether a character is male or female.

Zheztyrnaq is depicted as an evil creature. In particular, "Mythological Encyclopedia" (Meletynskii 2008, 214) says: "Zhez Tyrnak (Copper Nail), Kazakh evil demonic creature in the guise of a beautiful young woman with a copper nose and copper nails. Zhez Tyrnak has monstrous powers and the ability to kill animals and birds with her loud voice. Kazakh fairy tales demonstrate the character's insatiable cunning when Zhez Tyrnak wants to kill a human." Divaev recorded the tale that demonstrated that behavior (1903, 3):

And so before the sun has set, at the time when, having made a fire, he was boiling meat, a woman appeared before him. Tulebai batyr looked at her and, seeing she is young and very beautiful, offered her a piece of meat; she accepted the meat not with her bare hand, but with a rolled down sleeve of her dress. At this moment Tulebai batyr realized that a Zheztyrnaq sits before him and started devising a plan to defend himself. When Tulebai batyr, having eaten the meat, started wiping his hands with a piece of cloth, the woman sitting next to him said: "It is a waste to wipe tallow with tallow," and when Tulebai batyr began sucking the bones, she said: "Do not sharpen steel with steel."

After such suspicious words, Tulebai felt something would happen, so rather than sleep next to the fire, he placed a log there for the night and climbed up the tree. Zheztyrnaq came and jumped at it, embraced it and fell with it to the ground. In the opinion of researcher Inzhuna Karazahanova, this episode "carries obvious sexual connotations, perhaps suggests a homosexual anxiety, or a fear of being 'deceived' by a person who violates the norms of gender presentations and disturbs the rigid gender categories of heteropatriarchy" (2016, 51).

The presence of Zheztyrnaq in folk tales does not cause immediate recognition. Heroes (travelers or hunters) understand that something unusual is afoot when they hear a clang or see that a woman is hiding her hands.

The hunter looked at the woman: yellow face, angry eyes. She looked closely at the hunter. He was surprised and thought to himself: "Is this a human being, in his or her youth, who remained in abandonment by people in this place and became wild or some kind of other harmful creature?" The hunter removed the cauldron from the fire, stuck the tip of a large hunting knife into a meat, gave it to the woman and shouted loudly: "Take!" She without protruding arms from the sleeves took the meat and ate it. (Zhanuzakova 1983, 97)

Similar characteristics, such as seducing heroes and endangering them, are possible to trace in the next female monster—Albasty. Kondybai explains (2005) its origin—*Al* as ancient deity firstly perceived as female and *Abas* as autonomous term for designation of spirits, female demiurges.

Al and Abas were separate images and only with time did they become together in one single anthroponym—*al-abas—alabas—albas*. According to the mentioned scholar, the combination of two individual characters led to the appearance of a new spirit accepted as the progenitrix, the first mother. Adding the Turkic prefix *ty (ly)* demonstrated the existence of her children (a group of male and female spirits). With time the meaning changed, and the offspring of Albas were assumed to be representatives of demonic, lower mythology. (2005, 59–60)

In Kazakh folklore, she absorbed details of other monsters (Peri, Zheztyrnaq, Mystan Kempir). Her main nuance is habitat—lakes, rivers, water sources. She comes when a person is sleeping and presses their chest, causing the inability to move or breathe properly. Albasty visits pregnant women and steals their lung, which personifies a spirit of the parturient woman. Mostly shamans have power over Albasty and if they subdue her, she could help with the household, heal people who got sick because of her, and bring wealth to her owner. Like Zheztyrnaq, she can be dangerous to hunters and travelers or useful to them (as a donor or provider who gives a hero or heroine something useful that will help in a quest). She sends luck, gives her meat to eat, milk to drink. According to Fayzullina, Prokopova, and Ermakova (2019, 198–209), Albasty can charm men with her own expressed breast milk. A creature of the water element, she is also known for stories of having sexual contact with people. There is a recording where a spirit of lake—"bez shtanov" (without pants)—sits on a nose or at the feet of a music performer and interrupts music (Yadanova 2009, 174–185).

CROSSDRESSING MOTIVES AND PRACTICES

In his *Istoricheskie Korni Volshebnoi Skazki*, Vladimir Propp (1986, 108–111) dedicated a section to "travestism." He compares Baba Yaga and Witcher, continuing in the suggestion that a male rite performer disguises himself as a woman and becomes male-female. He gives an example of Melanesians who believed in a spirit—mother of all masks, Duk-Duk. He refers to Nevermann's description of a celebration at which strange figures appeared, and they had phalluses and female breasts and "seemed to an unwarned observer as hermaphrodites. But aborigines sharply deny such interpretation and stress that they always present themselves as men" (Nevermann 1933, 88). The person involved in the ritual kept his female secret name, as far as he imagined himself turned into woman.

Crossdressing motifs can be found in a Kazakh fairy tale named "Krasavitsa Malkhuan" ("Malkhuan the Beauty"), where the hero wants to take beautiful Malkhuan as his wife, but she is promised to one of the khans. So he decided to wear women's clothes and appear like Malkhuan, and nobody doubted the performative gender role of the crossdressed man. Even the sister of the khan did not recognize the serious substitution:

Even before this it seemed to Erkezhan that the love she felt was not for a [female] friend but her intended . . . because she saw in her sister-in-law a lot of masculine qualities when they spent time together alone. (Krasavitsa Malkhuan: "Malkhuan the Beauty") (Sidel'nikov 1971, 155–164)

In "Batyr Totan" one of the hero's helpers named Vetronog (Windyleg) dresses in Kunkei's clothes, female heroine.

> Totan was sad. He admitted to his comrades that on his way Zhalmauz-Kempir was waiting for him, to whom he had given the word to give Kunkei. Faithful friends grieved and began to think how to rid him of this scourge. They thought, thought and came up with an idea. Vetronog possessed extraordinary beauty, was thin and gentle, like a girl. When they arrived at Zhalmauz-Kempir's house, he was knitted with braids from a ponytail, dressed in the clothes of Kunkei and led to the witch. (Tursunov 1983, 126)

In another tale, "Doch' viziria" (The Vizier's Daughter), the heroine and her maids dress as men and join the khan's hunt. And again nobody has any suspicion—everybody saw only the brave archers. Further transgressive characters can be found in "Ezhigeldy" and "Dudar Kyz" (Radlov 1870, 279–287, 309–320), where Dudar disguised herself as a male hunter and Ezhigeldy as a male who stole *saukele* (a female wedding headdress) and impersonated a woman.

The story of Dudar in the fairy tale "Dudar Kyz" (Tursunov 1983, 43–50) is quite striking. For a long time, her parents could not have a child, but she was born after her father slaughtered a brown horse. In the compilation of fairy tales, her birth is described differently: a baby born by a women and by a horse. Dudar does not only disguise herself as a man but also purposely continues to perform herself as himself throughout the plot. When the *khan* (ruler) gives his daughter as a promised bride to a sharpshooter at a contest, where Dudar participates and wins, when the khan gives the young couple a separate yurt, nobody questions what is going on. Only after three days does the bride ask her youngest brother (*kainysy*) why she was married to a female, at which point the brother decides to check everything out. The magic light bay horse of Dudar warns her about the approaching examination:

> Dudar said: "What should I do?" The horse said: "Suggest to *kainysy* to race together." And she did that. Her light bay won the competition. She killed one *kulan* (wild horse) and took his bottom part. A lake was ahead. Dudar suggested: "Hey, relative, let's have a bath together. "Let's do that,"—he agreed. They both got naked, Dudar took the leg of the dead kulan and kept it between her legs. The kainysy saw it with satisfaction. When Dudar went off water she dropped the kulan's leg and took her clothes. They got onto horses and rode to khan's daughter.
>
> The kainysy told his sister: "Sister! You said he is a girl, but he is a man. I saw his genitalia." (Radlov 1870, 315)

Besides the queer scene, from the beginning, Dudar as a female character is not quite usual for numerous Kazakh fairy tales—it is an outstanding example. The name "Dudar" means curly, an affectionate way of referring to a *dzhigit* (young male) by a girl. Being in the womb of her mother, Dudar asks all the women to be shown out of her parents' yurt and then starts to talk to her father. The baby shares that she will come out only if she will be the only owner of her life and decisions. Her father agrees.

The girl keeps her name a secret even from her parents. Nobody knows it. When dzhigits come to the *aul* (village) to woo her, Dudar questions them about her name and says that if somebody knows it, she will agree to marry that person. Her mystery soon become solved by one man who was hiding his own secret—he turns into a werewolf. Dudar escapes him with the magical help of a talking horse and gets dressed in men's clothes. After she meets the lonely rider Er Tostik and presents herself as a male hunter, Tostik immediately decides to make his new friend his sworn youngest brother.

Next in the narrative, there is no need for Dudar to come out as a lady. She accepts that easily, without any doubt or discomfort. Suddenly Tostik and Dudar have news about khan's *toi* (celebration) and contest for the best sharpshooter. Dudar wins the competition and as a result receives the khan's daughter as a bride. And still there is no worry for the disguised hunter to disclose. She only comes out when she asks Tostik whether one of them would take khan's daughter (here it is possible to relate this to a tradition when the youngest brother cannot be married before the eldest). The twist comes when Dudar says that she is a female (she shows her hair and breasts at their joint hunt), but she does not make the heroine and the hero feel less comfortable with each other, and Tostik decides to take both ladies as his wives.

CONCLUSION

It is crucial to note that the queer scene of the recorded version of the fairy tale "Dudar Kyz" is presented only in Radlov's "Obraztsy." In other versions, for example, those printed in Soviet times and translated from Kazakh language to Russian, such as "Zolotaya Bita" or "Kazakhskie Narodnye Skazki," the motive is omitted. Why did the eradication of any transgression happen? Was it considered immoral or inappropriate? In search of an answer to this a meticulous archival study, expansive interviews with folklorists and ethnographers, communication with people in rural areas who remember fairy tales are needed. Herein a potential multiple layer arises for new researchers of Central Asian oratures from a queer and feminist paradigm. This is a promising quest to review habitual plot development and explore the enchantment of crossdressing and transgressing motives, as Kay Turner noted:

If fairy tales seem to hurtle headlong toward normative reunion, marriage, and social stability, often the route navigates topsy-turvy spaces filled with marvels, magic, and weird meet-ups. These do not simply contradict the normal but offer possibilities for fulfilling alternative desires that affect individual destinies. Crucially, the move into an enchanted realm stops the story's progress; it is the site of arousing decisive difference for the protagonist. (2015, 46)

It seems that in the case of transgressive and crossdressing practices for a hero or heroine in Kazakh folklore, it was very easy to change into another gender and make people believe and accept it. Here a question arises for further research about passability in different temporalities of fairy tales and popular imagination where the identification of gender identity from the past to present is characterized from simple to complex. Also, not less important is that folklore materials should be presented as they were recorded in the original language, translated without omission, and interpreted in new ways, allowing readers to see queer motifs. Nowadays transgender people feel the weight of the binary heteronormative matrix requesting from a biological woman and a biological man a number of layers to be recognized by and fit in the narrow gender system. What made this recognition so complex? One possible answer could be related to the tightened social control by the religious authorities in Kazakhstan, who, due to politico-historical challenges, have changed their attitude to many of the issues in Kazakh society that they were previously lax about.

I suggest we should not resist accepting alternative desires or the existence of female characters in Kazakh folklore who are transgressing their gender roles and bringing new experiences to the reader. It is time to rethink queer fairy tales which open up hidden meanings, fabulous transformations, and budding sexualities. It is possible to locate the faintest and sometimes the evident glimmers of gender variant interpretations, see in monstrosities the potentiality of empowerment and embodiment, modify docile bodies into active ones, and finally understand folklore as a form of provocation, resistance, and activism. Thereby we will keep continuing to tell the fairy tale.

NOTES

1. I am very grateful for the Publishing House "Aruna," which kindly allowed me to use the illustrations included in the chapter.

2. It should be noted that there was an intention to compile a separate study on the ethnography of foreigners of Russia, but RGO decided to develop special instructions for collecting ethnographic information on the foreign population and this program was not accomplished (it was not printed and delivered) (Maikov 1872, 49–50).

3. *Zhalma* (from Kazakh language)—devourer, *auz*—mouth, *kempir*—woman.

4. Ishanova, Assima, "Interview with Assima Ishanova." February 18, 2019. Email correspondence.
5. Ishanova, Assima, "Interview with Assima Ishanova." February 18, 2019. Email correspondence.

REFERENCES

Afanas'ev, Alexander. 1861. *Narodnye Russkie Skazki*. Moscow: Tipographiya Gracheva and Koni.
Alexeev, Nikolai. 1984. *Shamanism of the Turkic-Speaking Peoples of Siberia*. Novosibirsk: Nauka.
Alieva, Alla. 1995. *Skazki Narodov Mira*. Moscow: Detskaya Literatura.
Alma-TQ. 2016. "Violations by Kazakhstan of the Right of Transgender Persons to Legal Recognition of Gender Identity." Last modified January 1. https://afe5453 6-d925-4980-901f-33c45c005215.filesusr.com/ugd/feded1_e958b48313ea4138 9e9132ca3bc21975.pdf.
Andreevskii, Ivan, Konstantin Arsen'ev, and Fedor Petrushevskii, eds. 1894. *Entsiklopedicheskii Slovar Brokgauza i Efrona*. Volume 13. St. Petersburg. Last modified November 2. www.vehi.net/brokgauz/.
Bacchilega, Cristina. 1997. *Postmodern Fairy Tales: Gender and Narrative Strategies*. Philadelphia: University of Pennsylvania Press.
Basilov, Vladimir. 1976. "Shamanism in Central Asia from the Realm of the Extra-Human." In *The Realm of the Extra-Human*, edited by Bharati Agehanada, 149–158. Berlin: De Gruyter Mouton.
Berman, Steve. 2009. *So Fey: Queer Fairy Fiction*. Maple Shade Township, NJ: Lethe Press.
Chulkov, Mikhail. 1786. *Abevega Russkikh Sueverii, Idolopoklonnicheskikh Zhertvoprinoshenii i Svadebnykh Obryadov, Koldovstva, Shamanstva i Prochego*. Moscow: Tipographiya Gippiusa.
Cosquin, Emmanuel. 1886. *Contes Populaires de Lorraine, Comparés Avec les Contes des Autres Provinces de France et des Pays Étrangers*. Volume 1. Last modified October 4. www.gutenberg.org/files/57892/57892-h/57892-h.htm.
Divaev, Abubakir. 1903. *Etnograficheskie materialy. Sbornik Materialov dlya Statistiki Syr-Dar'inskoi oblasti*. Volume 9. Tashkent: Tipo-Litografiia Il'ina.
Donoghue, Emma. 1997. *Kissing the Witch: Old Tales in New Skins*. New York: Joanna Cotler Books.
Fayzullina, Guzel, Mayya Prokopova, and Elena Ermakova. 2019. "Zhenskie Demonicheskie Personazhi v Miphakh i Folklore Narodov Zapadnoi Sibiri: Genezis, Funktsii, Atributika." *Nauchnyi Dialog* 12:198–209.
Ford, Michael. 1996. *Happily Ever After: Erotic Fairy-Tales for Men*. New York: Masquerade Books.
Hatto, Arthur. 1994. "On Some Siberian and Other Copper-Crones." *Suomalais-Ugrilaisen Aikakauskirja Journal de la Société Finno-Ougrienne* 85:71–105.

Holden, William. 2010. *A Twist of Grim: Erotic Fairytales for Gay Men.* Maple Shade Township, NJ: Lethe Press.

Jurttyn Balasy. "Talk Show "Oz Oiym": Trans, Gays and Beauty Bloggers/Honest Review." December 6, 2018. Video. www.youtube.com/watch?v=dxZwJfhPOFs.

Karazhanova, Inzhuna. 2016. *Monstrous Femininity in Kazakh Folklore: Delineating Normative and Transgressive Womanhood.* Astana.

Kaskabassov, Seit. 2013. *Altyn Zhylga. Zertteuler men Makalary.* Almaty: Zhibek Zholy.

———. 2014. *Folklornaya Proza Kazakhov. Izbrannye Islledovaniya.* Volume 3. Astana: Foliant.

Kaskabasov, et al. 2011. *Babalar Sozi. Zhuuz Tomdyq.* Volume 75. Batyrlyq Ertegiler. Astana: Foliant.

Kondybai, Serikbol. 2005. *Kazakhskaya Myphologiya. Kratkii Slovar.* Almaty: Nurly Alem.

———. 2011. *Myphologiya Predkazakhov.* Digital Reproduction of Original Manuscript. http://otuken.kz/topics/serikbolkondybai/.

Krohn, Kaarle. 1926. *Die Folkloristische Arbeitmethode.* Oslo.

Maikov, Leonid. 1872. *Obozrenie Deyatelnosti Obshchestva po Otdeleniyu Etnographii. Dvadtsatipyatiletie IRGO* 49–50. St. Petersburg.

Meletynskii, Eleazar. 1990. *Myphologicheskii Slovar.* Moscow: Sovetskaya Entsiklopediya. Last modified January 3. https://bit.ly/2TcX5FK.

———. 2008. *Miphologicheskaya Entsiklopediya.* Moscow: Drofa.

Mignolo, Walter, and Madina Tlostanova. 2007. "The Logic of Coloniality and the Limits of Postcoloniality." In *The Postcolonial and the Global*, edited by Revathi Krishnaswamy and John Hawley, 109–123. Minneapolis: University of Minnesota Press.

Miropiiev, Mikhail. 1888. "Demonologicheskie Rasskazy u Kirgizov." In *Zapiski IRGO po Otdeleniiu Etnografiii.* Volume 10, no. 3. St. Petersburg: Tipographiya Kirshbauma.

Mode, Heinz.1973. *Fabulous Beasts and Demons.* London: Phaidon.

Mogil'ner, Marina. 2013. *Homo Imperii: A History of Physical Anthropology in Russia.* Lincoln: University of Nebraska Press.

Nadezhdin, Nikolai. 1850. "Protokol Zasedaniya Etnographicheskogo Otdeleniya." *Arkhiv RGO* 1(1).

Nevermann, Hans. 1933. *Masken und Geheimbunde in Melansien.* Berlin: Reimar Hobbing.

Novikov, Nikolai. 1974. *Obrazy Vostochnoslavyanskoi Volshebnoi Skazki.* Leningrad: Nauka.

Ostroumov, Nikolai. 1906. *Skazki Sartov v Russkom Izlozhenii.* Tashkent: Tipographiya Okruzhnogo Shtaba.

———. 1908. *Severnye Skazki. Zapiski Imperatorskogo Russkogo Geographicheskogo Obshchestva po Otdeleniyu Etnographii.* Volume XXXIII. St. Petersburg.

Poetry Paper. 2016. "'Ышшoodna'. Antiperiodicheskoe Antikommercheskoe Izdanie Gazetnogo Tipa." Volume 5. Last modified December 13. https://yadi.sk/i/eh83pgW2qfUyQ.

Propp, Vladimir.1986. *Istoricheskie Korni Volshebnoi Skazki*. Leningrad: Izdatelstvo Leningradskogo Universiteta.

Radlov, Vasilii. 1866–1907. *Obraztsy Narodnoi Literatury Turkskikh Plemyon Zhivushchikh v Yuzhnoi Sibiri i Dzhungarskoi Stepi*. St. Petersburg.

———. 1870. *Obraztsy Narodnoi Literatury Turkskikh Plemyon Zhivushchikh v Yuzhnoi Sibiri i Dzhungarskoi Stepi*. Volume 3. St. Petersburg.

Rogachevskaya, Ekaterina. 1998. *Entsiklopediya Literaturnykh Geroev. Russkii Folklor I Drevnerusskaya Literatura*. Moscow: Olymp.

Schlauch, Margaret. 1994. "Folklore in the Soviet Union." *Science & Society* 8(3):205–222. Last modified December 10. www.jstor.org/stable/40399614.

Sekerbayeva, Zhanar. 2021. Understanding Actors and Processes Shaping Transgender Subjectivities: Case Study of Kazakhstan. In *Trans Health: Global Perspectives on Care for Trans Communities*. Max Nicolai Appenroth and Maria do Mar Castro Varela. Bielefeld, Germany: Transcript Publishing.

Sidel'nikov, Viktor. 1971. *Kazakhskie Narodnye Skazki v Tryekh Tomakh*. Alma-Ata: Zhazushy.

Tokarev, Sergei. 1980. *Myphy Narodov Mira. Encyclopedia*. Volume 1. Moscow: Sovetskaya Entsiklopediya.

Turner, Kay. 2015. "At Home in the Realm of Enchantment: The Queer Enticements of the Grimms' 'Frau Holle'." *Marvels & Tales* 29(1):42–63. Last modified November 7. www.jstor.org/stable/10.13110/marvelstales.29.1.0042.

Tursunov, Edyge. 1983. *Zolotaya Bita*. Alma-Ata: Zhalyn.

Valikhanov, Shokan. 1904. *Sochineniya. Zapiski Imperskogo Russkogo Geographicheskogo Obshchestva*. Volume 29. St. Petersburg.

Vanderhooft, JoSelle. 2009. *Sleeping Beauty, Indeed & Other Lesbian Fairytales*. Maple Shade Township, NJ: Lethe Press.

Vaskul, Anastasiya. 2013. "Izuchenie Inorodtsev v Russkom Geographicheskom Obshchestve v Seredine XIX veka." *Mezhetnicheskie i Mezhkonfessionalnye svyazi v Russkoi Literature i Folklore* 1:115–126.

Veselovski, Alexei. 1872. *Slavyanskie Skazaniya o Solomone i Kitovrase*. St. Petersburg: Tipographiya Demakova.

Vilkoviskaya, Mariya. 2018. *Pod Odnoi Oblozhkoi. Sbornik Kveer Poezii*. Almaty. Last modified November 22. https://issuu.com/tonkayagran/docs/queer_poetry.

Warner, Elizabeth. 2010. *Russian Myths*. Austin: University of Texas Press.

Winner, Thomas. 1980. *The Oral Art and Literature of the Kazakhs of Russian Central Asia*. New York: Arno Press.

Yadanova, Kuzelesh. 2009. "'Vstrecha Okhotnika s Dukhami-Khozyaevami / Almyssom.' Opyt Ukazatelya Syuzhetov i Versii po Materialam Altaiskoi Folklornoi Traditsii." *Drevnosti Sibiri i Tsentralnoi Asii* 1–2(13–14):174–185.

Zhanuzakova, Farida. 1983. *Kazakhskie Narodnye Skazki*. Alma-Ata: Zhazushy.

Zhirmunsky, Victor. 1979. *Sravnitel'noe Literaturovedenie. Vostok i Zapad*. Leningrad: Nauka.

Chapter 8

"Pugacheva for the People"

Two Portraits of Non-Urban Post-Soviet Queer Performers

Kārlis Vērdiņš and Jānis Ozoliņš

In the broadening field of East European LGBTQ+ studies, there are various demographic groups which deserve more attention from scholars to draw the picture of post-socialist queers in a more inclusive mode. The field is dominated by studies of Russian culture, and it focuses mostly on urban space and its social issues, such as state-supported restrictions and violence, homophobia, and queer experience of the city. In the context of the emerging field of rural queer studies, it is worth looking at performances of queerness when they exist outside of big cities with their more or less established gay subcultures. The focus of our attention is the cultural practices performed by two non-urban Latvian queer men outside Riga, its capital. The creative output of poet Jancis and singer Gints is taking place outside the mainstream of Latvian culture production as well as outside the narrow niche of its gay and lesbian subculture, which is limited to very few places of entertainment in Riga and online activities. Their artistic practices encourage us to ask questions about popular culture in the post-Soviet region and the limits of its inclusivity, as well about the circulation of culture production and changes in gender dynamics in the region.

As results of several public opinion polls show, Latvia is one of the most homophobic countries in the EU, and progress in fighting for equal human rights and tolerance has been slow for the last thirty years (Mole 2011; Vērdiņš and Ozoliņš 2020). However, despite the majority's refusal to accept same-sex marriages or inclusive civil partnership law, Latvian society in general is not seen by itself as inclined to radical activities or violence toward any group of minorities. "Don't ask, don't tell" tactics are usually praised as the most relevant when it comes to complicated questions of identity politics.

As collections of queer life-stories show, this tactic is a common way to deal with one's homosexuality as both gay persons and their parents would rather choose silence over open confrontation (Ruduša 2014). Similarly, in the field of arts and entertainment, there are very few professionals who would openly align their creative practices with their queerness, as such a choice can be a serious obstacle for future careers, and an "open secret" solution seems to be one which keeps all involved sides satisfied. Commercially oriented or self-funded enterprises addressed to a wide audience would use queerness as cross-dressing performance for entertainment purposes rather than tolerate queerness as a personal trait of the performer. This situation becomes even more complicated if queerness travels from the biggest cities to the countryside.

RURAL QUEERS AND THE RULE
OF METRONORMATIVITY

As research work in the emerging field of rural queer studies shows, queerness is usually thought of as an urban phenomenon. John D'Emilio has linked the consolidation of homosexual identities and LGBT communities with the labor organization of capitalism in urban environments, which enabled individuals to have independent careers as well as separate living spaces (D'Emilio 1983). Eventual developments of queer studies as urban-centered discourse made J. Jack Halberstam coin the term "metronormativity" which describes the valorization of urban spaces in LGBT culture (Halberstam 2005). Metronormativity celebrates the city lifestyle as the only comfortable form of existence for gay and trans people while assigning negative value to rural space. As contemporary research shows, this binary opposition might be not correct, as rural space, with its different norms, might not yield to the stereotypes about its negative effects on the LGBT community:

> The term "rural" seems to imply certain things these days, not the least important of which is a stubbornly persistent attachment to highly traditional views regarding gender and sexuality and, by extension, an aggressive, sometimes even murderous, antipathy toward gender and sexual difference. [. . .] Yet, the supposed sharp borders between where overt hostility ends and moves to tolerance and eventually into celebration are less clear when thinking through the subject positions upon which the rural is constituted. As one heads out to the country, the institutional frameworks positioning subjects become more vague, more customary, more local, and more difficult to discern without insider knowledge. (Johnson et al. 2016, 11–12)

The different use of signs, as contemporary queer studies argue, serves as a survival tactic in specific circumstances where different rules of privacy and desire are valid, and the need for secrecy is a significant factor which influences the existence of members of the LGBT community (Johnson et al. 2016, 15). In Eastern Europe, the problem of secrecy is probably even more acute than in the west as it is considered to be relevant equally to urban and rural dwellers. However, almost every time queer scholars of the region invoke rural space, it gets labeled as particularly backward or lacking a supportive community for queers (Buyantueva and Shevtsova 2020, 94, 105, 191). While this might be true in terms of Western understandings of how proper LGBT communities should work, we argue that the lived experience of the East European gay community and its cultural production allows for a more generous view on rural space in the region, where ignorance and hatred might exist together with some degree of acceptance and curiosity.

In Latvia, the countryside has historically been a politically charged place, as the question of "Who owns the land?" has been crucial to agrarian economies, which were the most common source of income for the majority of Latvian families until the mid-twentieth century. Even when the process of urbanization took place throughout the twentieth century, the self-image of Latvians as "the peasant nation" whose existence is grounded in physical labor, folklore traditions and heterosexual divisions of "women" and "men" types of labor, is still persistent in the public discourse. As it is in other countries, the Latvian countryside is seen as the bulwark of "traditional" family values where ideas about sexual politics are relatively unchanging, while the fight for LGBT emancipation takes place in the capital, negotiated between the urban middle-class and political parties. Demographic aspects have to be taken into account as well. Latvia currently is one of the fastest shrinking countries in Europe, losing one percent of its population each year due to emigration to European countries with higher living standards and a negative birthrate (Vērdiņš and Ozoliņš 2020). The process of "dying out" is felt in the countryside as people move to bigger towns and cities as well to other countries to get better paid jobs, education, or access to social support and healthcare. As an answer to this process, the Latvian government shuts down schools and hospitals in sparsely populated areas while the region of Riga as well some bigger towns emerge as developing areas where the number of economically active people is growing. In such an uneven social context, the creative practices of Jancis and Gints take place.

Both Jancis and Gints spent their childhood and youth in Soviet Latvia, exposed to Soviet mass culture. From that time, they have both shared their admiration for Alla Pugacheva as the ultimate Russian popstar and a strong woman whose private life, marriages and relationship with politics, press, and other singers have provided exciting material for Russian mass media for decades. Their affective connection to the singer as the most striking example of Soviet popular music speaks to the taste of a big part of the ethnically divided population of Latvia which consumes both Russian and Western cultural production. In such a situation, performances that include transgender or non-normative sexuality easy also become "transnational" or "transcultural" performances and carry a cluster of other meanings unknown to the Western gaze.

In this chapter, we draw portraits of both Jancis and Gints, based on their life experiences and publicized accounts of their creative practices as well as interviews with them conducted in the form of both field work and e-mail correspondence. According to their wishes, their full identities are not revealed.

JANCIS: "THE INTERNET RUINED MY LIFE"

Since March of 2018, Jancis lives in a care home for elderly people in rural Latgale, in the Eastern region of Latvia. Before his health deteriorated a few years ago, he was living in his parents' old house in Latgale and writing sentimental poems about his life experiences and people he observed in his surroundings. Before his first self-published collection of poems was published in 2012, he had tried his hand at various different trades and hobbies. Our research is based on the analysis of Jancis's work, especially his autobiography, self-published in 2013, as well as other self-reflective materials (including articles, blogs, poems, song lyrics, and interviews) and field work carried out in October 2013 at his country home.

Jancis was born in 1960 in a rural area in East Latvia, where his father worked as a forester and his mother was a farmhand at a collective farm. As he likes to recall, as a child he already desired to be creative and tried different arts. At the age of fourteen he started designing and sewing "stylish" clothes for himself. Later, he applied to study at the Applied Arts College in the nearby town of Rēzekne; however, he failed the mathematics exam and was not accepted (Baltjancis 2013, 39). He then worked as tailor apprentice in Rēzekne for some months, but he quit that job because of the heavy drinking that took place in the company. Later, sewing for friends and neighbors became his opportunity to earn some pocket money while still living with his parents; it made him somewhat of a local style icon, at least for his friends, and boosted his wish to become famous. When he was twenty, he pulled himself together to send some poems to the youth newspaper "Padomju Jaunatne" to be published but received advice to work harder. Not taking it too seriously, he decided to try singing instead and went to Riga—his plan was to meet the manager of the State Radio Orchestra and apply for a position as an orchestra singer and pop recording artist. His effort ended in the foyer of the Radio House when he was denied entrance (Baltjancis 2013, 67–68). Political issues are also touched upon in his autobiography, especially his refusal to do the obligatory military service in the Soviet Army that resulted in a short-term imprisonment in a mental hospital in the nearby city of Daugavpils (Baltjancis 2013, 80–83). He also stresses his pride in being Latvian and his dislike of growing up and spending his youth in the USSR. However, Pugacheva and other Russian TV personalities and pop stars have constantly occupied his mind.

Beyond those unsuccessful efforts, it is hard to hide Jancis's queer sensibility with a taste for kitsch and sentimentality, as well as his wish to form intimate friendships with men. In his autobiography, he permits himself to mention some male friends who have been important to him without clearly stating the status of their relationship. The first openly gay episode takes place in the mid-1980s when he visits the Kalngale gay beach on the coast of the Gulf of Riga and is careful enough to pretend to distance himself from its frequent visitors:

> Once [. . .] I reached Kalngale where another surprise awaited me: a gay beach. However, this misunderstood and disdained part of society did not evoke antipathy in me, because, in my opinion, everybody has the right to live his life as he pleases and as nature has determined, as Mother Nature has created each of us. Probably the term "nature" is not the right one, because our destiny is created and dictated by forces higher than us. God rules everything! (Baltjancis 2013, 108–109)

As Jancis recalled in 2013, the Vecāķi nudist beach actually was the place where his first sexual experience took place when a man showed him a gay porn magazine, thus finally making Jancis aware of his sexuality. Other "adventures" followed at the Vecāķi beach and also at the unofficial gay beach at Kalngale.

After the USSR collapsed in 1991, Jancis, still living in his parents' house, used the new possibilities of free communication and started correspondence with foreign pen friends who sympathized with the poor ex-USSR citizen and sent him various presents. As he recalls, in 1992, he received sweets, an electronic calculator, eau de cologne, music records, an audio player, clothes and other things from his pen friends. Occasionally, a small sum of money was added to letters from his new friends, which Jancis spent on clothes and more sweets (Baltjancis 2013, 142–143). Some of these friendships did not last long because of Jancis's poor English skills. In his autobiography, he happily gives an account of every gift received and feels lonely and betrayed in periods when the stream of presents dries up. Eventually Jancis's contacts with foreign gay individuals, organizations and publications became a way for him to earn some money. Without revealing it to his elderly parents, Jancis started a business. A variety of different goods—gay magazines and books, porn movies, condoms, et cetera—started to flow to Jancis's mailbox to be re-sent to his acquaintances and clients all over Latvia and in its neighboring countries. In 1993, his activities became noticed by gay activists in Riga: the newly established Latvian gay newspaper "Loks" in its first issue sneeringly announced that a gay club "Jancis & Co" had been established in Latgale, as they had learned from advertisements, posted by Jancis in the foreign gay magazines "Gay Times" and *"Männer Aktuell,"* offering to find Latvian boyfriends for a fee (Loks 1993, 1, 3).

In 1994, Jancis started to publish an underground gay zine. In spite of its changing name[1] and appearance, his zine survived almost fifteen years until 2008 and still can be called the most prolific printed gay publication in Latvia. The zine was put together by Jancis in Latgale, then Xerox-copied by his Swedish friend in Stockholm and sent back to Latgale to be distributed further to its subscribers. The last two years it was published as a CD which contained articles and photos to be read on computers. The magazine consisted of a few original contributions, mostly by Jancis himself, erotic and pornographic pictures reproduced from foreign gay magazines, stories of Latvian celebrities borrowed from official newspapers and magazines, as well as dating ads. Since the magazine was distributed privately by mail, it was not easy for it to reach its potential readers. Its circulation, as Jancis remembered, rose to more than 100 copies while the files of the editor included around 500 addresses of gay men in Latvia and abroad who either corresponded with Jancis, bought various things from him or put their dating advertisements in the magazine. Dating ads were free for Baltic men and paid service for others. Answering these ads was a pretty complicated process: at the end of the text there was a code, and the interested reader would send a letter to the editor with the code and some money in another envelope to let Jancis send the letter to the addressee. "Loks" met Jancis' publication with another sneer by stating that this is "not a real magazine" for it contained only dating ads, cut-outs from other magazines and pornographic pictures (Loks 1(3) 1995, 14). In the next issue of "Loks," Jancis's angry defensive response was followed by his accusations to the editor of making his name public and praising himself for making a magazine that carefully selects the best from other publications. The editor of "Loks" AinārsLočmelis added to this letter an ironic comment reminding Jancis that his use of other publications' materials violated copyright laws and that sending such publications to foreign people could "degrade the prestige of the whole country" (Loks 2(4) 1995, 34–35).

As this exchange shows, Jancis always preferred to do things his own way, holding a rather high opinion of his lonely activities even if they received harsh criticism by urban gay activists. The thought of collaboration with the editors of "Loks" never crossed his mind. "Everybody wants to make something himself, everybody wants to be the big star," he told us in 2013. The position of editor made Jancis a kind of minor celebrity in Latvian gay circles. As he recalled in 2013, "I could not even go to Kalngale beach any-more—if somebody who was a reader of my zine would recognize me, oth-ers too would come to stare at me to see what Jancis looked like." However, soon his activities were met by a bigger challenge than smirking urban gay activists: the internet.

In 1999, the internet site *Gay.lv* was launched, and similar sites appeared in other Baltic countries. Besides news and occasional featured stories, it had an extensive section of dating ads which allowed the users of the site to contact each other immediately. Other online dating sites were established, posting ads from both straight and gay people. Also, pornography became available through the internet, and a significant part of it was for free. In such circumstances, Jancis's magazine lost many readers and supporters. "The Internet ruined my life," complained Jancis in 2013. However, he did not sur-render and tried to attract new audiences with original content. One attraction of the zine was its annual readers' vote for the best looking man in Latvia. The results were published as a chart, and it included many local celebrities, mostly hetero-identified young men that seemed appealing to the remain-ing readers of the zine. Soon Latvian tabloids noticed the chart and started to republish it, thus making the results of voting visible to the mainstream public (Pakalns 2003; Vakara Ziņas 2005). Not all the winners were happy about such recognition. As Jancis remembered in 2013, when the famous pop singer Mārtiņš Freimanis, whose sexuality was an object of speculation for a long time, got to know of his leading position in the chart in 2003, he called Jancis and protested.

From 2002 to 2007, Jancis was in a relationship with Jānis, a young man twenty-three years younger than Jancis, who had some musical education, played synthesizer and wrote romantic tunes. Jancis resumed his career as a poet and lyricist, and together they started a pop duo. Their band was initially called "Buča" (Kiss), and its repertoire included adapted songs by Pugacheva as well as cover versions of well-known Latvian pop songs of the Soviet period, sometimes with alternative lyrics by Jancis. Their Swedish friends helped the new band with computer programs and sound recording tools, making it possible to record their material at home. From 2002 to 2009, the band recorded and released eight home-made and privately distributed albums; however, their efforts did not gain the desired popularity. In 2004, the duo decided to get wider recognition and made their song "Varavīksnes karogs" (Rainbow Flag)[2] available for listening on the *Gay.lv* website. It was intended to be the Latvian gay anthem and mentioned various male names, friends of the band members, in addition to celebrating the raising of the rainbow flag (Gay.lv 2004). The reaction of the website's users was mostly hostile: the band was accused of dilettantism and poor performance; Jancis again was called a disgrace to the Latvian gay community. After such a disappointment the band changed their name to "Jāņunakts" (the Latvian word for Midsummer night, the main festivity in Latvian pagan rites) and avoided immersing themselves in explicitly gay subjects. Their highest achievement was the number one song on Radio SWH, the biggest commercial radio station at that time, humorous top "Radio Lāga" in 2010, another disappointment for Jancis who had written the lyrics of the song "Jel piedodiet!" (Forgive me!) to the tune originally performed by Pugacheva as his life story and meant it to be taken seriously. Before that happened, in 2009 Jānis broke up their relationship and moved to Riga, leaving Jancis with broken heart. After the latter's musical career was over, he resumed his career as a poet.

In his self-published books,[3] Jancis collects his sentimental poems, usually written in rhymed quatrains. He is one of many amateur poets in Latvia who post their new poems on Facebook and on the Latvian social networking service Draugiem.lv, as well as release self-published books or collaborate with vanity presses. The most common subjects of such poems are the beauty of one's native land, town or rural area, the beauty of nature, dedications to close people, poems with wishes for luck and success, poems influenced by wisdom quotes as well as occasional humorous poems. Jancis's opinion on poetry is strict. In 2012, the local newspaper "Ezerzeme" quoted him stating: "I do not understand modern, philosophically oversaturated poetry! I have no intention of rereading the poem many times to understand what the author really wanted to say. I need everything to be clear in a moment!" (Roga 2012). However, Jancis has something to add to the simple rural lowbrow poetry: the theme of homoeroticism. "Baltais sapnis" contained poems about his relationship and split-up with his boyfriend, while "Saldais citrons" included some poems, previously available on his blog for restricted readership including his trusted gay friends, which were dedicated to men who have sex with other men under the influence of alcohol or a closeted homosexual guy who desires other men but nevertheless marries a woman and leads a miserable family life.[4] In more recent editions, Jancis tries to separate his "mainstream" poems from his homoerotic work. In 2019, a whole collection of homoerotic or, as Jancis calls them, "freethinking" poems named "Svelme" (The heat) was published to be distributed privately among Jancis's friends through previous subscription.

As can be seen from these tactics of publicity, Jancis still sees himself as operating on the border of two different audiences: (1) mainstream culture of rural Latvia with a base of supposedly heterosexual supporters who like and share his posts on social networks and who are offered mostly poems on more general and "safe" subjects; and (2) a virtual community of gay users who are selected to read Jancis's "spicy" poems, posted online for a restricted audience or published in a separate edition of poems. It is likely that his "mainstream" supporters actually know his sexual orientation, and it is not an obstacle for them to enjoy his literary production; however, Jancis's artistic attempts still linger between his desire to queer the scene of amateur poetry and his need to keep his "open secret" untouched for his "mainstream" readers. On the few occasions he was interviewed by national or local media, he held back from talking about being gay, for example, in his 2014 interview for "Delfi," the leading Latvian news portal.[5] His attitude to his sexuality is still ambivalent even in private communication: in an e-mail written to us on June 15, 2015, he regrets his period of gay activism because, as he thinks, it has irrevocably type-cast him in public opinion.

Jancis is the only prominent example of a single person in post-Soviet Latvia who has refused to enter urban LGBT circles and to adapt to their habits of consuming and creating cultural production, employing "do it yourself" tactics to work independently outside the usual state-supported or commercially oriented modes of production. On the one hand, his example encourages us to ask about the openness and inclusiveness of the commercial gay subculture in post-Soviet space (Kondakov 2019, 410). On the other hand, by distancing himself from urban heteronormativity and homonorma-tivity and aligning his creative practices with the rural amateur culture, Jancis shows the limits of inclusiveness and tolerance of this culture which is open to embracing people's creative efforts as far as they are not seen as speaking against the "traditional" values of countryside. If the common story about the queer experience is, as Halberstam has put it, "the metronormative story of migration from 'country' to 'town'" within which "the subject moves to a place of tolerance after enduring life in a place of suspicion, persecution, and secrecy" (Halberstam 2005, 36–37) then Jancis's story shows the reverse or, should we say, failed side of this narrative. The countryside, with its relative tolerance to alternative lifestyles and amateur creative practices proves to be more friendly place for a person like him than urban space, with both rules of cultural production and circulation and rules of LGBT subculture with its tendencies toward homonormativity and exclusivity. Different dynamics have shaped the life experiences of Gints, our second hero, leading him to somewhat similar trajectories.

GINTS: NOT IN AMERICA, I NEED IT HERE!

Gints was born in 1962 in the Northern part of Latvia in a family that loved music. He studied music since he was a child and graduated from Valmiera Music School. In his youth, he discovered as an unusual singing talent: his vocal range stretches for four octaves, making him able to sing parts of bass, tenor, alto, and soprano (PBK 2012). In his youth, he started to sing at private home parties and episodically joined local bands as a lead singer.[6]

His powerful voice was appreciated by several professional musicians; however, Gint's lifelong dream about the big stage could not be fulfilled easily. Despite his wide range, he prefers to sing soprano and alto repertoire, mostly covering songs by female pop artists,[7] because he sees them as fitting the possibilities of his voice the best. As he is not writing songs himself, his career could not advance without the help of songwriters and producers. In the early nineties, he became a part of a recording duo together with Ivars Rutmanis, a local singer-songwriter who rose to national fame in the 1980s with a couple of successful pop ballads. They recorded two albums of songs, written mostly by Rutmanis,[8] presenting themselves as a duo of two different male performers. Rutmanis, singing in his husky masculine voice, sported a moustache while Gints, singing his parts in higher pitch, resembled a female both vocally and physically with bleached hair strands and tinted glasses.[9] Such a duo challenged the expectations of the Latvian audience, which was used to pop duos consisting of male and female artists who represented the ideals of beauty and style of Soviet popular music as well as conformed to the mandatory celebration of heterosexuality, sexual difference and gender norms.

Gints continued to perform with other musicians at local parties and festivities as well as trying his luck with national TV music competition shows. In the 1990s, he participated in amateur singing competition "Dziesma manai paaudzei" (Song for My Generation); in 2009, he joined in "Koru kari" (Choir Wars) together with Valmiera Town Choir as their principal male singer; in 2012, he entered into the singing talent competition "Golos" (The Voice), organized by the Baltic Russian TV channel; and, in 2017, he applied for the Latvian edition of the "X Factor" competition. These competitions provided him with short-term recognition, but he never passed the initial selections of participants and his singing career did not advance. These rejections confused him and make him wonder about the reasons for downplaying his singing talent. As he guessed in 2017, the evaluation of his talent might be influenced by his appearance, his unusual vocal qualities, as well as his years—he was fifty-five when he applied for the "X Factor," while the majority of his competitors were half his age (VTV 2017).

In the late 2000s, Gints's singing career took another turn: he started to perform in drag. Unlike many performers in the west, Gints sang live, finding his vocal range perfect for embodying female pop stars. And, unlike those performers, Gints's main audiences were local people of Northern Latvia, mainstream rural audiences who found his drag performances (or, as he calls them, parody acts) funny and entertaining. Among his impersonations are global pop stars Madonna, Lady Gaga, and Tina Turner as well as Alla Pugacheva and Latvian Russian singer Laima Vaikule. As Gints recalls, his first parody act was a performance impersonating Pugacheva at the House of Culture of the Valmiera District, and it was met with great enthusiasm by the audience. Since then, Gints has performed his "parodies" for more than ten years, and the audience, according to his words, are always supportive (VTV 2017). This seemingly surprising acceptance of drag by such audience needs a more detailed explanation.

Unlike in Western countries, the populations of republics of the former USSR do not experience such cross-dressing as a part of LGBT subculture and do not necessarily connect such practices with a performer's gender identity and sexual orientation. Instead, we can speak about cross-dressing as a cultural phenomenon which can contain different meanings. Crossdressing was a part of the fertility rites of Baltic peasants when masked processions went from one farmstead to another with singing, dancing and playing music. Cross-dressing by both women and men played a significant role then, because demons and fertility gods were imagined to be able to perform their magic only if they were creatures of two sexes or androgynies (Jansons 2010, 300). Of course, such cross-dressing was a part of the annual collective rites rather than expressions of an individual gender or sexual non-normativity. Even if the biggest Latvian cities in the twentieth century were witnessing the growing blending of gender stereotypes and occasional cabaret acts or theater performances that included crossdressing, this practice never entered the mainstream of the local culture. As Julie A. Cassiday has argued, the collapse of the USSR created a drag renaissance in the Russian entertainment industry that affected both highbrow and popular performances (Cassiday 2018, 274); however, she sees that the conditions under which such practices surfaced to the mainstream culture were different from those in the west. Crossdressing comedians, who regularly appeared on Russian TV on shows like "New Russian Grannies" or Verka Serduchka, depicted femininity "visibly past its prime" and did not strive for conventional beauty or glamor but provided ironic overidentification which was supported by misogynistic and homophobic attitudes: "Drag acts in Russia's mainstream media aim not for gender camp, which creates community through fantasies of leveling and inclusion, but for gender kitsch, which discriminates between 'us' and 'them' via condescension and exclusion" (Cassiday 2018, 275). After 1991, besides some comedies and farces in Riga theaters, the only prominent example of such gender kitsch in Latvia was the comedy show "Imanta—Babīte atkal pietur" which, similarly to the "New Russian Grannies" show, made fun of two elderly naïve rural women through male impersonations. Crossdressing is considered to be funny and "safe" as long as it does stay within the realm of kitsch and does not approach camp.

As Gints's experience and comments by the audience of these rural drag performances show, actually the border between cross-dressing as kitsch or camp might not be as strict as Cassiday's division suggests. In the conservative and homophobic post-Soviet space, there is a part of the audience for whom any transgressing of gender boundaries serves as a red flag. As Gints recalls, sometimes after such performances he had to cope with name calling as individual persons from the audience did find his act too provocative (VTV 2017). After his appearances on TV shows, Gints's performances have been subjected to the harsh criticism of internet users who constantly accuse him of looking and singing "like a woman" (PBK 2012). To avoid an open confrontation with the audience, he takes several precautionary steps. As Gints explained to us in 2018, he aspires to impersonate his heroines in a very accurate manner, not making caricatures of them, and always makes sure his acts are "cute and enjoyable, and never vulgar." The problem of appearing "vulgar" is caused by the fact that, as Gints contemplated in 2017, not all of his favorite divas are equally good objects of parody. Pugacheva, with her stocky figure, loose-falling stage costumes, abundant hairstyle, and frank way of communication with the audience is a gratifying object which does not demand that the impersonator erase all his manly features. Whereas Madonna, with her more fragile frame and tight, elegant costumes is a hard task for Gints: as he revealed in an interview in 2017, he is not satisfied with his Madonna impersonation act because it turned out a bit "vulgar" (VTV 2017). Gints's impersonations visually seem to be on the "safe" side of gender kitsch while his physical and emotional involvement shifts them to the risky side of gender camp, especially for a sympathetic queer gaze. And his rural audience is most likely to enjoy his performances if he uses the typical tools of gender kitsch which encourage the audience to take his drag acts as mere jokes, masquerades, parodies.

Another step of precaution for Gints seems to be emphasizing his "unique" voice as the foundation and reason for his artistic practices. His choice of high-pitched songs, originally sung by female artists, as well as his involvement in drag performances is always explained by the particularity of his voice as if it "demands" such practices. He even has a mystic explanation of how he could be born with such an atypical voice: his musically gifted grandmother could not properly develop her singing skills because of World War II, and her singing talent just "went over" to Gints when he was born (VTV 2017). On the other hand, his "feminine" appearance in his daily life, which includes flamboyant haircuts, earrings and jewelry, are never explained, nor is the silence surrounding his private life: he is presented as a loner who has committed both to his singing talent and his daily job as a hairdresser, and whether he has any significant others is not a part of his story. The erasure of his private life from his interviews and TV appearances serves to mask his daily performance of gender camp, replacing it with an identity of a versatile performer who boasts about his capacity to both confirm to traditional gender norms when singing "Love Me Tender" in deep bass or performing in a duo with female singers and also his successful impersonation of female pop divas. As Gints revealed to us in an interview in 2018, his Pugacheva "parodies" might even cause collective delusions of his audiences:

> Alla is welcomed everywhere, in every possible Latvian celebration, both a wedding and a corporative event. The attitude is always very positive. Sometimes they put me inside a limousine and drive me to the place of event, they would even provide me with two body guards. People see this show as a professional performance, and sometimes they are even ready to believe that what they see is the real Alla herself. People are always waiting for me; they know this performance will be the highlight of the whole show.

Even if his account of the effect on his audiences might be exaggerated and even if his audiences see him mostly as somebody similar to the kitschy women impersonators on Russian and Latvian TV shows, his role as a drag artist, impersonating Pugacheva, can still be seen as transgressive in at least three ways: (1) he is a male who aspires to pass for a female performer; (2) he is a Latvian, celebrating the glory of Russian pop; (3) his performances take place in the twenty-first century while imitating an artist who is mostly associated with the Soviet "estrada" music which nowadays is employed by the cultural industry of Russia to bring about feelings of nostalgia for the Soviet period. A part of the audience probably sees the pleasant memories of their youth in the image of Pugacheva, and the power of their memories makes them believe in her "realness."

Like his peer Jancis, Gints has his ups and downs as his feelings about his singing career is constantly swinging. As he told us in the beginning of 2020, he is busy with singing for audiences both in Latvia and Southern Estonia, where people respect him and welcome his repertoire of Western pop songs from the 1980s as well as popular songs from the Soviet period. In other moments, his view on his creative efforts has been less optimistic. In 2017, he complained that his artistic ambitions have never been taken too seriously, and his drag performances sometimes seemingly overshadowed his "real" artistic output (which actually consists mostly of covering pop hits by female artists in masculine appearance). He and his supporters tend to interpret his lack of major success as evidence of the smallness and defectiveness of the local pop industry. As he told the enthusiastic local TV reporter: "People keep telling me: if you were not here but in London or in America, you would definitely be as big as Britney Spears. But I don't need it in America, I need it here!" (VTV 2017) He is aware that, as he approaches sixty, his competition with younger and more attractive singing talents is getting increasingly hard. That makes him feel torn by a wish to either organize one last grand performance in his local house of culture and quit the stage afterwards or to wait until fame will finally come to him and he would be allowed to sing at least one song on a "big" stage together with professional singers (VTV 2017). Until now, Gints has managed to maintain his optimism. Contemporary queer theorists might say that his optimism is cruel.

CONCLUSION: RURAL QUEERS AND THEIR CRUEL OPTIMISM

According to Lauren Berlant's concept of cruel optimism and its dangerous attachments (Berlant 2011), the lives of both Jancis and Gints are affected by the double burden of such attachments: living in the demographically shrinking (or "dying out") Latvian countryside with limited social, financial and cultural opportunities goes hand in hand with living in their fantasy world of approaching fame. Going through several moments of "impasse" when another encounter with reality challenges their dreams of stardom interchanges with periods of hope and activity when they are trying their hand in new creative projects which hopefully will bring them more recognition and eventually also fame and fortune. However, before we write off their attachments as delusional or immature, it is worth remembering the view of rural queer theorists "that it is elitist and reproductively hegemonic to dismiss bad attachments simply because they are bad by normative standards, particularly given the fact that bad attachments are often the best attachments that many people can afford" (Johnson et al. 2016, 14). Rejected by professionals of arts and show business, they pursue their creative careers in their rural environment which, as their experience shows, turns out to be more inclusive and accepting than we would probably assume. Of course, this inclusion is by no way unconditional as the relationship between the respectability of rural heterosexuality and queer existence in the East European countryside is still a strained one. As George L. Mosse stated, speaking about the conditions on which a homosexual can be accepted in society: "Solitude was the price exacted for abnormal behavior, and the outsider [. . .] was supposed to live a lonely life and die a lonely death. If he attempted to enter society, he had to pay the price of admission" (Mosse 1985, 186). Both Gints and Jancis are paying the price, adapting their creative practices for their supposed audiences and carefully shaping their public personas to appeal to desired mainstream audiences without giving up their queer sensibilities; however, their imagined "actual" entrance into society has always been suspended.

Their creative practices are taking place in a period when people in Eastern Europe are increasingly informed both about the gender plurality and fluidity of the West and the conservative, homophobic politics of Russia and some other countries of the region, including Russia's ban on "gay propaganda" in 2013 and the declaration of "LGBT-free zones" in rural Polish counties. In this context, acts of queer performances can both invite the audience to show their support (or, at least tolerance) for expressions of non-normative gender and sexuality, and it can also provoke homophobic and transphobic reactions toward such performers. As the life-stories of our heroes show, a set of different tactics of adaptation is still needed for them to be tolerated by their audiences. In Jancis's case, it is the separation of his cultural production intended for straight and gay audiences while, for Gints, it is balancing gender camp and gender kitsch to lead the audience away from inspecting his private life too closely.

And probably one of the most appealing qualities about them both is their openness: they are always open to fail to show their emotionality and to share their dreams. If their audiences keep believing in their sincerity, their creative work will still have supporters in spite of not being flawless. Rather than seeing them as sexual and gender dissidents, their audience is interested in their modesty and their closeness to the local communities in which they dwell. Hiding beyond the poly-semantic figure of Pugacheva, they add to the Latvian countryside a pinch of emotional comfort which for different people might invoke diverse feelings, like pleasant memories or hopes for better future and good life.

NOTES

1. "Zilā GAYsma" (Blue light, 1994), "GAYsma" (1994–95), "Elwis" (1996–2003 and 2006–08), and "Jancis" (2003–05).

2. Accessible on: www.youtube.com/watch?v=sOSqySMTz6U

3. Jancis's books: "Baltais sapnis" (The white dream, 2012, poems), "Es nāku pie jums" (I come to you, 2013, memoirs), "Saldais citrons" (The sweet lemon, 2015, poems), "Atgriešanās" (The return, 2019, poems), "Es" (Me, 2019, memoirs and poems), "Svelme" (Heat, 2019, erotic poems), "Basām kājām uz laimīgo ostu" (Barefoot to the happy haven, 2020, poems).

4. The book includes also some translations of Jancis's poems in other languages, done by his friends, for example, this English translation of the poem "I Love You" by Indriķis Sīpols: "—I love you!/I wish to say it every day!/—I love you!/Distance separates us. How to make it go away?/—I love you!/I will once dress you up in rose petals, too!/—I love you!/I will give my all to you!/—I love you!/With kisses your velvety cheek will cover./—I love you!/I will get wild, passionate and tender./—I love you!/Come my way, even if it's just a little bit!/—I

love you!/The knot between our fates: we have to tighten it!/—I love you!/The ship of dreams will soon be done!/—I love you!/A common journey will make us one!" (Baltjancis 2015, 135)

5. The article on Baltjancis was posted in the section "Melomania" and titled "Latvian people's Pugacheva—poet and musician Baltjancis." It introduced him as "one of the favorite figures among the users of social networks in Latvian show business," "a poet, a lyricist and a musician," who is "obsessed for twenty years with Alla Pugacheva" and who "continues to entertain his fans with methods, well-tried by the Russian diva" (Delfi 2014). The article, published anonymously, also included Jancis's complaint of living a poor life in the countryside. The article's comments section soon became a battlefield of Jancis and his relatives or neighbors who anonymously accused him of using his disabled mother's money for his needs and leading a parasitic lifestyle. Jancis fought back with quotes from his poetry and words of wisdom by Pugacheva.

6. According to practices of Soviet cultural organizations, pop bands were officially classified as dance orchestras and usually attached to some collective farm, factory or local "house of culture." For example, Gints sung with such collectives as the band of Valmiera Furniture Factory and the band "Varavīksne" (Rainbow) of the collective farm "Nākotne" (Future) in the Jelgava rural district. He has been a restaurant singer as well.

7. Among his highlights are such songs as "Memory" from Andrew Lloyd Webber's "Cats," a medley of "ABBA" songs, and "I Will Always Love You" by Dolly Parton.

8. "Gaisma" (Light 1994) and "Sauc mani atpakaļ" (Call me back 2004).

9. Their album's artwork is available on Ivars un Gints (2017).

REFERENCES

Baltjancis. 2012. *Baltais sapnis [The White Dream]*. Mana grāmata.
———. 2013. *Es nāku pie jums [I Come to You]*. Mana grāmata.
———. 2015. *Saldais citrons [The Sweet Lemon]*. Mana grāmata.
Berlant, Lauren. 2011. *Cruel Optimism*. Durham, NC: Duke University Press.
Buyantueva, Radzhana, and Maryna Shevtsova, eds. 2020. *LGBTQ+ Activism in Central and Eastern Europe: Resistance, Representation and Identity*. New York: Palgrave Macmillan.
Cassiday, Julie A. 2018. "Glamazons en travesti: Drag Queens in Putin's Russia." In *Russian Performances: Word, Object, Action*, edited by Julie A. Buckler, Julie A. Cassiday, and Boris Wolfson, pp. 272–281. Madison: University of Wisconsin Press.
Delfi. 2014. Latviešu tautas Pugačova—dzejdaris un mūziķis Baltjancis [Latvian people's Pugacheva—poet and musician Baltjancis]. www.delfi.lv/izklaide/pop-muzika/ melomanija/latviesu-tautas-pugacova-dzejdaris-un-muzikis-baltjancis.d? id=45120634.

D'Emilio, John. 1983. "Capitalism and Gay Identity." In *Powers of Desire: The Politics of Sexuality,* edited by Ann Snitow, Christine Stansell, and Sharan Thompson, pp. 100–113. New York: Monthly Review Press.

Gay.lv. 2004. "Sevi piesaka duets "Buča" [Duet "Kiss" Makes Its Debut]." February 6, 2004. https://sonichits.com/artist/Bu%C4%8Da.

Halberstam, J. Jack. 2005. *In a Queer Time and Place: Transgender Bodies, Subcultural Lives.* New York: New York University Press.

Ivars un Gints. 2017. "Ivars un Gints, "Sauc mani atpakaļ" (Playlist)." November 14. www.youtube.com/playlist?list=PLPCZ934dQc8T3Njea3ovBxsh_XzrOVut4.

Jansons, Jānis Alberts. 2010. *Latviešu masku gājieni [Latvian Masked Processions].* Rīga: Zinātne.

Johnson, Colin R., Brian J. Gilley, and Mary L. Gray. 2016. "Introduction." In *Queering the Countryside: New Frontiers in Rural Queer Studies*, pp. 1–21. New York: New York University Press.

Kondakov, Alexander. 2019. "Rethinking the Sexual Citizenship from Queer and Post-Soviet Perspectives: Queer Urban Spaces and the Right to the Socialist City." *Sexualities* 22(3):401–417. https://doi.org/10.1177/1363460717737770.

Mole, Richard. 2011. "Nationality and Sexuality: Homophobic Discourse and the 'National Threat' in Contemporary Latvia." *Nations and Nationalism* 17(3):540–560.

Pakalns, Juris. 2003. "Mārtiņš Freimanis – Latvijas geju topa līderis [Mārtiņš Freimanis – The Leader of Latvian Gay Top]." *Privātā Dzīve*, July 22, pp. 18–19.

PBK. 2012. "Gints – bas, tenor, al't i soprano." *Pirmais Baltijas kanāls*, September 27. www.youtube.com/watch?v=RZKdPmNqIa0.

Roga, Juris. 2012. "Talantu daudz, taču kur lai tos dēstu? [I've Got Many Talents But What's the Use of Them?]." *Ezerzeme*, August 28.

Ruduša, Rita. 2014. *Forced Underground: Homosexuals in Soviet Latvia.* Rīga: Mansards.

TV3. 2009. "Liene Šomase un Valmieras koris, "Jai ho"." *Koru kari 2*, October 4. www.youtube.com/watch?v=hoPzjTNZFO4.

Vakara Ziņas. 2005. "Latvijas geju elku tops [Top of Latvian Gay Idols]." *Vakara Ziņas*, 2005, 29. jūlijs.

Vērdiņš, Kārlis. 2013. "Interviews with Jancis, October 4–6, Transcripts in Author's Archive."

———. 2016. "Interview with Jancis, August 8, Transcripts in Author's Archive."

Vērdiņš, Kārlis, and Jānis Ozoliņš. 2020. "The Latvian LGBT Movement and Narratives of Normalization." In *LGBTQ+ Activism in Central and Eastern Europe: Resistance, Representation and Identity*, edited by Radzhana Buyantueva and Maryna Shevtsova, pp. 239–264. New York: Palgrave Macmillan.

VTV. 2017. "Vidzemes Televīzijai cetrutdaļgadsimts." *Vidzeme TV*, July 1. www.youtube.com/watch?v=w8N9GRzIvuo.

Chapter 9

Religious Experiences in Life Stories of Homosexuals and Bisexuals in Russia

Polina Kislitsyna

ARE RELIGION AND QUEERNESS INCOMPATIBLE?

Russian religious institutions, as is well known, are hostile to LGBTQ people. In conditions of clericalization or desecularization of contemporary Russian society, governmental gender and sexual politics are formed with active support from the Orthodox and other churches. As Healey demonstrates, the federal law banning the spread of propaganda of non-traditional sexual relationships and the discourse of traditional Russian values are the results of a mixture of secular and religious homophobic ideas about homosexuality (Healey 2018). Before him, considering Russian homophobia in the context of politics and democratic values, Kon (2010) named the Russian Orthodox Church the main motivating force behind the informational campaign that demonized homosexuality in the public discourse. He claimed the church's hostile attitude to homosexuality is based not only on religious canon but also political motives. In this way, the church tries to consolidate conservative forces around itself.

According to the Russian Public Opinion Research Center, in 2019, 63 percent of the Russian population adhered to Orthodoxy (VCIOM 2019). Among persons aged over sixty, the proportion of Orthodox believers is much higher, accounting for 74 percent of the population. Given the popularity of Orthodoxy, members of Parliament enlisted the support of the Russian Orthodox Church to lobby for the law about propaganda (Healey 2018; Sozaev 2014). At the same time, less powerful churches like the Russian Union of Christians of Evangelical Faith demonstrated their solidarity with the government by gathering signatures for this law, as Sozaev (2014) has shown. Other religious groups, such as Muslims and Catholics, also have expressed homophobic attitudes to LGBTQ people in Russia and most post-Soviet states (Mole 2019).

In such conditions, there is an assumed polarization of Russian society where LGBTQ and faithful people are at opposite poles, as Sozaev states (2017). On the one hand, he writes, "the monopoly of authoritative religious opinion makes an impression that any religion unequivocally condemns homosexuality" (Sozaev 2016, 5). Most queers don't know that some religious movements affirm LGBTQ people and their rights. On the other hand, there is a popular point of view that non-heterosexuals and non-cisgenders need to renounce religion. This perspective is based on the negative religious experiences of many queers who faced hate, emotional or even physical violence, and condemnation in the religious sphere. Most religious doctrines are assumed to harm queers' well-being as far as they urge people to overcome the sin of homosexual desire and thus cause their self-hatred. Also, in most cases, conversion therapy (a form of psychotherapy aimed at altering a patient's sexual orientation from gay to straight and recognized as unethical and inefficient) is founded on religious beliefs.

All of this led to the consideration of religion as incompatible with the successful acceptance of one's queerness. This view has a theoretical elaboration in the American context. Harris (2014) offers the concept of gaytheism. Using queer theory, he criticizes both conservative and liberal branches of Christianity for hierarchical, heterocentric assumptions. In his opinion, even liberal denominations like the Metropolitan Community Church and deinstitutionalized forms of religion are inherently heteronormative. So, as he writes, "queers should demur from religion as a reactionary framework . . . they should cease attempts to rehabilitate forms of religion and seek forms of community and ethical sustenance outside religious structures" (Harris 2014, 26). Harris mentions deinstitutionalized forms of spirituality only superficially, without any specifics, and omits the ethnography of such communities that have existed since the 1990s, like radical faeries, for instance. This gay male subculture is positioned in opposition to fundamentalist forms of Christianity, appropriating rituals from non-Christian cultures (Celtic, Greek, Egyptian, and other). Egalitarianism and non-normative gender are emphasized in their cultural practices, so this movement, as researchers demonstrate, has a subversive potential (Barrett 2017).

The complex relationships between being queer and being religious are considered by some researchers in American society (e.g., McQueeney 2009; Samerau 2012, 2013; Wilcox 2009; Wolkomir 2006). Using similar methods to this chapter, Samerau et al. (2016) write about transformations in American Gay Christians' sexual and religious experiences. The authors apply Goffman's concept of moral career and demonstrate the following turning points of Gay Christians' moral career: essentializing religious belief (description of one's belief as inherent part of oneself), emotionalizing painful early religious experience, spiritualizing one's coming out process (mentions of God's help, e.g.) and sexualizing coming back to religious participation (linkage between one's sexual identity and religious feelings). Though I do not use the concept of moral career, in this chapter, I consider how my participants describe their religious experiences and take into account their rhetoric.

Currently, there is no systematic study about the religious experiences of LGBTQ people in Russia. This chapter is the first attempt to describe diverse scenarios of Russian queers' religious experience, from religious oppression to empowerment from belonging to LGBTQ religious communities. Using the biographical method, I reveal the role of religion in life stories of Russian homosexuals and bisexuals. I consider the narratives about religion in relation to social and cultural contexts that have been changing in the past thirty years. Besides, the social situation varies significantly in different regions of Russia. The chapter does not purport to give an exhaustive description of the religious life of Russian queers. Rather, based on particular cases, I explore in what systems of social relations Russian non-heterosexual believers are incorporated and how they verbalize their experiences. The body of the chapter is divided into two parts, the first of which is devoted to negative impressions of religion, and the second reports positive experiences of the coexistence of queerness and faith in the Russian context.

The chapter is a part of a broader research project devoted to constructing biographical narratives of non-heterosexuals in Russia. My main methodological framework is a biographical and narrative analysis. From these perspectives, I consider the strategies that Russian non-heterosexuals use in talking about their sexuality and life paths. The source material for this study consists of forty-seven interviews and thirty-seven written life stories collected from gays, lesbians, and bisexuals aged from eighteen to sixty-four. For the study on religious experiences, the cases where the relevant topics were discussed were selected from the whole corpus of materials. All names of the participants are withheld.

As I have observed, within Russian communities of queers and LGBTQ activists, religiosity in general is sometimes perceived of as a sign of ignorance or "backwardness." LGBTQ believers particularly face misunderstandings. For example, on the Russian social networking site "VKontakte," in an LGBTQ group, under a post about a public coming out of a Russian clergyman, is the following comment: "Why would these people, who are perverts and sodomists from the religious perspective, confess a religion or even become a priest?" For the author of the comment, any religion and especially priesthood are irreconcilable with homosexuality, although it was the clergyman of the True or Genuine Orthodox Church, a movement within Orthodox Christianity that separated from the mainstream Eastern Orthodox

Church and is regarded as more tolerant. Nonetheless, the position of the gay priest is unclear for many Russian queer people. He is seen almost like a traitor who took the side of the enemy, the church, which, as they assume, hates homosexuals.

Another case from my fieldwork was a workshop on Christianity, homosexuality, and LGBTQ activism in Russia organized by Timothy Sozaev, gay activist, researcher, and founder of LGBT ministry *Nuntiare et Recreare* in Saint Petersburg. He talked about his Orthodox experience in childhood and youth, the creation of his project *Nuntiare et Recreare*, queer theology, and the foreign churches that affirm homosexuality. At the end of the workshop, during the final discussion, it became clear that the most pressing issue for the audience was what kinds of arguments can be used in disputes with religious fundamentalists. Most attendees appeared to be atheist or agnostic who were seeking out any information to use as a weapon in the struggle against religious homophobia.

These cases are not precisely about the hatred of religion; rather, they demonstrate that faithful and especially Orthodox communities are perceived of as "other" and "dangerous" by most Russian queers. At the same time, this contributes to stereotypes of a homogeneous and egalitarian LGBTQ community in which there are no believers. Within this process in Russian society, there are traces of homonationalism, Puar's term. It is an interconnection between LGBTQ rights and a nationalist ideology (Puar 2007). Homonationalism is closely related to prejudices about the "non-Western" world as homophobic and dangerous and the "West" as egalitarian. From this perspective, a homosexual true Orthodox believer seems as improbable as a queer Sikh, the example Puar uses. Homosexual identity is supposed to be modernized and westernized, while a fundamentalist religion like Orthodoxy is considered non-Western and backward. Of course, Orthodoxy is a mainstream religion in Russia, so the term homonationalism that initially conceptualized instrumentalization of LGBT rights by politicians must be used carefully. Nevertheless, this concept may be helpful as a critique of the homogeneous image of the Russian LGBTQ community where LGBTQ believers are a minority within a minority.

EXPERIENCING RELIGIOUS OPPRESSION

The average age of my participants was 33.6, and most of them grew up in the 1990s. At that time, Russia was experiencing a period of so-called "religious revival" after the removal of restrictions on religious activities at the end of the 1980s (Krindatch 2004). While atheism was an important part of official Soviet ideology for nearly seventy years, in the 1990s in Russia, the number of religious organizations and religious diversity in general increased. Not only did the Orthodox Church become more popular, but various Protestant denominations and churches which were not present in Soviet times, many of which were the product of foreign missionary initiatives, also appeared. As Krindatch reports, between 1990 and 2003 the total number of religious communities in Russia raised from 6,600 to 21,000, which covered places of regular worship, monasteries, religious missions, administrative centers of religious organizations, religious brotherhoods, and theological educational institutions. These processes are reflected in the life stories of my participants.

Many participants first learned about homosexuality just as something negative, wrong, and pathological. The "sinful" nature of homosexuality was frequently included in this perspective. For example, one of my participants read about the existence of homosexual relationships in Orthodox books, where it was said that sodomites did not inherit the kingdom of God. He didn't know then that this related to him but kept in mind. He recognized his homosexual desire over time and after this had believed that he was a sinner who would never be saved. This led him to suicidal thoughts.

In some cases, any sexuality appeared to be linked with sinfulness or dirtiness. It is worth noting, as the participant emphasizes in the following quote, that his feeling of guilt was caused by sex in general, but not his homosexual experience in particular.

> It was my first gay sex, we both were fourteen. I remember that, after the first pleasant and sweet feeling, I felt guilt and shame. It seemed to me there was some dirt, sin or something like this on me. I even wanted to tell someone from my family and repent. However, the problem was not that I did "it" with a boy. The problem was exactly that I did "it." My family was puritan: talking about sex was not accepted at all, and this silence caused the assumption that sex is dirty. (gay male, thirty-three)

Feeling guilty for their "sin," the participants turned to God in their prayers for help in getting rid of their homosexuality. This practice is often mentioned by those who grew up in religious families and were deeply concerned about their "purity" and morality in the sense that their religion offered them. My research shows that these themes are common in the biographical narratives of faithful or ex-faithful queers. In these prayers, as participants described, homosexuality was considered to be a "sin," "disease," or "temptation," in other words, something apart from the subject of homosexual desire. Participants were afraid of their own desires, and they were asking God to deliver from all of this. As one participant, a twenty-six-year-old gay man, described, "Well, I yelled out of the window in my childhood, asked God: 'I wish I weren't like that!'" Another said,

And every time, after masturbating and viewing gay porn, I prayed and asked God to help me get rid of this "disease" and to forgive me for doing sinful things. (gay man, nineteen)

In some cases, these prayers are mentioned alongside various self-destructive things like suicidal thoughts or self-harm. Guilt about the sinfulness of homosexuality because of religious assumptions is described as what induces people to search for ways to escape from wrong thoughts and feelings. In the following quote, a gay man who grew up in the Muslim tradition of the Chechen Republic writes about the Christian websites where he read stories about curing homosexuality. This case stands out among my materials, and I will elaborate on it later. It is remarkable that his seeking solutions to the problem had a super-ecumenist character as he turned to the expertise of another religion to meet the demands of his faith. Perhaps it was due to the fact that most practices of conversion therapy are based on Christian customs, although there are similar activities among Islamic specialists (Jahangir and Abdul-Latif 2015).

In my arsenal there were prayers, self-destruction (usually I beat my head against the wall because I wanted to deprive myself of memory), abstinence from sleep, viewing lesbian porn, reading Christian sites about people who were wonderfully cured of homosexuality, Internet search for medications, and so on. (gay man, twenty-five)

Growing up and living in a religious atmosphere does not always mean belonging to a religious community and regular church attendance, but several stories contain such experiences. Given that the adolescence of many participants coincided with the appearance of various Protestant churches, in three biographical narratives, the beginning of one's sexual recognition and acceptance was interrupted by attending church. All of these stories begin with unproblematic homosexual or near-homosexual experiences. For example, one lesbian described how she and her sisters wore boyish clothes, fell in love with girls, and discussed their feelings among themselves: "It was natural for us to tell each other about our sympathies. And since an early age, these were always girls. . . . We looked like boys: short hair, boyish or unisex style. In Soviet times!" (lesbian, forty).

However, when she was fourteen, her family was engaged in the Protestant community where homosexuality wasn't acceptable. During the ten years she belonged to the Protestant church, she rejected her homosexual desire. Then, as she said, she was tired of the church where the priests repeated the same words. The participant was twenty-five before she first attended a gay party and met her girlfriend; in other words, she returned to the acceptance of her sexuality and began her lesbian life.

Another participant, a gay man, had sexual experiences with a young man in his adolescence, which were described as happy and pleasurable experiments. Then, when he was seventeen, his mother involved him in the Baptist church, and after this, his sexuality is appeared to become problematized: "One of the Christian doctrines said that God is against homosexuality. So my slow struggle with myself began" (gay man, thirty-three).

After a few years of life surrounded by Baptists, he was sure that he had gotten rid of homosexual thoughts and planned to get married, but later he fell in love with his neighbor who was a parishioner of his church. Their relationships were not successful because my participant's partner repented of their sexual activities in front of their older brothers in faith. This led to the participant's expulsion from the church since he refused to repent and redeem himself. His homosexual desire and identity were emancipated, and he left the church and renounced the religion which oppressed his sexuality.

A third story is very similar, with the main difference being that the participant wasn't concerned about the religious ban of homosexual relations, but his partner was, resulting in their separation and disenchantment with religion. In all these stories, coming to church hindered the understanding of one's sexual desires, delayed self-acceptance, and caused traumatic experiences of exclusion, shaming, or loss.

In some cases, the participants faced the oppression of their faithful relatives who wanted to cure homosexuality with religion. The older members of their families were trying to convince my participants that same-sex relationships are sinful and to insist on their church fellowship. My data demonstrate that the agents of such "care" were my participants' mothers, although it is not a representative sample. However, some researchers state that Russian women are far more religious than men (Greeley 1994; Krindatch 2004). This even led to the novel situation of gender authority within the patriarchal Orthodox churches when women began to be religious professionals and participate in religious education as teachers (Ladykowska and Tocheva 2013; Kizenko 2013). Under such circumstances, it is not surprising that it is women who try to fix their children's sexuality by religious rites or conversations with priests. Also, it may be related to the fact that any care is women's responsibility (Kittay 1999). Since faithful relatives see their tactics as a way to "save" their children and as manifestations of love and care, such religious oppression is initiated by women.

It is noteworthy in the following quote, the mother turned to religion after she sent her daughter to a psychologist. The psychologist did not reach the mother's goal insofar as she didn't try to correct my participant's sexuality and held therapeutic sessions instead. When psychotherapy didn't meet her expectations, the mother's next step was using religious arguments. It may mean that in this case religion appeared to be just an instrument for the disposal of homosexuality, among other things, like psychotherapy or medicine. In addition, this case illustrates how religious oppression intersects with emotional violence and subordination in interactions between homosexuals and their parents.

> Then she brought the "heavy metal"—the church—into play, namely taking me to monasteries and priests. And I had no force or even wish to resist, so I consented silently to this violence on myself. Now I understand that all she did was a cruel violation of my personal boundaries and was the result of her own psychological trauma. But I was so scared that she would abandon me, and I used to believe in her claims that my life is a sin, I would never be happy, I should have fought who I am, all lesbians are only people who were imprisoned, and so on. (lesbian, thirty-one)

The next case demonstrates the usage of near-religious or spiritual practices in attempts to normalize sexuality, although it is not the personal experience of the participant. She described the situation in Buryatia in the 1990s. As she wrote, the mothers of her friends turned to both Orthodox churches and midwives or Shamans to cure their children's homosexuality. Such practices correlate with the religious landscape of this Russian region where Orthodox believers, Buddhists, and Shamanists coexist and alternative medicine is very popular (Darieva 2008).

> No one was fine: from eighteen to forty-five years old, all of them had problems. The mothers used to take the young women to churches to cure them, namely exorcize demons. There must be *tema* [lesbians] among Buryats, but I don't know whether they were taken to Buddhist datsans. Both Russians and Buryats crossed paths at the home of Natasha, the midwife who healed alcohol addiction of both nations by *zagovory* [verbal folk magic]. I have never met a recovering lesbian, but there were about five persons in "treatment" as I remember. (lesbian, about forty)

As I mentioned before, in my materials there is a story of a gay man from the Chechen Republic which stands out among other biographical narratives. Chechnya is characterized by a high level of militarization and prevalence of dogmatic Islam, and in 2017, unofficial prisons for men deemed to be homosexual where the victims were tortured were discovered (Kondakov 2018). Such a difficult and volatile situation is reflected in my participant's autobiography. He described himself as a totally closeted gay man who told nobody about his homosexuality except in some cases through Internet communication on gay dating sites. Religion is a very important context of his life because his surroundings suppose that he is Muslim and he needs to meet their expectations and thoroughly hide his homosexuality.

> I am an agnostic. And I am grateful to all heaven's forces that I don't accuse myself of all sorts of evils as some faithful gay men do. Judge for yourself! A man believes that God created him the way he is, but he is afraid of God's wrath because he was born gay. There is no logic here at all. Therefore, freedom from religious bonds gives me a little chance to breathe more freely. Sure, it is diffi-cult when you live in the Islamic republic where everyone asks you whether you pray. In those moments I avert my eyes. I can't answer: "My friend, I stopped believing in these oriental tales since I was 17." Although there were times when I begged God to rid me of this punishment and make me a normal guy the same as my friends who sat for a long time and chatted with their girls, whom, however, they forgot after a couple of months. But it was not what I wanted. My homosexuality made me more independent from the behavior of the crowd. Although I wish I didn't want to spend the evening hugging my friend. Because it is so low to be friends with the man who sees me as a friend and brother and want to have romantic relationships with him. However, religion surrounds me everywhere so I try to pay no attention to it and say in time: "Everything is in the Hands of the Lord." In any case, it is a part of my nation's culture so I don't see anything wrong in my participation in religious rites, though there is no faith in my soul. (gay man, twenty-five)

Unlike most of the participants who experienced religious oppression, he can't renounce their religion openly without leaving his homeland. He has to follow Islamic rites and pretend to be a believer to secure himself in Chechen society. Remarkably, he describes this necessity as an almost unproblematic routine thing. In so doing, he emphasizes that his inner freedom of religious conscious absolves him from feelings of guilt and shame. This case illustrates that strategies of resistance to religious oppression are deeply contextualized and depend on social conditions.

Many Russian non-heterosexuals need to feign that they are hetero-sexual. Most participants hide their relationships from their parents and colleagues, and some of them tell a lie about their non-existent heterosexual relationships or even introduce their friends of the opposite gender as their boyfriends or girlfriends in order to establish an alibi. One participant told me that he and his partner could not live together and need to rent differ-ent apartments in one building and pretend to be merely neighbors. In this perspective, pretending to be a believer turns out to be just one way of mask-ing one's true identity for safety. Yet nobody else reported similar cases to me. It is difficult to say whether it means that such dissembling is limited to Islam. Rather, it depends on how far religion is influential in the family, community, or region.

EXPERIENCING RELIGIOUS EMPOWERMENT

As far as my research has shown, there are at least two queer religious groups in Russia: the LGBT ministry *Nuntiare et Recreare* (in Latin: herald and strengthen) in Saint Petersburg and the Christian community *Svet Mira* (Light of the World) in Moscow. While the Moscow community is designed for members of all Christian denominations, the Saint Petersburg ministry unites LGBT believers of different religious and confessional affiliations (not only Christian) and also people who are not affiliated with any organized forms of religion. Both of them arrange meetings of faithful people for communication and collective worship, hold seminars and other educational events, and publish educational literature. Moreover, *Nuntiare et Recreare* uses some of the spiritual practices of the afore-mentioned Radical Fairies, like the heart circle. This is a speech event with organized turns at speaking which other participants keep silent and listen carefully; in these circles, participants exchange their emotional and spiritual experience (Barrett 2017, 65). Hence, *Nuntiare et Recreare* extends beyond the usual religious denominations, turning to the experiences of the combined non-Christian spiritual movement.

Both Saint Petersburg's and Moscow's communities promote queer or affirmative theology, which reinterprets the Bible and other religious texts positively and constructively from the perspective of queer theory (Cheng 2011). In the view of such theology, homosexuality, as well as other forms of sexuality and gender beyond heteronormativity, is not a sin but an important part of a human, God's creation. This approach reclaims the place of homosexuality in religious thoughts and cultures (Loughlin 2009). There are many controversies in queer theology, one of which is between those who focus on identity groups and essentialist categories and those who try to overcome essentialism and identity politics. These debates are essential to the broader context of LGBT theology and have been discussed in greater detail elsewhere (e.g., Cornwall 2011; Schneider and Roncolato 2012 for reviews).

In my data, two life stories described engagement in communities of faithful LGBTQ people. Both stories start with the oppressive religious experiences mentioned before. In both cases, fellowship in homophobic churches predates discovering affirmative religious communities. The first case is the story of a woman who left the Protestant church at twenty-five and accepted her homosexuality. Ten years later she found the community of LGBT

Christians, and this helped her to solve the conflict between religion and homosexuality and finally find balance. The affirmative approach to religion gave her a way to be a lesbian and a believer at the same time. She named her entry in the community of LGBT Christians one of the most important events of her life.

> I had an internal conflict. On the one hand, I understood that it is a sin, but, on the other hand, I didn't. I couldn't understand. And I found the community of LGBT Christians. . . . It struck me when, over time, they said that it's not written anywhere that being an LGBT person is a sin. . . . And they talked about how you could see yourself and your life in general. (lesbian, forty-two)

The second case is about a man who came to the Protestant church with his partner and lost him due to the religious ban on homosexual relations. He described his first time attending an LGBT Christian event as a very dramatic moment because he found information that could have saved his previous relationships and prevent his painful loss.

> Once I met a man who helped me to solve my main problem later. Just then I understood what LGBT community and LGBT Christians are. I first learned there were churches that interpreted the Bible not literally but from different perspectives. God appeared to love all people equally and not condemn homosexuality. When I arrived at the LGBT Christian forum, I attended a lecture about how God accepts us the way we are and does not condemn us, homosexuals. After this, I was crying for an hour for the first time in my life. Why didn't this happen in due time? Why not before? This could change a lot! (gay man, forty-two)

Both stories demonstrate that leaving the church the participants did not resolve the conflict between their religious feelings and sexuality. Internal contradictions and doubts, as my participants described, stayed with them. Queer theology and communities of LGBTQ believers supported them and contributed to their empowerment and emancipation. All of this helped them to finally get rid of the religious oppression that they experienced before. Belonging to queer faithful communities also led these participants to civil activities and to struggle for their rights. Beginning to be a member of LGBTQ faithful communities, they engaged in the organization of different events, discussion of social exclusion and inequality, and the development of the LGBTQ movement.

In addition to the previous cases, it is worth noting the usage of queer theological rhetoric in biographical narratives. The following quotes are fragments of written autobiographies. Their authors didn't concretize what role religion played in their life. They didn't mention any churches, denominations, religious communities, spiritual experiences and feelings, or anything of that nature in the rest of the text. However, these participants turned to theological arguments when they claimed their identity and right to be who they are. They explained their sexuality as a result of God's will. In other words, as they said, they were created homosexual or bisexual. This kind of rhetoric partly tends to be close to essentialism (or belief that sexual orientation is an inborn characteristic of people) because it conceals the possibility of choice. One young bisexual woman stated, "God created me this way and said that I have a right to be, but humans think that something is wrong with me." As another put it, "Faith in God gave me strength. Knowing that God loves me the way he created me" (gay man, age unknown).

An essentialist view on homosexuality or bisexuality is very popular among my participants. Many of them tend to think that they were "born this way." Essentialism can be useful as a way to accept oneself and explain it to people, especially in religious circumstances. In this case, biological determinism intermingles with religious naturalism: the rhetoric of "born this way" mixes with the "God created me this way" argument. Walters (2014) writes about this phenomenon in the American context. She estimates such argumentation is a trap because it leads to a denial of choices. From this point of view, only these whose sexuality is immutable and inborn deserve a tolerant attitude. Furthermore, essentialist and determinist approaches to homosexuality entail serious risks for queers.

We cannot know whether these participants are aware of queer theology and communities of LGBTQ believers. It is possible that they didn't read or hear about these, and their appeal to religion is motivated by their self-image and amateur rethinking about religious doctrines. In any case, such affirmative rhetoric in the narratives attests to the positive religious experience of Russian queer persons. The participants mentioned their faith and, within these life stories, it does not contradict their sexuality.

CONCLUSIONS

In contemporary Russia, faithful and queer people are opposed to each other discursively. This is underscored by the homophobic rhetoric of fundamentalist churches and the assumptions of queer people about religion doing harm to their well-being. Such polarization of Russian society leads to a homonationalist view on the LGBTQ community which is understood to be homogeneous. Any religion is seen as hostile, and LGBTQ believers appear to be misunderstood and excluded. My materials demonstrate the diversity of religious experiences among Russian lesbians and gay men where religion is not only an oppressive institution, but where some forms of religious consciousness and communities can also support queer believers and help them to see themselves without contradiction with their religion.

Nevertheless, most of the participants who shared their religious experiences faced many forms of oppression. Assumptions about the sinfulness of homosexuality are deeply rooted in Russian culture, and my participants discovered the existence of homosexual relationships and guilt because of it simultaneously. Religious perspectives aggravate feelings of shame shared by many queers because faithful young LGBTQ people thought that they would never be in harmony with their God. Most of the stories about feelings of guilt and shame that were caused specifically by religious oppression are from men. Although the volume of data is too small to extrapolate findings for all Russian society, this pattern may be rooted in the fact that male homosexuality is mentioned in the Bible more frequently and has served discursively as a bigger sin. It is worth noting here that gay men and lesbians were treated differently throughout Russian history and especially during Soviet times. Male homosexuality was criminalized and considered as a crime while female homosexuality was understood as disease and subject of psychiatry (Healey 2001, 2018; Stella 2015), although Clech (2019) demonstrates that it could be difficult to draw a line between them because some homosexual men were subjected to compulsory treatment and some lesbians were imprisoned. Nevertheless, different images of gay men and lesbians in public discourses could influence the perception of them in the religious sphere.

Since most of my participants grew up in the 1990s when the so-called religious revival began, they were involved in religious communities that condemn homosexuality. This exacerbated the already complicated process of understanding and acceptance of their sexuality. All of them left these communities but it was not always a solution to the internal conflict between their faith and self-consciousness.

In some cases, religious oppression came from relatives who tried to "fix" the participants' sexuality through religious or spiritual practices. In all cases I have collected, the agents of such oppressive care were women, as they are usually caregivers and responsible for childrearing. The objects of this oppressive care were also women in most stories. Without claiming representativeness of my findings, one could suppose that this may reflect the more dependent position of young women in Russian families, unlike young men.

The wide religious landscape of life determines strategies of interaction with religious communities. The high level of fundamentalist religiosity in the region forces queer people to pretend to be believers without sincere faith to secure themselves. Such strategies of hiding combine with a silenced rethinking of religious doctrines.

Empowering religious experience relates to belonging to communities of LGBTQ believers. In Russia, there are such communities in Saint Petersburg and Moscow, and they also have websites that promote information about affirmative or queer theology. Access to such information and social networks within LGBTQ communities contributes to successfully resolving an internal conflict between religious demands and one's sexuality. Affirmative religious communities support queer believers who are misunderstood by members of other churches and atheist queer people. Also, the religious queer communities often involve their members in LGBTQ activism.

In some stories, some traces of affirmative rhetoric can be observed, although their authors didn't describe their participation in religious communities or just faith as an important part of their life path. However, they appealed to divine creation when they explain their identity and life course to potential readers. These data may testify there are positive experiences of coexisting religious conscious and LGBTQ identities beyond communities of queer believers.

In Russia, LGBTQ individuals face religious oppression on different levels. There is internalized religious oppression, exclusion from religious institutions or communities, relatives' abuse, and wide cultural suppression in the regions where fundamentalist religions determine most social relations, like the Chechen Republic. In spite of this, there are believers in Russian LGBTQ communities, as well as the cases of the successful coexistence of non-heteronormativity with faith.

REFERENCES

Barrett, Rusty. 2017. *From Drag Queens to Leathermen: Language, Gender, and Gay Male Subcultures.* New York: Oxford University Press.

Cheng, Patrick S. 2011. *Radical Love: An Introduction to Queer Theology.* New York: Seabury Books.

Clech, Arthur. "Between the Labor Camp and the Clinic: Tema or the Shared Forms of Late Soviet Homosexual Subjectivities." In *Soviet and Post-Soviet Sexualities,* edited by Richard Mole. London: Routledge, 2019, pp. 32–55.

Cornwall, Susannah. 2011. *Controversies in Queer Theology.* London: SCM Press.

Darieva, Baira. 2008. "Health, Gender, and Religion in a Russian Province in Transition." In *Health Capital and Sustainable Socioeconomic Development,* edited by Patricia A. Cholewka and Mitra M. Motlagh. Boca Raton, FL: CRC Press, pp. 19–32.

Greeley, Andrew. 1994. "A Religious Revival in Russia?" *Journal for the Scientific Study of Religion* 33(3):253–72.

Harris, William C. 2014. *Slouching Towards Gaytheism: Christianity and Queer Survival in America.* New York: SUNY Press.

Healey, Dan. 2001. *Homosexual Desire in Revolutionary Russia: The Regulation of Sexual and Gender Dissent.* Chicago: University of Chicago Press.

―――. 2018. *Russian Homophobia from Stalin to Sochi.* London: Bloomsbury Publishing.

Jahangir, Junaid B., and Hussein Abdul-latif. 2015. "Investigating the Islamic Perspective on Homosexuality." *Journal of Homosexuality* 63(7):925–54.

Kittay, Eva F. 1999. *Love's Labor: Essays on Women, Equality, and Dependency.* New York: Routledge.

Kizenko, Nadieszda. 2013. "Feminized Patriarchy? Orthodoxy and Gender in Post-Soviet Russia." *Signs: Journal of Women in Culture and Society* 38(3):595–621.

Kon, Igor. 2010. "Homophobia as a Litmus Test of Russian Democracy." *Russian Social Science Review* 51(3):16–37.

Kondakov, Alexander. 2018. "Chechnya, Detention Camps In." In *Global Encyclopedia of Lesbian, Gay, Bisexual, Transgender, and Queer History*, edited by Howard Chiang and Anjali Aronekar. Boston: Charles Scribner's Sons, pp. 315–18.

Krindatch, Alexey D. 2004. "Patterns of Religious Change in Post-Soviet Russia: Major Trends from 1998 to 2003." *Religion, State and Society* 32(2):115–36.

Ladykowska, Agata, and Detelina Tocheva D. 2013. "Women Teachers of Religion in Russia: Gendered Authority in the Orthodox Church." *Archives de Sciences Sociales des Religions* 162:55–74.

Loughlin, Gerard, ed. 2009. *Queer Theology: Rethinking the Western Body.* Oxford: Blackwell Publishing.

McQueeney, Krista. 2009. "'We Are God's Children, Y'All': Race, Gender, and Sexuality in Lesbian-and-Gay-Affirming Congregations." *Social Problems* 56:151–73.

Mole, Richard. 2019. "Constructing Soviet and Post-Soviet Sexualities" In *Soviet and Post-Soviet Sexualities*, edited by Richard Mole. London: Routledge, pp. 1–15.

Puar, Jasbir K. 2007. *Terrorist Assemblages: Homonationalism in Queer Times.* Durham, NC: Duke University Press.

Schneider, Laurel C., and Carolyn Roncolato. 2012. "Queer Theologies." *Religion Compass* 6(1):1–13.

Sozaev, Valeriy. 2014. "V Epicentre Konflikta: *Khristianstvo I* Gomoseksual'nost' v Nachale XXI veka" [In the Epicenter of Conflict: Homosexuality and Christianity in the Beginning of 21st century]. In *Gomoseksual'nost' i Khristianstvo v XXI Veke: Sbornik Statey Raznykh Let* [Homosexuality and Christianity in the 21st Century: A Collection of Articles from Different Years], edited by Valeriy Sozaev. Saint Petersburg: Nuntiare et Recreare. (In Russian).

―――. 2016. "Ot Sostavitelya" [Preface of the Editor]. In *Religioznyy Fundamentalizm i Sindrom Religioznoy Travmy: Materialy dlya Psikhologov i Aktivistov* [Religious Fundamentalism and Religious Trauma Syndrome: Materials for Psychologists and Activists]. Saint Petersburg: Nuntiare et Recreare.

―――, ed. 2017. *Predstavleniya Svyashchennosluzhiteley Khristianskikh Denominatsiy Sankt-Peterburga po Voprosam Gomoseksual'nosti i Transgendernosti: Rezul'taty Issledovanija* [Views on Homosexuality and

Transgenderness of Christian Clergy in Saint Petersburg: Results and Conclusions].
Saint Petersburg: Nuntiare et Recreare. (In Russian).

Stella, Francesca. 2015. *Lesbian Lives in Soviet and Post-Soviet Russia: Post/
Socialism and Gender Sexualities*. Basingstoke: Palgrave Macmillan.

Sumerau, J. Edward. 2012. "Mobilizing Race, Class, and Gender Discourses in a
Metropolitan Community Church." *Race, Gender, and Class* 19(3–4):93–112.

Sumerau, Jason E., Ryan, T. Cragun, and Lain A. B. Mathers. 2013. "'Somewhere
Between Evangelical and Queer': Sexual Religious Identity Work in an LGBT
Christian Church." In *Selves, Symbols, and Sexualities: Contemporary Readings*,
edited by Staci Newmahr and Tom Weinberg. Thousand Oaks, CA: Sage, pp.
123–34.

———. 2016. "'I Found God in The Glory Hole': The Moral Career of a Gay
Christian." *Sociological Inquiry* 86(4):618–40.

VCIOM. 2019. "Orthodoxy and Baptism." Accessed February 14, 2019. https://wc
iom.com/index.php?id=61&uid=1697.

Walters, Suzanna D. 2014. *Tolerance Trap: How God, Genes, and Good Intentions
Are Sabotaging Gay Equality*. London: New York University Press.

Wilcox, Melissa M. 2009. *Queer Women and Religious Individualism*. Bloomington:
Indiana University Press.

Wolkomir, Michelle. 2006. *Be Not Deceived: The Sacred and Sexual Struggles of
Gay and Ex-Gay Christian Men*. New Brunswick, NJ: Rutgers University Press.

Conclusion

Emily Channell-Justice

This volume came out of a panel at the 2018 American Anthropological Association, entitled "Decolonizing Queer Performance, Practice, Experience: Examples from Post-Socialism," which I organized when I became curious about how LGBT+ rights intersected with leftist activist priorities in Kyiv, Ukraine. I used that panel to think further about how to frame the discussion that now appears in chapter 4 of this volume, and several of the panelists have contributed chapters as well. Those that did not are still represented through their influence on that panel and with references to their work. I relied on their knowledge to expand my own reading in Queer studies, particularly as it relates to the post-socialist world.[1]

The panel and the ensuing volume came out of the idea that scholars of and from Eastern Europe and the Former Soviet Union (EE/FSU) should push back against the hegemony of Western-dominated Queer studies. While much of this research remains canonical, the experience of LGBT+ people in EE/FSU has shown that the categories established in North American and Western European Queer studies do not map easily onto those regions. Rather, as several authors in this volume have argued here and elsewhere, insisting that Western-style gay rights is immediately applicable to the newly post-Soviet world is a kind of colonizing process, taking one of at least two directions. It can force activists to organize themselves around what they think will be appealing to Western audiences who are likely to fund their groups, or it can make researchers evaluate the success and failure of LGBT+ activism based on how those groups have moved through the Western world. Of course, this colonizing process can do both of these at the same time.

How does the present volume contribute a decolonizing framework? First, the authors have drawn from grounded methodologies—ethnography, interviews and life histories, analysis of artistic production, and archival

189

research—to consider LGBT+ communities on their own terms. The chapters move away from and critique large-scale survey data that attempts to quantify attitudes toward issues such as gay marriage, the legality of which is often the standard by which "success" is measured in regard to LGBT+ activism. While all of the chapters deal in some capacity with violence toward LGBT+ people—an unfortunately unavoidable theme in this field— they complicate LGBT+ people's responses to violence. They consider how LGBT+ people find solace in religion, how differently they might interact with police and surveillance, or how they create communities for themselves to reject socially dominant acceptance of that violence. They ask us to take seriously the creation of hegemonic narratives in art and storytelling that exclude some LGBT+ people while privileging others. They show that this burgeoning field has so much more to contribute to Queer studies as a whole.

On the one hand, these chapters show that the experience of state socialism in each of the examples has had a strong influence on LGBT+ communities, both during and after the end of socialism. While in many ways, socialist states paid attention to gender equality in a way that many Western capitalist democracies did not (Ghodsee 2018), LGBT+ populations were not part of the narratives of socialist progressivism that Communist Parties attempted to spread throughout the world. As I have discussed elsewhere (2020), and as Tamar Shirinian discusses in chapter 2, after 1989 and 1991, many Western feminists assumed that newly independent women would throw off their socialist yokes and join the women's movement that asked for equality in the workplace and reproductive rights, dominant themes in Western Europe and North America. Such assumptions have led to backlash against feminism across EE/FSU, though feminism has become a site of contention in many of these countries in recent years.

We can see a parallel trend in the expectation of LGBT+ activist movements in EE/FSU after the end of state socialism. Many scholars assumed that these countries would develop gay rights movements that demanded visibility and specific rights, such as marriage equality and anti-discrimination legislation. Some groups making these demands do exist across the post-socialist region, and my point here is not to detract from their work. Rather, I wish to point out that, as the chapters in the present volume show, many of these groups understand that they are working within a Western-dominated framework, within which they create their own spaces and their own communities. While many scholars continue to assess the status of gay rights in EE/FSU with specific measures, members of the community themselves often value their own work much differently. In the example of Ukraine, my own fieldwork context, activists attend Pride Parades even as they create spaces and groups devoted to critiquing the mainstream gay rights agenda. They find empowerment in creating communities on their own terms, even as their so-called rights are not secure.

It is necessary to mention here that perhaps these communities do not put their faith in the law to protect them. Returning to the question of gender equality in the Soviet Union, for instance, legislation ensured women had equal access to jobs, including political representation. Yet in reality, women's jobs were often underpaid, and few women actually attained positions of real power in the government. It should come as no surprise, then, that in the post-socialist context, people do not necessarily believe that laws do what they are supposed to for people. In comparison to many other post-socialist countries, Ukraine has progressive legislation regarding gender-based violence. Yet gender-based violence remains extremely prevalent in Ukraine, because laws can easily be ignored, powerful people can pay off judges who might otherwise convict them or their families, and law enforcement is not motivated to resolve domestic conflict in a way that protects those who experience violence.

Among LGBT+ activists, many people understand that rights and laws will not prevent violence, so why should they be exclusively focused on these goals? This is certainly not to say that rights are not important, or that activists should not be focused on legal protections. Rather, activists should be free to define their own priorities based on their communities' needs, rather than framing their work around external expectations. Further, the law has been operationalized by the opposition in numerous cases in the region, most explicitly in the so-called "gay propaganda" law in Russia (Kondakov 2019) and attempts to replicate such legislation in places like Ukraine. Thus, a distrust of the use of law for protection rather than harm is understandable.

This volume has also shifted the focus of discussions of LGBT+ experiences away from activism. While some of the chapters are about activists, they do not all assume that members of the LGBT+ community must be activists in order to be worthy of attention (Buyantueva and Shevtsova's 2020 volume also makes this important shift). This move again relies on the self-description of LGBT+ people, meeting them where they are, using methodologies that prioritize their own stories. Such research diversifies the representation of LGBT+ people in the post-socialist world, hopefully resonating not just with Queer studies scholars but with LGBT+-identified residents of the region more broadly.

Finally, several of the authors in this volume contribute to an important discussion of researcher positionality. The process of decolonizing any field of study must reckon with who is contributing to the representation of the community at hand. For this reason, the volume includes authors based at institutions around the world, researching in their own countries and communities or researching others. These varied researcher positions show that multiple viewpoints creates greater, better representation and complicates the discussion around LGBT+ experiences in the post-socialist world in ways that I firmly believe are fruitful and generative.

WHAT NEXT?

While the chapters in this volume attend to a wide array of issues, communities, and people, it also neglects certain topics that will be of increasing importance in post-socialist studies, Queer studies, and the disciplines of the authors, such as anthropology and history. Here, I address a few of those ideas, thinking about not only research priorities but also the priorities of the communities at hand. As we pointed out in the introduction, these stories are never detached from the human, lived experiences of LGBT+ people who are claiming space in their worlds.

First, the rise of right-wing populism and nationalism across Eastern Europe and the Former Soviet Union has a significant impact on LGBT+ futures. Many scholars have already written or begun to research the direct connections between right-wing movements and anti-LGBT+ action, but I see no indication that this issue will decrease in importance in the near future. How governments respond to the demands of right-wing groups—which often seek to gain representation in those governments—and the demands of LGBT+ rights groups will be an important indication of how researchers should proceed.

A second area of attention should address the intersection of LGBT+ with displacement and migration. While several scholars have discussed LGBT+ experiences in diasporas, such as the Russian diaspora in the United States or Israel, with more and more movement around the globe, Queer studies must continue to develop a focus on displacement and migration. Further, those scholars studying displacement and migration must consider LGBT+ identities within those spheres; Queer themes cannot be marginalized for the sake of coherent narratives. Marusya Bociurkiw's film *This Is Gay Propaganda: LGBT Rights and the War in Ukraine* highlights the stories of displaced Ukrainians who identify as LGBT+, recognizing the overlapping struggles of those people featured in her film. More systemic research at this intersection across disciplines is essential.

In all, what Queer studies needs is simply more: more research on Eastern Europe and the Former Soviet Union, more representation of diverse groups of people and their life experiences, and more scholars willing to take on the task of in-depth, dedicated research in LGBT+ communities. More panels at conferences where the scholars who laid the groundwork for this volume can hear from and connect with the young researchers who are contributing to this burgeoning field of study. Queer studies in EE/FSU remains a risky endeavor, so scholars in a position to take risks must prioritize these themes and support students and junior faculty who are committed to them, as well. I look forward to seeing the future volumes that come from these efforts.

NOTE

1. I thank Samuel Buelow, Jennifer Carroll, Roman Leksikov, Alexandra Novitskaya, and Tamar Shirinian for their contributions to this panel.

REFERENCES

Bociurkiw, Marusya. 2015. *This Is Gay Propaganda: LGBT Rights and the War in Ukraine*. Winds of Change Production. Documentary in Ukrainian, English, and Russian with English Subtitles.

Buyantueva, Radzhana, and Maryna Shevtsova, eds. 2020. *LGBT+ Activism in Central and Eastern Europe*. London: Palgrave Macmillan.

Channell-Justice, Emily. 2020. "Gender, Feminism, and Nation: Contributions of the Socialist and Post-Socialist Worlds." *Feminist Anthropology* 1(1):24–31.

Ghodsee, Kristen. 2018. *Second World, Second Sex: Socialist Women's Activism and Global Solidarity During the Cold War*. Durham, NC: Duke University Press.

Kondakov, Alexander. 2019. "The Influence of the 'Gay Propaganda' Law on Violence Against LGBTIQ People in Russia: Evidence from Criminal Court Rulings." *European Journal of Criminology*. https://doi.org/10.1177/1477370819887511.

Index

About the Authors

Emily Channell-Justice is director of the Temerty Contemporary Ukraine Program at the Ukrainian Research Institute, Harvard University. She received her PhD in 2016 in sociocultural anthropology from the Graduate Center, City University of New York. Her research has focused on self-organized political activism in the context of the Euromaidan protest movement in Ukraine in 2013–2014, specifically among leftist, feminist, and student activists in Kyiv.

Feruza Aripova is a PhD candidate in world history at Northeastern University and center associate at the Davis Center for Russian and Eurasian Studies at Harvard University. Currently, she is working on completing her dissertation, tentatively titled, "Silencing of Same-Sex Desire in the Post-Soviet Space: Deconstructing the Soviet Legacy."

Vitaly Chernetsky is associate professor of Slavic languages and literatures and director of the Center for Russian, East European & Eurasian Studies at the University of Kansas. He is the author of *Mapping Postcommunist Cultures: Russia and Ukraine in the Context of Globalization* (2007) and numerous articles on Russian and Ukrainian cultures where he seeks to highlight cross-regional and cross-disciplinary contexts, as well as a translator of Russian and Ukrainian writing.

Tjaša Kancler is an activist, artist, post-doc researcher, and associate professor of Media Arts and Gender Studies at the Department of Visual Arts and Design—Section for Art and Visual Culture, Faculty of Fine Arts, University of Barcelona. They are a co-founder of t.i.c.t.a.c.—Taller de Intervenciones

Críticas Transfeministas Antirracistas Combativas (www.intervencionesd ecoloniales.org)—and a coeditor of the journal *Desde el margen* (www.desde -elmargen.net).

Polina Kislitsyna is a PhD student at the European University at Saint Petersburg. The theme of her dissertation project is "Biographical Narratives of Non-Heterosexuals in Contemporary Russia: Rhetorical Strategies and Self-Understanding." It concerns how Russian non-heterosexuals talk about their lives, what events and recollections are considered as significant and important by them, what categories are used by them. She has a Master's degree in anthropology and ethnology from European University at Saint Petersburg in 2017.

Roman Leksikov is an early stage researcher who works on the intersection of criminology, criminal justice studies, sociology of violence, and gender and sexuality studies. He graduated with a Master's degree from the University of Alberta, where he defended his research thesis dedicated to the problems of hate crimes policing. Roman currently collaborates with the Ukrainian Center for Law and Crime research and resides in Montréal, Canada.

Jānis Ozoliņš is a researcher at the Institute of Literature, Folklore, and Art of the University of Latvia (ILFA), lecturer at Art Academy of Latvia, and currently a PhD candidate at the University of Latvia. He is editor of the book *Andra Neiburga: Language, Gender, Narrative and Image* (ILFA, 2018), coeditor of the book *Queer Stories of Europe* (2016). His fields of expertise are narrative theory, queer and masculinities studies, as well as Soviet litera- ture and film.

Zhanar Sekerbayeva is the co-founder of the Kazakhstan Feminist Initiative "Feminita." She is a feminist, powerlifter, and poet. In 2014 she enrolled at the European Humanities University (Lithuania) MA program in sociology with focus on gender and culture, and she defended her PhD at the University of Tsukuba, Japan. Her doctoral dissertation focuses on the processes of shap- ing identities of trans people in Kazakhstan.

Tamar Shirinian is a postdoctoral fellow in the Department of Anthropology at the University of Tennessee in Knoxville. She received her PhD in cultural anthropology, with a certificate in feminist studies from Duke University in 2016. Her research has investigated the tensions between queer activism, right-wing nationalism, and geopolitics in the postsocialist world, especially in the Republic of Armenia.

Syinat Sultanalieva completed her PhD the University of Tsukuba, Japan. In her academic research, she focuses on studying feminist narratives and

LGBTQ activism and narratives from a decolonial point of view. She is a recipient of the MEXT Japanese governmental scholarship, as well as the Fall 2020 CAAFP Fellowship at the George Washington University. Prior to academia, Syinat has been actively involved in LGBTQ activism in Kyrgyzstan and Central Asia.

Kārlis Vērdiņš is a PhD candidate in comparative literature at Washington University in St. Louis, and a researcher at the Institute of Literature, Folklore, and Art of the University of Latvia. His publications include the monograph *The Social and Political Dimensions of the Latvian Prose Poem* (2010) and the edited volume *Queer Stories of Europe* (with Jānis Ozoliņš, 2016).